THE HARD WAY

SURVIVING SHAMSHUIPO POW CAMP
1941–45

THE HARD WAY

SURVIVING SHAMSHUIPO POW CAMP
1941–45

MAJOR VICTOR STANLEY EBBAGE
MBE BEM
EDITED BY ANDREW ROBERTSHAW
IN ASSOCIATION WITH THE ROYAL LOGISTIC CORPS MUSEUM

Cover Images: *Top*: Photograph of Captain Ebbage, taken from his identity card (RLC Museum). *Bottom*: Photograph of Prisoners of War. The back of this photograph reads: 'Shamshuipo, Hong Kong. Singapore & Siam. At last camp, Hiroshima Camp No. 3. Taken early September 1945. 1. Jack Hart. 2. Jack Emberson. 3. Joe Grossen. 4. Harry Hobson. (RLC Museum)

Back cover: Card sent from Captain Ebbage to his son Kenneth from Camp 'S' Shamshuipo. (Collection of Miss Ebbage)

First published 2011

Spellmount, an imprint of
The History Press
The Mill, Brimscombe Port
Stroud, Gloucestershire, GL5 2QG
www.thehistorypress.co.uk

British Library Cataloguing in Publication Data.
A catalogue record for this book is available from the British Library.

ISBN 978 0 7524 6064 2

Typesetting and origination by The History Press
Printed in Great Britain

Dedication

This book is dedicated to all members of No. 6 Section, Royal Army Ordnance Corps who served in Hong Kong 1939-45, and in particular to those who gave their lives while fighting the Japanese, or while Prisoners of War, or who succumbed after release. For all were 'Gentlemen of Ordnance'. And also, in grateful thanks to the Red Cross, to whom so many who survived captivity owe so much.

Note: The numbers making up the Section in Hong Kong at the outbreak of War with the Japanese was about 150.

DISCLAIMER
The text of this book is true to Captain Ebbage's original typescript. Only slight changes have been made for consistency and readability, but his original sentence structure has been retained. Any additions in square brackets are to enhance the meaning of certain sections and have been added by the Publisher or Editor.

Contents

Editor's note

One of the advantages of being a museum curator is the opportunity to see artefacts and archives that have not previously been seen by the public. In the past when items were donated by members of the public, a record was created and, all too often unless it went on display, the item was put into storage. The fact is that all museums have more objects than they can display and the archives consist of so many documents, photographs and other items that have to be kept in temperature- and humidity-controlled stores. However, one part of the mysterious work of museum curators and archivists is systematically going through collections, correctly cataloguing the items so they can be of use to current and future historians. In doing this occasional 'gems' are found: objects or collections that stand out and are so remarkable that they clearly cannot simply stay in store. This was the case with the collection of documents and photographs belonging to Major Ebbage which was brought to my attention by two museum staff members, Adam Culling and Melanie Price, when they were looking for information about the activities of the predecessor Corps of the current Royal Logistic Corps in Hong Kong. Subsequently Gareth Mears, the Archivist, located other items related to Major Ebbage and specifically his period as a Japanese Prisoner of War (POW) in Hong Kong.

As I read Major Ebbage's story of his early life, career and time as a POW I was struck by many coincidences that linked my non-military life with his military career. He was born in Leeds, where I spent my early years and he was sent by the army to Shanghai, Hong Kong and Beijing, places to which I have travelled and know well. This gave me some idea of his travels, but nothing could prepare me for his account of life in Shamshuipo POW Camp, Hong Kong, between 1941 and 1945.

He survived a battle in which his commanding officer and many other comrades died, and tried to evade capture, but was forced to surrender. Within hours of being taken prisoner, he was acting as liaison officer between his comrades and captors, travelling with them to the site of a battle in which he had been a lucky survivor, and then having tea and a chat with Japanese officers in a hotel with a sea view, all in the same day.

He then found himself responsible for the other ranks of Number 6 Section Royal Army Ordnance Corps (RAOC) in camp 'S' (Shamshuipo), when the other officers were sent elsewhere. For four years, despite starvation, privation, brutality and ill-treatment from his captors he did some remarkable things. Not only did he keep the men busy, but moreover he did so with useful activity. No opportunity for improvising appears to have been missed and if today 'recycling' and 'sustainability' are the watchwords of modern society, it is quite clear that the Major and his men were well ahead of the rest of us.

He is modest about his attempts to maintain morale and also acknowledges the efforts of those of his captors who attempted to be fair. Critically he praises the work of others, especially the Red Cross, in ensuring that the prisoners survived. It is a telling point that after his release in 1945, one of his first acts on his return to the United Kingdom was to write to the relatives of every man in the section who had been killed or died.

I never met Vic Ebbage, although I wish that I had – it would have been a fascinating meeting. He wanted his story to be told, but for various reasons his account was not turned into a book in his lifetime. This publication, seventy years after the fall of Hong Kong, allows this to happen. I hope that his account of resilience, fortitude, good humour and humanity will be of interest to an audience who are perhaps more familiar with celebrity status and glamour than duty and self sacrifice.

acknowledgements

This book is the result of the hard work and dedication of its author, Victor Stanley Ebbage. The Royal Logistic Corps Museum is grateful to him for his decision to deposit the typescript in our archive in the expectation that the museum could at some future date get it published. This process was greatly assisted by the author's daughter, Miss Joyce Ebbage, who gave her full support to the project and provided the editor with additional genealogical information and a number of photographs.

The starting point for the book was a search of the museum's archives by staff who were looking for information about the experiences of members of the Royal Army Service Corps and the Royal Army Ordnance Corps as POWs. It was Adam Culling and Melanie Price who brought the material to my attention and they deserve my gratitude for their diligent research. As parts of the book used a large number of Chinese place names, some of which are now spelt differently than they were in the 1930s, I recruited Shirong Chen, an old friend from the BBC to help with translation. Tony Banham, expert on the defence of Hong Kong and the experience of the POWs between 1941 and 1945, generously shared his knowledge, having been contacted by me, 'out of the blue', and was an extraordinary resource. A final thanks goes to the staff of The History Press who recognised the value of Major Ebbage's account and agreed to its publication.

Major Victor Stanley Ebbage MBE, BEM

a Brief Military Biography

Victor Stanley Ebbage was born in Beeston, Leeds on 13 August 1901, the son of Thomas Henry and Rose Monica Ebbage (née Grimshaw).[1]

Thomas Ebbage worked as a clerk for a local railway goods company and according to the 1911 Census the family also had a daughter, Phyllis, who was just a year old. Their address at this time was 20–21 Lanes End, an area of terraced housing and industry which did not survive German bombing in the Second World War or the post-war redevelopment.[2]

Victor had an aptitude for learning; however the death of his father in 1912 from tuberculosis, aged just thirty-four, meant that like most children of his background and generation, he left school in July 1914. He was able to leave school aged nearly thirteen because he was ahead of most of his classmates and had acquired the required standard of elementary education.[3] He found work as an office boy in the office of his uncle, Sidney Grimshaw, and his income would have been welcome for a now fatherless family.[4]

Victor was witness to the momentous events of the Great War on the home front, which broke out only a month after he started work. Leeds was the scene of effective recruiting drives throughout 1914 and 1915 and many of the young men who joined the Leeds' Pals Battalion and other local units would have been well known to him. He was, however, too young to serve as the conflict ended before his nineteenth birthday which would have given him the opportunity to volunteer or be conscripted.

After the war Victor's mother was able to gain employment as a book keeper for a woollen merchant and this provided Victor with the opportunity to take up a new and more challenging career.[5] After just less than six years of office life he enlisted into the Royal Army Ordnance Corps (RAOC) as Private 7576720 in his home city on 1 March 1920.[6]

His initial period of training was at No. 2 Section RAOC Tidworth in Wiltshire. He was sent for his first overseas service on 13 October 1920 in what was then Mesopotamia, today Iraq.[7] In 1920 the region was controlled by Britain as a Mandated Territory under the terms of the Treaty of Versailles. In the spring of 1920 there was a revolt against British rule, which started in the capital Baghdad. During the unrest that followed over 500 British and Indian troops were killed. Victor served in and around Basra (the focus of events in a more modern conflict involving British soldiers). Within a year, on 1 December 1921 he was promoted to Lance Corporal without pay,[8] although he had to wait until July 1923 before his promotion to Lance Corporal with pay.[9] For his overseas service he was awarded the General Service Medal (GSM) with the Iraq Clasp.[10] On his return to the United Kingdom he was posted first to Bramley in Hampshire[11] and then on promotion to Corporal for two and a half years to No. 10 Section RAOC Burscough in Lancashire.[12]

It was during this time that he demonstrated the academic promise of his younger years, which had been frustrated by the premature end to his education in 1914. He generously ascribes this success to the care of various Army Schoolmasters and others.[13] He was promoted to Lance Sergeant in October 1925 and gained a 2nd Class Educational Certificate in December of the same year.[14] By June of the following year he had gained a 1st Class

Educational Certificate, having distinguished himself in mathematics, and was eligible for the examination for promotion to Sergeant.[15] He passed the examination and was promoted to Sergeant in March 1927.[16]

A month later he was, once again, sent overseas. This time the destination was the Far East, as part of the newly created Shanghai Defence Force.[17] In early 1927 the International Settlement in Shanghai was in danger of being captured by warring Chinese armies and the local forces available were insufficient for the task. The British government sent a division to secure the settlement and protect British lives and property. This force included elements of the Royal Army Service Corps and RAOC to deal with stores and ammunition. Presented with this show of force the situation rapidly stabilised without serious fighting and it was possible to withdraw all but a single British battalion which remained as the Shanghai garrison.

On his return home, in 1928, he saw service at a series of Ordnance installations including Hilsea in Hampshire, Stirling in Scotland, Barry Camp in Wales, Didcot in Oxfordshire, Woolwich Arsenal and Chilwell in Nottinghamshire. He had clearly been intending to marry for some time as he applied for married quarters in August 1927,[18] but was still on the waiting list when he married Elsie Iddon on 23 April 1930 at Ormskirk in Lancashire, not far from her family home.[19] Their first child, Elsie Joyce, was born a little under a year later on 19 February 1931, while the family were quartered at Stirling, Scotland.[20] It is during this period of his service that he is frequently mentioned in the journal of the RAOC in connection with not only success at billiards, but also organising events such as dances and other music events.[21] Mrs Ebbage is not absent from the accounts of sporting accomplishment and in July 1934 she won the Married Ladies Race at the Didcot sports meeting.[22]

By September 1933 shortly before the family moved from Stirling to Didcot in Oxfordshire, Ebbage had passed the examination required for promotion to the rank of Warrant Officer Class II (Staff Quartermaster Sergeant).[23] This promotion did not occur until 29 January 1936.[24] However, in the same year he was awarded the Medal of the Military Division of the Most Excellent Order of the British Empire (RAOCG now known as the BEM) and promoted to Warrant Officer Class I (Sub-Conductor).[25] The award of the BEM was related to a one year period which he spent at Woolwich in connection with, the then very innovative development of, machine accounting.[26]

The expansion of Japanese influence into China from 1937 during the Second Sino-Japanese War directly threatened British interests in the region. In addition to Hong Kong there were British units in Shanghai, Tientsin and Peking (Beijing), as well as a rest camp at Shanhakwan. On 24 February 1938 with the threat of war growing, Sub-Conductor Ebbage was drafted for service in Hong Kong and his farewell concert was held at Chilwell.[27] He and his growing family (Mrs Ebbage was heavily pregnant) went to the Far East on His Majesty's Transport (H.T.) *Dilwara*.[28] A son, Kenneth, was born on 19 July 1938 shortly after their arrival in Hong Kong.[29] More good news followed when he was promoted to Conductor in October 1938[30] and received his Silver Medal for Long Service and Good Conduct from Major-General A.E. Grasett, DSO, MC in March 1939.[31]

By now, the family had settled down in Hong Kong, buying furniture and securing the services of a local Amah (nanny) for the children. In July Conductor Ebbage in company with Staff Sergeant Morries travelled to Japan for a three-week 'holiday', staying in Kobe.[32]

The outbreak of war with Nazi Germany led to the expansion of British forces and the need for additional officers. On 12 February 1940 he received an emergency commission as a Lieutenant, almost twenty years after he entered the RAOC as a private.[33] His first appointment was as a member of staff for the General Officer commanding Shanghai. His post was

Deputy Assistant Director of Ordnance Services, Shanghai and Tientsin. This brought with it the responsibility for removing large quantities of small-arms ammunition held in the magazines at Beijing, which due to the removal of British troops were no longer required. However this ammunition was needed at Singapore and Hong Kong.[34] Once again his small family was on the move and aboard the vessel *Wo Sang* they arrived in Shanghai. The family initially lived in the Palace Hotel at a time when shootings and public disorder were all too frequent.[35]

In March, Lieutenant Ebbage was sent by ship to Tientsin, North China via Weihaiwei. From there he travelled by rail to Beijing. Having made initial visits to the magazine where the vital small-arms ammunition was stored, he returned to Shanghai to report the situation and get permission to attempt a 'rescue' of all the useful ammunition.[36] Whilst back in Shanghai he tried to make arrangements for his family to move into their own accommodation. Shanghai was now an extremely dangerous city, surrounded by the Japanese, and European forces had established concession zones which were run according to their own rules.[37]

A second visit to North China in late spring took Lieutenant Ebbage to the British rest camp at Shanhaikwan on the coast and then back to Peking. Here he survived an attack from a mob by taking refuge in the American Embassy, and managed to persuade a Japanese delegation to examine ammunition stored in the magazine at the British Legion. Some of the mortar bombs had been damaged in flooding and Lieutenant Ebbage managed to eventually persuade the Japanese that to prevent a potentially catastrophic explosion it should all be removed and dumped at sea.[38]

Having returned to Shanghai to report his success he also finally secured a home for his family. During another journey to Peking Lieutenant Ebbage was able to supervise the removal of the ammunition from Beijing and the dumping of the dangerous elements into the sea. The ship involved then headed to British territory still carrying thousands of vital rifle and machine gun bullets under the noses of the Japanese against whom they would later be used.[39] Yet another journey to North China was followed by the apparent opportunity for a family summer holiday in Korea, away from the increasing confusion and violence in Shanghai. These plans came to nothing and following the evacuation of many of the British families from Hong Kong it was decided to also evacuate those British families in Shanghai to safety. Mrs Ebbage and the children embarked on SS *Tanda* bound for Australia on 23 August 1940.[40]

Following a final, farewell journey to Beijing, Tientsin and Shanhaikwan, Lieutenant Ebbage returned to Hong Kong in September 1940 as part of No. 6 Section RAOC. He was promoted to Captain and became Officer in Charge of Provisions and Local Purchase.[41] He was sharing a flat in 3 Gap Road with Captain Burroughs, who was later killed during the fighting on Hong Kong Island.[42] The Japanese attacked the Colony of Hong Kong on 8 December 1941. Once the Japanese breached the defences on the mainland the main Ordnance Corps depots came under attack and some storehouses were destroyed. Although the magazines were under shell fire and aerial bombardment, the bulk of the explosives were moved to safety. Captain Ebbage had a lucky escape on the morning of 10 December when a Japanese shell exploded close to where he, Colonel MacPherson, Captain Burroughs and Lieutenants Hanlon and Sutcliffe were gathered in an office 15 yards away.[43] By early on 13 December all British troops had withdrawn from the mainland. This however exposed the Lyemun Magazine and Married Quarters to heavy Japanese fire across the narrow straight of water separating the island from Kowloon. Captain Ebbage was directed to take charge of a party which transferred all the stores from the Married Quarters to the Ridge on 11 December.[44] He was in command there until the later arrival of Lt Colonel MacPherson.

The Ridge was a key position in the defence of the island as it lay on the route between Repulse Bay and Wong Nei

Chong Gap, both places at which heavy and prolonged fighting took place. The work of moving the stores was carried out under heavy shell fire and the RAOC drivers involved were all volunteers.[45] Most of the stores were in position by 17 December and some ammunition was handed over directly to gunners at gun positions. Although the initial Japanese assault on 15 December was beaten off with heavy losses they managed to make their first landing on a broad front on the night of 18/19 December.[46] Parties of Japanese soldiers moved rapidly inland cutting off various units and occupying the vital Wong Nei Chong Gap. From here they were able to advance on Repulse Bay, Shouson Hill and Little Hong Kong, cutting the island in two. The first Japanese soldiers were seen near the Ridge on the 19th and a party of their soldiers was engaged with machine-gun fire with some effect. By now a mixed party of Royal Engineers, Royal Army Service Corps, Hong Kong Volunteer Defence Corps and Royal Army Ordnance Corps were defending the Ridge.

These troops, numbering about 280, used nearby houses and bungalows as improvised strongpoints with the men divided between these, and a proportion of officers allocated to each. A party of men under Lt Colonel Frederick, RASC, attempted to leave on the morning of 20 December but were attacked and many were killed or wounded. Some returned to the position on the Ridge and a few escaped to the hills.[47] The remaining men on the Ridge were joined by the remnants of a Chinese battalion and other stragglers.[48] On the evening of the 20th instructions were received for the personnel on the ridge to break into four groups. Two parties of eight officers and eighty other ranks were detailed to help hold the position, allowing the third group to make for Repulse Bay. The last group including Captain Ebbage was detailed to wait until the road to Repulse Bay had been cleared and then evacuate the Ridge.[49] By the following day it was virtually impossible to move because of heavy Japanese fire and the order was received to stay at the Ridge because Canadian troops would be arriving. Around sixty members of the Canadian Royal Rifles arrived during the night under command of Major Young.[50]

Captain Ebbage reported that although it was possible to receive messages by telephone these were now in French as it was believed that the lines were being tapped by the Japanese.[51] With the weight of fire increasing from machine guns, mortars and artillery, casualties began to increase. At 5pm on 22 December the commander of the detachment, Lt Colonel MacPherson decided to surrender but told those who wished to make their own way to Repulse Bay.[52] Despite a flag of truce, firing continued and Lt Colonel MacPherson was mortally wounded around 3pm.[53] Some officers and men managed to slip away, but the men under Captain Ebbage found it impossible to leave House No. 1 which was 'continually riddled with machine gun fire'.[54] After dark a party under Captain Ebbage left the position at 7.40pm with the intention of making their escape to the relative safety of Repulse Bay. Although the party headed by Captain Ebbage made for the Repulse Bay Hotel, only three – Armament Sergeant Major R.A. Neale, Quarter Master Sergeant (QMS) James Edward Cooper and Ebbage himself – made it to the hills. This small group remained hidden from the Japanese until the following night, 23 December, when in an attempt to get past the Repulse Bay Hotel, Sergeant Major Neal was believed to have been killed. This was confirmed by the two remaining men around 8pm on the following evening when his body was found.[55] Although there was evidence that other members of the party from the Ridge were in the area, the two made their way into the hills to avoid the Japanese. At the time of the official surrender on Christmas Day, QMS Cooper and Captain Ebbage were trying to evade capture. The two of them survived without food or water for three days before they finally surrendered at 8.30am, 28 December.[56] During this time many of his fellow officers believed that he had died in the fighting on the Ridge. He was also not aware until he was reunited with his comrades that of fifteen officers and 132 other ranks of the RAOC who were in the garrison of Hong Kong, only ten officers and eighty-nine other ranks had survived. This represented a casualty rate of 33 per cent, higher than any other unit in the Command. Many of the prisoners and wounded on the Ridge were massacred after the collapse of resistance and few like Captain Ebbage were able to escape.[57]

As a POW he was held in Shamshuipo POW Camp (Camp S) from 30 December 1941 until the Japanese surrender on 16 August 1945. Although he spoke no Japanese he became the liaison officer with his captors and remained with the men of No. 6 Section RAOC in Shamshuipo Camp.[58] During this time many fellow prisoners had reason to be grateful for his efforts to make life in the camp more bearable. On his release from captivity he returned to the United Kingdom by sea, to Liverpool, where he was reunited with his family after a separation of nearly five years.[59] After debriefing he was posted back to 14 Battalion RAOC at Didcot. One of his first tasks on his return was to write personally to the relatives of all the members of No. 6 Section RAOC who had been killed in the defence of Hong Kong in 1941 or who had died in captivity.[60] His services whilst a POW were rewarded by his appointment as a Member of the Order of the British Empire (MBE) in April 1946.[61] Captain Ebbage survived a car accident near Didcot in 1948[62] and was made a Major in June 1949.[63] In 1952 he was appointed to the War Office as Deputy Assistant Director of Ordnance Services (DADOS) and he finally retired on 1 September 1956.[64] He was then re-employed as a Retired Officer in the Ordnance Directorate until his final retirement, after nearly 46 years' service, at the age of sixty-five in 1966.[65] Earlier that year he had returned to Hong Kong with fellow former POWs to attend a commemorative service and reunion.[66]

In retirement he kept in contact with the Corps and old friends, attending functions for as long as he was able. He devoted his spare time to gardening and voluntary work, and for many years was President of the Woking Branch of the Royal British Legion and member of the Far East Former Prisoner of War Association. The Royal British Legion Sheltered Housing Association built a block of flats in Woking and named it Ebbage Court.[67] He died at home in Woking on 8 August 1990, aged eighty-eight, leaving a son, Kenneth, and daughter, Joyce, who had cared for him in the final years of his life.[68]

Foreword

Major General G.L.F. Payne, CB, CBE
Former Director of Ordnance Services and Colonel
Commandant Royal Army Ordnance Corps

I have known Major Vic Ebbage for a number of years – since 1954 in fact – when we began a close association in Whitehall. I always had the most excellent advice and support from him, and from other Ordnance Executive Officers of the Royal Army Ordnance Corps, and I eventually became Director of Ordnance Services and subsequently a Colonel Commandant.

They were a fine body of men, and an outstanding example is that of the 'Chief Clerk' in this book. Not only was Major Ebbage a true professional in the best sense, to whom many came for advice, but he presented a most likeable and cheerful personality to all of whatever rank who came into contact with him. He was indeed a legendary figure.

Readers of this book will no doubt conclude that he must also have appeared in a similar light in the prison camp in Hong Kong, where he represented the needs of the prisoners, in attempting to make life under the Japanese as bearable as possible. Knowing him as I do, I am not surprised at the modest way in which he hints at the trials and tribulations with which he was faced in all his dealings with the Japanese. The prison guards no doubt did their utmost to degrade and denigrate their prisoners as much as possible, and what they did was made easier for them by Japan not being a signatory to the Geneva Convention.

From the very factual account in this book of what life was like for the prisoners under these conditions, one can but have the very greatest regard for the bravery, fortitude and inventiveness of these men, and the men of No. 6 Section, Royal Army Ordnance Corps were not least in these respects. A number of these men who showed such skill and inventiveness had been, in 1942, transferred to the Royal Electrical and Mechanical Engineers, but this fact was not known at that time. At all times Major Ebbage's thoughts must have been first for the men of his own corps, including those who were subsequently transferred to Japan. There must be many who were prisoners then, who remember his attempts to make life more bearable for them with gratitude. Later, after the war, others like myself regarded it as a privilege to have known such a gallant gentleman as Major Vic Ebbage.

> Major General G.L. Payne, CB, CBE, Retd
> Fishbourne,
> West Sussex
> February 1986

Preface

Author's Note

In the early 1950s when my retirement from the army was drawing near, much thought was given to the future, how and where my family would live, and how I should spend my time.

Three things stood out; I wanted to have a house and a garden, do some voluntary work, and write about my life in the Army. As the day of my departure from service life grew closer, the realisation I had no home, or money, and insufficient pension settled the issue. If I wanted a home I needed a job to pay for it. So for nearly ten years after retirement from the Regular Army writing had, perforce, to take a back seat, but during this period I was able to concentrate on my garden and voluntary work. In any case my writing, in the shape of an autobiography would be of little interest outside my own family, for whom it had primarily been intended, after my death. My literary ability was nil, while my grammar reflected my lack of educational background. I had left Junior School just prior to my thirteenth birthday in 1914 for work as an office boy, and had progressed from there, with some help from army schoolmasters and others, and an ever widening knowledge of the world.

There might be a tale worth telling, but there were limitations on my ability to tell it! During that extra ten years of work I was able to look at matters from a different angle. I now had a house and nearly a third of an acre of garden; was immersed in voluntary/social work; had an ailing wife, and one or two problems with my own health. *The History of the Royal Army Ordnance Corps 1920–45* did not contain any reference to periods spent as Prisoners of War. For that reason I resolved to give this part of my story priority; even more so because others gave me much encouragement to do so. As a result I reserved the three coldest months of the year (when confined to the house) to writing, research, typing, etc. What I thought would take but a few weeks became months and then years; the task seemed never-ending, and instead of being a simple straightforward biography, the work was becoming very much more!

As writing progressed I came increasingly to appreciate two factors:

a. The great talents, ingenuity, unselfishness, courage and loyalty of men of my own, and other units who, while Prisoners of War were prepared to do so much for others. No. 6 Section, Royal Army Ordnance Corps, to which I belonged, included many officers and men who had been officially transferred to the Royal Electrical and Mechanical Engineers on its formation in 1942, but who remained 'RAOC' and wore this cap badge until the end of 1945, when they returned home.

b. Of the work done by the Red Cross to alleviate our lot, under the most difficult and trying conditions they had to face in Hong Kong, and the Far East. They receive so little praise (and do not ask for it). Had it not been for the supplies of food, clothing, etc which came into Shamshuipo Prisoners of War Camp in November 1942, and kept us going for many months, I feel sure there would have been very many more deaths, and I might well have been one of them! If therefore, my comments in the following pages appear harsh, ungrateful, and possibly unjust to the Red Cross and its representatives, my praise for them is unstinting and wholehearted - for, by their effort they saved many lives!

Individuals have not been mentioned by name, but some may be alluded to in different ways; nor are the sequence of events necessarily in the correct chronological order.* The account is as accurate as I can make it, taking into consideration that the happenings related occurred many years ago. I did not keep a diary, just a few notes, but have had access to records, papers, etc and the benefit of details supplied by my friends, which also enabled me to refresh my memory.

I have written my memoirs because I think that the story I have to tell might be of interest and benefit to others. It was written without thought of personal gain or aggrandisement, and for this reason it will not be published in my lifetime. In my advancing years, and when I was not physically capable of more exacting work, it has provided me with an outlet, or therapy, for my still active and fertile brain. The account is as factual as I can make it, taking into consideration that the happenings I have related occurred many years ago. I did not keep diaries, and indeed there were times when this was not possible; in particular, my sojourn in a Japanese Prison Camp, but I have had access to certain papers and the benefit of details supplied by friends, in particular about Shamshuipo,[1] which have enabled me to refresh my memory.

Most of my adult life has been spent in the service of the Crown; nearly forty-six years in all, from very junior Private Soldier to Commissioned Rank.[2] It is natural therefore that most of my story deals with my life in the army. My unique career covers a wide variety of experiences and activities; during the run down after the First World War; preparations for the second; a personal narrative of the defence of the Ridge during the war against the Japanese in Hong Kong; and the aftermath of the Second World War as well.

---

* The editor has taken the liberty of identifying a few of the individuals mentioned in the account by name and provided a chronology of the principal events of the author's life in the form of a brief biography.

This part of my story may have particular interest to those who serve the Crown now, or may do so in future, and especially those members of the RAOC[3] in which it was my honour to serve for so long. I hope it will bring no benefit or comfort to the enemies of our country.

I have called my story 'The Hard Way' because that is just what is was. The climb from obscurity to a position of power, if not in rank, was not easy. The pitfalls were great and the hazards constant and the struggle was hard, yes, very hard indeed on both myself and my wife. It is my wish that on my death, my daughter, if she wishes, will hand the manuscript over to the Historical Committee of the RAOC so that it may be kept in the RAOC Museum.[4] If it is decided that all or part could, with advantage, be published, then I should like any profits to be given to the Red Cross, to who owe so much and to the RAOC Aid Society, in equal portions.[5]

*****

Very early in 1940 I was commissioned in Hong Kong after what seemed an interminable length of time; it was an event for which I had planned and worked for over twenty years, but nevertheless the improvement in my status, if not in my finances, proved a considerable uplift. I was there at last; now I began to wonder how I should make out, how I would conduct myself, and how I would be accepted amongst those I had served. I need not have worried about the latter, everyone was most helpful and many gave me advice and guidance about my conduct and my new position. One brother officer had made for me a small leather covered stick, a symbol of my new rank, which I was to carry at all times when in uniform. It felt a bit like a Field Marshal's baton and quite apart from keeping my hands out of my pockets became perhaps my most treasured possession until I had to exchange it for a rifle a couple of years later. It seemed like a magic wand and I came to regard it as such. I replaced it some years later but the new ones were never the same, the magic had gone.

My uniform was 'made to measure', my shirts were tailored, I now qualified for 'Servant Allowance', acquired a 'Camp Kit' and had my visiting cards printed. An Officer I now was; could I qualify as a gentleman as well? I left the first of my visiting cards at Flagstaff House, the home of my General and signed the visitor's book. This would ensure that at some later date my wife and I would be invited to functions there. I thought very highly of this particular General; as a Conductor (Senior Warrant Officer Class I) I had been working closely with his staff and he had been my proposer when I joined the Hong Kong Jockey Club. (The Chief Justice was my seconder). Similarly, the leaving of cards and the signing of the visitor's book at Government House, the residence of the Governor, followed. These matters of protocol and etiquette were viewed in a new light now I could appreciate their usefulness. There is a duty to those one likes, and dislikes, a responsibility to 'keep up one's position' as a representative of His Majesty the King, to keep one's subordinates 'in good order and discipline', to obey Orders and Directions given according to the Rules and Discipline of War, to act in the best interests of one's country.[6]

My experience thus far had been in a minor executive role; but I was now about to embark into an administrative sphere as my first appointment on commission was on the staff of the GOC[7] Shanghai as Deputy Assistant Director of Ordnance Services, Shanghai and Tientsin Area. I was on my own; there would be no one to ask for day-to-day guidance about my own particular job, only broad policy directions. I was 'briefed' by a Senior RAOC Officer in China Command HQ about my departmental duties. There would be no one to take over from as my predecessor had already left so I would be free to do things in my own way. There were two main points, however, on which I was to give most of my attention. They were: the running down of stocks in North China to realistic levels should the closing down of

the installations in North China if and when the two infantry battalions there be taken away; and the removal of a large
quantity of ammunition held in Tientsin and Peking which,
due to reductions in the garrison, was not now required.[8]
There was, however, an urgent need for it elsewhere! I should
examine these two situations on my arrival and consult with
the GOC Shanghai and his staff on the agreed action to be
taken. For the second time I disposed of my private furniture
and effects in Hong Kong and, with my wife and two children, plus our Cantonese Amah, sailed for Shanghai in the SS
Wo Sang, flagship of the local shipping line![9]

The cabin, etc was palatial when compared to 2nd Class
troopship accommodation and we dined at the Captain's
table! I studied with care the elaborate anti-piracy devices
and grills, and the sickly looking guards who were to protect us, and in my cabin my own capacity to defend family
and myself. Piracy on this run was a regular occurrence.[10]
Each ship carried large numbers of Chinese passengers
with mountains of luggage and every conceivable kind of
utensil and cooking pot and charcoal burner in the well
deck, so it was easy for the 'pirates', at a given signal, to try
to take the ship over. Most times they seemed to succeed
but this time all was quiet and at last we sailed past the
forts at Woosung and into the Whangpoo River. Shanghai:
international city of teeming millions, of Concessions and
settlements, poverty and plenty, vice and affluence, gang-
sters and godly men, of Russian princesses and opposing
forces, and where 'men from the sea foregather'. I had seen
it before in 1927/28 when I came out with the Shanghai
Defence Force, and again in 1939 when passing through en
route for Japan, so to me it was not new.[11]

A suite of rooms had been booked for my family in the
Palace Hotel, a corner site on the first floor with windows
overlooking the Bund and Nanking Road – 'Palace, the
first place after you have stepped ashore and where you
are sure to meet a friend'. It was full of American tourists, but very, very expensive for a newly commissioned

Lieutenant. I reported to headquarters, left my cards at all the appropriate places and inspected my Shanghai Depot. This was housed in the upper floors of the racecourse stables in Mohawk Road, immediately behind the racecourse and the recreation ground where the Seaforth Highlanders were stationed. They provided the guard on my depot. Not much in the way of stores, thank goodness, chiefly warlike items. No ammunition or barrack stores, the two Battalions and Barrack Officers took care of them. Not much of a task evacuating Mohawk Road if and when the time came. The small depot was well run and the accounts quite satisfactory. The single members of staff lived in depot premises but ate with the Seaforths. Demands for stores, which we could not meet, were forwarded to Hong Kong for direct supply. HQ would try to find me a house. Quite good, I mused, on my way back to the Palace Hotel. I had hardly got into the hotel when all hell was let loose outside and as I looked down from my first floor vantage point I witnessed my first street gun battle between two opposing forces. The streets cleared as if by magic as the antagonists fought it out from behind pillars; it was a vicious affair while it lasted but it was quickly brought to a halt by the Shanghai Municipal Police who arrived with machine guns blazing, cutting down the protagonists from either side. They heaved the dead bodies into the back of a truck and within seconds all was back to normal, just as if nothing had happened. This eye opener was an abject lesson for me as it became the pattern of daily life in the big city and made me even more concerned about the safety of my family. A bad start, too, for my wife, but she never complained, just gathered her offspring around her. Our Amah[12] was upset and determined to leave for the land of her ancestors at the earliest moment![13] Having made my acquaintance with the Commanding Officer [CO] and Officers of the Seaforth Highlanders, who made me an honorary member of their Mess, I proceeded next day to lunch with the Commanding Officer of the East Surrey Regiment in their Mess where again I was invited to become an honorary member. As I had no Mess of my own, these gestures were much appreciated and I was at home with both units. The East Surreys were manning the British sector of the perimeter and doing one hell of a job when in the company of their CO I visited them on the banks of Soochow Creek.[14] The adjoining sector was manned by Italians with whom, at that time, February/March 1940, we were at war. How strange it seemed that two countries at war with each other should be defending the same perimeter, side by side, contradictions I was soon to become accustomed to. Germans, too, there were in plenty in the settlement but each nationality, though at war, kept strictly apart. You did not partner them on the tennis courts, or drink together at the bars, but just maintained a rigid and distant politeness, observed and respected by both sides. What an Alice in Wonderland set up! I wonder what Gilbert & Sullivan would have made of it?[15]

It had been suggested at Shanghai HQ that I arrange my first visit to North China as early as possible in the company of the CO of the East Surreys who had one company stationed in Tientsin[16] and a detachment at Peking[17]. It would help me get to know the people I would need to rely on and I would get to know the ropes when dealing with the Japanese and other unfriendly, and friendly, nationals in the easiest possible way. I should give my first priority to getting the ammunition out, if possible – it was needed urgently in Singapore. In this connection I should first make contact with the Political Officer at Tientsin who would give me advice, guidance and help as to who was privy to what was required. At this stage I was told that the French had in their Concession a quantity of ammunition which they too wanted to get out of Tientsin to bolster up their stocks in Indo-China. This introduced a new dimension to the problem. The Japanese who controlled everything that went in and out of both Concessions and who were in occupation of the surrounding territory were the main obstacle. They made constant searches, confiscating anything they did not like.

A passage was booked for both of us on the next ship
going to North China. It was fortuitous that this should
be a very small tramp steamer which plied regularly
between the ports of North China and was well known
along the China costs; her officers and crew had long
experience of the east and of the ways of both Chinese
and Japanese. We made our way slowly up the coast, the
ship being completely blacked out, calling at Tsingtao,[18]
which had been a German Concession until the World
War and then Chefoo,[19] where we took on board a large
quantity of prawns in barrels. I have never seen such large
prawns before or since; they were reputed to live on the
dead bodies washed down by the rivers to the many sand
banks but they tasted wonderful and we feasted on them
for most meals. I had another look at Wei Hai Wei,[20] used
as a Naval Anchorage and torpedo testing area, where
I had spent some weeks recuperating in 1928, with its
wonderful silver sand beaches. We disembarked at Taku[21]
to continue our journey by train. The ship, the *Lee Sang*,
would be unloading part of her cargo there to lighten the
ship and then make it possible to go up the Hai Ho River
as far as Tientsin. It was only a short journey but we were
watched constantly and questioned as to why we were
going to Tientsin[22] and what our business there was. Would
we be calling at Japanese HQ? We had plenty of evasive
answers to give. Quite obviously, we would be watched,
right throughout our journey. I had met this kind of thing
before, when I went for a holiday to Japan in 1939. From
the time we entered the Oriental Hotel in Kobe, wherever
we went and until the time we left, our personal spy was
in attendance. It is quite a game! But serious too, as one of
my friends had found out in Japan when he took a photo
of some lovely flowering shrubs and was promptly arrested
and then found out they were camouflage for a gun![23]

On arrival at Tientsin Railway Station we were 'taken
over' by our representatives there, the OC[24] East Surrey
Regiment went to their Officer's Mess while I went to my

hotel, each going his separate way. The Court Hotel was an extremely Victorian establishment and lived up to its name and reputation; it was the kind of place with a long history where government officials could feel secure and where their baggage would most likely not be rifled while they slept or were away at breakfast; where snipe, quail and woodcock regularly appeared on the menu and bridge was played after dinner. I imagine it had not changed since before the Boxer Rebellion![25] It was the scene of much previous glory! I settled in quickly and was whisked off (by car) to inspect the Ordnance Depot, Tientsin. This was a small but efficient Tun Depot, part of an old barracks with an extensive parade ground and an apparatus for disposing of unwanted explosives in minute quantity. There was a small staff headed by a Sub-Conductor and one Ammunition Specialist; they were obviously pleased to see an officer of their own corps as I gathered they had for a long time felt 'out on a limb'. I enjoyed talking to each individual, listening to their problems (all were minor) and gave them some hope that they were not forgotten even though there was a war going on at the other side of the world. They were all doing a really good job and it was obvious they had gone to great pains to impress me. I had confidence in all of them as did the units they served. I inspected the whole of the depot most carefully and in particular the magazine area, which housed quite a lot of serviceable small arm ammunition.

Some of the ammunition had been damaged by floodwater and was subsequently condemned. It was currently being broken down but it was a slow process in so confined a space. The Ammunition Specialist briefed me on the position at Peking, which he also covered, making periodic visits there. I dined with the East Surrey Regiment in the evening, meeting all the officers who were tireless in their efforts to impress upon me the peculiar situation under which they were living and their hospitality. No evening was complete without a visit to the Cabaret in the adjoining French

Concession! The OC, East Surrey Regiment, told me of his visit to Japanese HQ where he had left cards for both of us. At least the Japanese knew we were there and why, even if their spies had not told them – he to visit his unit detachments in Tientsin and Peking whilst I would be visiting my installations in Tientsin, Peking and Shanhaikwan.[26] The next day I met the Political Officer to make my number. He was a very pleasant, capable and helpful chap, well versed in the ammunition situation, and the provider of much good practical advice, particularly about the position at Peking, and the difficulties I might encounter there. We agreed to meet again on my return. Train reservations were made for Peking and I was duly escorted to the station early next morning, dressed in my best uniform and carrying my stick. I had been made aware that, on arrival at the station I should meet pleasant Japanese who would ask 'all the usual questions' and that someone would take my photograph for the local Japanese Rogues Gallery. Sure enough, he was there, occupying a strategic position, and my escort drew my attention to him as we waited. In a matter of a minute or so 'Smiler' was at my side. 'Was I going to Peking?', 'Was I on business or holiday?', 'Where was I staying?', 'And for how long?', 'All the British are leaving – why had I come?' etc, etc and I could see the photographer trying to get in position. I suggested to 'Smiler' that I could see a man who obviously wanted to take my picture; if he would move over I could pose and provide a better likeness; I didn't want to be mistaken for someone else! The banter went on until I boarded the train. 'Smiler' wished me a safe and pleasant journey and then retreated to his strategic position ready to meet the incoming and outgoing passengers on subsequent trains. On a later occasion I actually asked to see his 'visitor's book' of important persons and read with much amusement the captions that went with the pictures. What the Japanese could make of it all I leave to the reader's imagination. We were all there – the Generals, the Colonels, the Captains – and myself! The journey to Peking was interesting. I was seeing

new lands and surroundings and I was being 'well supervised' by the Train Conductor; these characters seemed just
to hand you on one to another for as long as this was possible, picking up lost trails as and when opportunity offered.
I had been advised to take a rickshaw from the station to
the Grand Hotel Des Wagon Lits and this I did. It was a
relatively short journey from Station to Hotel through the
Ch'ien Men Gate[27] of the Walled Tartar City and into the
Legation Quarter, which is also surrounded by another set
of walls. The walls of the Tartar City are forty feet high and
thirty-four feet wide at the top. The Legation Quarter has a
history and background that would provide a tale all on its
own but it did house Embassies or Legations of many countries, business houses and banks, amongst which were those
of Great Britain, France, USA, Germany, Russia, Japan, Italy,
Netherlands, Spain, etc. It was in the British Legation that
my small Ordnance Depot was situated.

The Hotel des Wagon Lits was comfortable and I was
quick to sense at the reception desk that much was known
about me already. When there were lots of tourists the hotel
was a most popular place, now it was more or less deserted
so the upper floors had been taken over by the Japanese as
part of their headquarters. Their Legation was sited a little
lower down Can Street and nearly opposite our own. The
British Legation was extensive with many buildings and
offices necessary for the transaction of government business: extensive military barracks, an officer's mess, quarters,
a football field, training area and all the ancillary requirements needed to support and defend British people in the
surrounding area of Peking. It had been under siege and
flood before, as indeed had the whole Legation Quarter,
and survived. My little Ordnance Depot and Magazine was
commanded by a Sergeant, and a detachment of the East
Surrey Regiment was currently supplying the Legation
Guard. It seemed laughable that though our country was
at war there were probably small pockets of troops like this
tied up throughout the world, all doing a necessary job for

Britain, and what is more, doing it well. They had of course their own local war to contend with. They talked of home, trips to the Western Hills, the Ming Tombs and the annual visit to the seaside at Shanhaikwan, and then again of home and of Nationalists, Communists, War Lords and Japanese for whom Peking was the main goal. It was indeed an eye opener for me. The place had been going for 3,000 years, a long history and many beautiful buildings and works; I was near to the Forbidden City, The Temple of Heaven and The Thieves Market, all waiting to be explored as they had been by so many good men of my corps who had the fortune to do a tour of duty in North China, and now perhaps I was to be the last of a very long and distinguished line, probably closing down the best station (or one of the best) our corps ever had. Well, no point in dreaming about the past or the future. My job was to concern myself with the present. Not much to worry about from a stores point of view; I felt that I could have moved the lot with the aid of a hand cart in two or three hours, the quantity seemed so small. There were of course barrack stores which were 'out in use' but the ammunition and the magazine were a very different question; again there was not really so very much but it was just 'awkward'. The magazine was of a conventional type, having been purpose built and below ground because of its close proximity to other buildings, and more or less in the centre of the Legation premises. It had been flooded before, but most recently two or three years before when the whole of Peking had been under water for quite a long time. I walked down the steps of this Aladdin's Cave and with my Sergeant opened the heavy iron doors, it looked much like the scene from a children's pantomime. The effects of the relatively recent flooding were now plain to see from the outside, but when the doors were opened the results of the flooding on the rows of boxes was obvious. The place smelt and the contents looked shocking! Not a bit like the clean, dry, airy stores I had been accustomed to see through my service in various arsenals, and much worse than conditions I had seen in Mesopotamia in the twenties.[28] However, only the mortar bombs were considered to be 'unserviceable' and had been condemned. Even so, they were not regarded as being particularly dangerous, but certainly, in time, would become 'unreliable' unless something was done with them. I gathered that when there was ammunition for repair or disposal at Peking it had been the custom to send it back to Tientsin where arrangements were made for it to be dumped in the sea if the task of recovery, or breaking down, was not possible. It seemed there had already been a number of attempts to get rid of these mortar bombs but all had been frustrated by the Japanese who steadfastly refused to allow them to be sent to Tientsin, or for that matter anywhere else. It was stalemate, or so it seemed. We wanted the small arms ammunition out of that magazine to make use of it and get rid of the mortar bombs as well. That dank stinking magazine certainly looked and felt forbidding! There seemed only one realistic solution to the problem, to get the Japanese to 'ease up'.

I did a little sightseeing round the Imperial and Forbidden Cities, ate Peking Duck with a Signals friend at the Hotel de Peking, and took my problem back to Tientsin where I discussed it again with the Political Officer. Means must be found to get the ammunition out of Peking. It was an embarrassment where it was, but moving it to Tientsin, even if this were possible, would not provide a complete solution to the problem, we still had to get both lots out of North China. A possible way out appeared to be to convince the Japanese that the bombs were dangerous, their condition would not improve with keeping, and if and when we did depart we should perforce have to leave them behind. The alternative seemed to be to persuade the Japanese to let them out while they could still be moved and dump them in a deep channel in the sea. Perhaps if we could get the ammunition to Tientsin, and then bring a small ship right up into the Concession, we could load her there with the ammunition and other surplus stores from both Peking and Tientsin, in fact anything there was to go. Any search by the Japanese, when the ship moved down the river, might be more perfunctory if they knew it was carrying suspect Peking mortar bombs, the disposal of which had been agreed by them and they were fully aware of what was going on, and why, and were able to see for themselves. The French, too, might like to take advantage of this opportunity. The scheme seemed to have possibilities! I would discuss the matter at my headquarters in Shanghai while he would do his 'homework' at this end. Sometimes the seemingly impossible works, and sometimes the obvious does not seem so 'obvious'.

My family were pleased to see me when I got back to Shanghai with my picture postcards of the 'sights' of Peking; my daughter had been enrolled at the Cathedral Girls School and was equipped with her straw hat and new uniform, and my wife had found her way around the shops and watched the 'shadow boxing' practiced by so many on the Bund. They were settling down, but my wife did not care for hotel life and was a bit restless for a place of her own and had forebodings about Shanghai in general. So had I. But she accepted her lot and made the best of it. Certainly she never complained. There had been one or two more 'shoot ups' but not under our hotel window. All was well at Mohawk Road. During my periods of absence, the Barracks Officer signed 'my papers' and I resolved the minor irritations caused by having a 'stranger within the gate'. We were good friends and so were our wives, which helped to make matters easier. I gathered there was a house in the offing for me but it was not quite ready and there was likely to be a problem of 'key money'. Negotiations were proceeding. I gave my report to headquarters on my visit to North China. The proposals found favour and would be examined in more detail. That at least seemed to be that, for the moment. I could concentrate on Shanghai and make official visits to all the units, making certain their wants so far as ordnance stores, etc were taken care of, and getting

them to disgorge anything for which they had no immediate use, thus mitigating the problem should we ever have
to leave. The hospital seemed to have a super abundance of
gear, much of it not War Department property, and a most
capable and efficient quartermaster with whom I became
great friends. He was already occupying a house near to the
one suggested for me, and of a very similar type, so I got to
know all about it. I worked very closely with every unit;
some, like me had their families with them while the others
– the two infantry battalions, etc were without families who
had been left behind at their previous stations. I ruminated
often on the merits of having one's family present, and not.
In the case of Shanghai, it seemed better for them to be
away. However, I now entered the social life open to us
and my wife was able to accompany me to functions, races,
sports, etc where, as was to be expected, women were made
very welcome. We attended the 'At Homes' and the cocktail
parties and tried our best to join in the fun. I was not really
finding very much work to do. For years I had put in a full
working stint with civilian employees in the various installations in which I served, but now I was 'looking for work'.
This can be a serious disadvantage where staff is concerned;
I found it better to say what I wanted done and then to get
out of the place until the job had been finished, but I must
admit this was much easier said than done. However, all was
working out very well indeed at the small Shanghai Depot
so I spent more and more time with units. It was while
returning from one of these visits in a rickshaw and following two or three more, that I noticed a sudden commotion
right in front of me and at the entrance to my depot. Two
or three thugs on the pavement had attacked the leading
rickshaw boy and his passenger with knives and they had
been severely injured. We gave what help we could, called
an ambulance and sent them off to hospital. I quickly found
out that the white man in the leading rickshaw was no
other than the announcer on the local American radio station, 'Voice of America', a man of outspoken views who

gave the populace much to laugh about with his pungent comments and pro-American views. He certainly could, and did, put it over; it was quite uplifting to hear him lashing opponents right and left, but it was a risky business too, he knew it, but never seemed to care or take any notice.

The days were passing quickly and soon it would be time for me to make preparations for my next visit north so I determined to try and get the housing question settled. It seemed that building and negotiations were going well. The houses was situated in Route Fergusson, right at the very far end of the French Concession, the end one of a row and with a large open space on the un-built side. It was about the right size with three bedrooms, two living rooms and the usual offices. There was a high-walled yard back and front topped with burglar deterrents and with a wrought iron gate to be kept permanently locked. It was a little fortress in its own way but with rogues, thieves and vagabonds around who stopped at nothing to secure their ends, and with political opponents twice as ruthless and well armed, the more precautions there were the better. What a contrast to the safe days of England where you could leave your back door open all night, your wife and family would be safe from molestation and your property would be respected. There was plenty of excitement here in the life of a soldier! When I spoke to the Barrack Officer he told me the house owner was prepared to let this desirable empty dwelling to the British Army, but there was one snag: he wanted twelve thousand dollars (Mex)[29] key money and I should be expected to provide this amount; he might as well have asked for twelve million so far as I was concerned. However, I gathered this was the opening bid, he would come down, and we were hopeful. We would need furniture as well as the place was unfurnished so my wife and I set about looking, and pricing, suitable items. When I next visited headquarters, key money and my inability to pay were high on the agenda. The general was very sympathetic; so too was the general's wife when she heard about it! The paymaster, financial adviser and everyone who could lend a hand did. The asking rate dropped to ten thousand dollars, then to nine, and after I had left again for the north, down to eight thousand. I gathered afterwards that at this stage resistance stiffened. The vendor had reached a level from which he would not budge. I had already made the point that I could not afford to pay anything and if I was to occupy that or any other house the government would have to pay, not me. The future looked somewhat bleak, but at least my family would be remaining in hotel accommodation for the moment which was some relief as I was about to leave on my next visit to North China.

On this occasion, the ship I was taking was en route for Chinwangtao,[30] a small but up to date port on the Gulf of Liaotung,[31] and on the direct railway line through Tangshan and on to Peking. Tangshan is well known as the centre of the coal mining industry in North China, a place subject to earth tremors and earthquakes with sickening regularity and where the loss of life through these causes was enormous. Enormous, too, was its contribution to the economy. Much of the coal produced was shipped southwards from Chinwangtao. Chingwangtao was also very close to my depot at Shanhaikwan which made it a good starting point. We sailed into the harbour early in the morning, everywhere seemed bleak and the wind was bitter; certainly uninviting, even in the warmest of fur caps. The mountains looked brown and cold and I could see the Great Wall of China threading its way over them and down to the sea. The golf course, too, was as brown as the mountains, there was not a bit of green of any kind in sight, only ice and that bitterly cold wind. I was thankful for my leather jacket and greatcoat and my long johns, in fact anything that would keep me warm. I was quickly away to the railway station and my short journey from there to Shanhaikwan, where I was met by my representative and taken down to our own private railway. So far as I was able to gather, one of the conditions of the settlement of the Boxer uprising was that all the countries represented at Peking and Tientsin should have a similar training and summer camp, close to the sea, where their soldiery could holiday and get away from the summer heat of Peking. The British seemed to have led this idea; at any rate we had the camp furthest away from the main railway line, right at the point where the Great Wall of China ran into the sea and with a most lovely beach down below. The means of communication was by a narrow gauge single line (Decauville) railway track[32] which ran the full length (some three or four miles) and having double or loop lines as it passed each Concession – French, Italian, Russian, etc. The line was British owned and, because of this, protocol demanded that we should always have right of way. Priority was ours. The trucks were of platform or box type and were pulled by Mongolian ponies and in the centre of each truck was a small flag pole, about six feet high, from which the various nationals flew their flags whenever they travelled on the line. We had small Union Jacks, about nine inches by six inches, and one of these was duly hoisted and away we went. It was a slow journey and bitterly cold, but for me there were new things to see and to have explained as we passed the various loop lines. Our troops usually came down in the summer months and in winter there was hardly anyone there but one or two countries, namely the Italians with whom we were at war in Europe, were currently in occupation of their camp. Sure enough, as we approached, an Italian truck, loaded with men armed to the teeth, was coming down the line in the opposite direction; we stopped within a yard or two of each other and there was a confrontation. The Italians, I gathered, did not intend to go back and it would be a complete loss of face for me to do so. Here we were, at war with each other and the nearest other British soldier some 100 miles away and me armed only with my leather covered stick and the authority of the Union Jack. What a crazy situation! But we should just have to sit it out. The respective drivers argued, my Chinese representative gesticulated, and I just sat. Inevitably, the commotion was heard in the Italian Camp and soon a Lieutenant Commander of the Italian Navy appeared. We exchanged courtesies, the Italian ponies were re-yoked the other way round, the truck retreated to their own loop line and I continued uneventfully for the rest of the journey.

I gave a lot of thought to that encounter; it showed me how much we counted, in what esteem we were held, even by our enemies, how correct and fair we were. I was even more proud to be British. The Italians knew I was there; perhaps I would have an easier ride back! I have described the site of the depot. The general layout was in the shape of a summer camp where tents could be erected, supported by more permanent amenities, cookhouses, etc. There was a very large flagstaff, which dominated the whole area. It was the custom, when we were in occupation, to fly a Union Jack from this pole. The flag was always kept there so our first task was to hoist it. I am sorry there was no band or photographers, just a simple ceremony with one British officer, with stick under arm, and a few pro-British Chinese employees. It was quite touching; I am sure, for all of us. The flag remained flying throughout my visit, purely as a symbol, for all to see and respect. There was quite a lot of stuff held in this small camp depot but it chiefly comprised wooden and metal items which would not deteriorate and on which little maintenance, except for painting and preservation, was required. Chairs, forms, tables, bedsteads, tent poles, picks, shovels, etc – all of it was part worn. All the textile items like sheets, blankets, tentage, etc was returned to Tientsin for repair and refurbishing at the end of the camping season. When the time came, if it was not required and could not be sold, we could always set fire to it without any danger. It was sad, thinking about these things and what too might happen to the loyal Chinese staff if ever we left. I bade them goodbye, we stood to attention while the flag was lowered, I boarded my small truck still with its flag flying and the Mongolian pony started off on the return journey to Shanhaikwan.

The Italians just stood and watched as we passed down the line without incident.

That night I stayed at a hotel in Shanhaikwan that had seen better days. It was full of Japanese, some civilian, some military, who trailed their swords with them wherever they seemed to go. I had no one to talk to and the oriental food was not to my liking. I should be glad when I was aboard the train for Tientsin. I was early on the platform next morning, standing at the place where my guide assured me the first class compartment would stop, and with my small leather stick under my arm, when who should arrive but the Italian naval lieutenant commander I had seen at the Italian camp previously. He was in full war paint, complete with sword and pistol and accompanied by an escort of two fully armed naval ratings and a certain amount of kit. They stood a little distance away. As the train drew in, sure enough there was a first class compartment right opposite where I was standing so I picked up my small case and was quickly aboard. There was only one person in the compartment; a Japanese general slumped in his corner with his jacket and shirt undone and without his boots, which stood by his side. I indicated I proposed to sit in the seat diagonally opposite to him and he grunted something I took for approval as I put up my case and stick on the rack and sat down. At least this was perhaps better than sharing a compartment with the Italian and all the other compartments had seemed to be pretty full. It was then I realised that perhaps this particular compartment was 'Reserved' for the Japanese general but if it was there was nothing to show so I stayed put. Some minutes later the lieutenant commander also appeared; it seemed he had been unable to secure a seat elsewhere; though a little red faced, he too came into the compartment and decided to sit opposite the Japanese general with his two armed ratings just by me, out in the corridor. No words passed and I settled down to ponder, once again, on the strange circumstances that brought us together. However, somewhere between Chinwangtao and

Tangshan the party was complete. A breezy officer of the American army joined the compartment and sat opposite me. He too was fully armed, literally bristling with hardware of various kinds, and he too had an escort of a couple of GIs also fully armed, who joined the Italians in the corridor. Of course they were not at war with anybody then. He looked me over, including my cane, introduced himself and said 'Say, guy, pretty low company you are keeping' and kept up a barrage of loud and lurid comments, many with oblique references to our other two travelling companions. It seemed he was going to the bank with the canteen takings and then would draw pay for the GIs he had 'on Station'. That was the reason he had to be fully armed, otherwise he might have been as 'naked' as I was! He wanted to know what I was doing in these parts, what my ribbons were for and where my wife was. He told me all about himself, if indeed he was telling the truth, about his medals, one for shooting and other for boxing, or something like that, that he was single and would shortly be returning to God's Own Country, the USA. He certainly made me laugh at his blunt comments and forthright manner, and I was glad of his company on the journey. At Tientsin we parted company and I renewed my acquaintance with the Court Hotel and my problems there.

Great strides had been made in preparing all surplus items for transfer elsewhere at the appropriate time. I was also expecting there to be some happenings on the matter of the mortar bombs at Peking. I was not, therefore, surprised to learn that the Japanese would come and have a look at these bombs: at least there was nothing to lose and perhaps a decision the way we wanted might emerge so I adjusted my programme to fit in with the Japanese ability to meet us. A day and time were fixed. My party would consist of myself and my Ammunition Specialist with whom I had a very lengthy discussion and briefed him on what he should say. He would comment only on the technical aspects and then only when asked. He preceded me to Peking, staying in the Legation. The Japanese party would be three, one of whom I assumed would be an Ammunition Technician. I duly left for Peking a day or so later after much cross-questioning at the Station from 'Smiler'. He seemed quite nonplussed when I said I was going to Peking to meet the Japanese; I suspected he was aware of this already. I had a comfortable journey to Peking but when I got out of the station, I was appalled at the size of the reception committee. There were literally thousands of people milling about in the square, with much shouting and hand waving. An enormous poster was being put up right across the Ch'ien Men gate, which said only:

'EXCLUDE THE BRITISH'

and that was what all the disturbance was about. They could not even spell! At this particular time we were at the height of the 'Get Rid of the British' campaign. Here I was in my best uniform, complete with stick and weekend case, and facing a howling mob that were inspired and backed by the Japanese. I wondered if I should stay in the railway station until things quietened down or make my way as quickly as I could to the Hotel des Wagon Lits. I literally could not wait and the longer I delayed making the decision, the worse matters might get, so out I went into the station yard to try and get transport of some kind. No taxi or rickshaw driver would accept me and I was just contemplating walking when I think it was then that 'Smiler's' opposite number came to my aid. 'Where did I want to go?' He spoke to the rickshaw pullers and eventually I struck a bargain with one of them to take me to my hotel. He was reluctant, and so was I, but it was no good hanging about, when all is said and done, the Japanese knew I was coming, and why, so they had some responsibility.

Away we went; I was surprised at the way the great crowded parted to let us through the station square and soon we were right under that poster 'Exclude the British' and through the Ch'ien Men gate. The crowds lessened as we turned into the road leading to the Legation Quarter, I breathed again, it was only a few hundred yards now to the hotel! Unfortunately, coming in the opposite direction was a roving gang of Chinese, obviously bent on making trouble. However, on we sped, it was not possible to turn back and my rickshaw puller was trying his best to get to the gateway of the American Legation where the full guard was deployed at the entrance, while I was urging him on, like a jockey in the Derby. We nearly made it and were only a few yards short when we met the mob head on. The puller was knifed, dropped the rickshaw shafts and I was catapulted out into the dusty road, clutching my stick. It all happened in seconds and so did the prompt action of the American guard who quickly came to my aid, picked me up, plus the rickshaw puller, his rickshaw and my case and dragged us into the Legation Guard room. I was badly shaken and had a couple of cuts and a dirty suit but I still had my cane! The rickshaw boy had a few stab wounds which the Americans dressed while I had a stiff brandy and a wash and brush up while we waited for proceedings to cool down. The Legation gate had been closed and there was a howling mob outside. I gathered that everyone was on the alert for expected trouble so they were not surprised at what had just taken place; in fact they had been expecting it. The Chinese had suddenly become inflamed with hate and I had arrived at quite the wrong time! When I was fit to proceed, and things quietened down, the Americans offered me an escort to my hotel, which I gladly accepted. I said goodbye to my rickshaw puller, reimbursed him as best I could for his injuries, and tendered my heartfelt thanks to the Americans for coming so speedily to my aid.

It was a shaken but thankful man who walked up the steps of the Wagon Lits. The Southern Chinese have a proverb 'Kind Friends are Better that Unkind Brothers'. The following day I was due to meet the Japanese and my feelings for them were not exactly fraternal; on the other hand, I had a job to do. I had managed to clean myself up and looked reasonably presentable. Bodily I was alright and I hoped I was mentally alert! I waited for them at the Legation gates while my Ammunition Specialist remained close to the magazine. The three of them arrived punctually and we went through the usual process of greetings. As I expected one was an explosives expert, one an interpreter and the third presumably a staff officer. I am sure they all spoke and understood English but only one would conduct the conversation with me, the others asked their questions through him. We made our way, in procession, to the magazine where I explained to them all about the mortar bombs and their dangerous condition and how they came to be in their present state. I called my Ammunitions Specialist over and introduced him and together we went down the steps to the doors of the magazine. The Japanese were reluctant to come with us and it seemed to me that they had fear of a trap or something of the sort. We unlocked the doors, opened them and went inside. Even then they did not seem to want to come but were arguing amongst themselves. Naturally, I took no part, just standing there waiting for them to make up their minds. At last they decided to come down and from the look on their faces it was obvious they thought the stuff would blow up any second. I wondered if we had overplayed our hand, but perhaps they were just being suspicious of something they did not understand, perhaps a booby trap. I have already described what the magazine looked like; it was even more uninviting today. It smelt even worse, the boxes looked even dirtier and more mud stained than ever, and the place spoke for itself, it did not need any assistance from me, quite the reverse. My Ammunition Specialist offered to open one of the boxes so they could see the contents inside. Would they please choose one? Not on your life, they were all for getting out and up the stairs, but a box was chosen and carried up the steps for a more detailed examination. My man displayed his skills and gave a short but competent and convincing lecture. They began to take to him and respect his professional ability to handle the stuff without fear. What sort of an explosion would it make? For how long would it be safe to move? Why did we want to throw it away? They explained to me that they had no authority to decide but would be prepared to listen to any suggestion or proposals I might have to make. I countered that we had repeatedly asked for permission to move this ammunition to Tientsin with a view to dumping it in the sea but all previous requests had been refused. We now proposed to make the bombs as safe as we could and leave them in the magazine. I was glad they had been able to see the problem. In fact, I assumed this was the reason they had come today. On the other hand, though we liked the idea less, the more time went by, we would still welcome their co-operation in getting the bombs dumped at sea while they could still be moved and while my Ammunition Specialist was available to me. They then asked, in a most roundabout way, a number of questions. In the main they boiled down to: 'What did we consider the safest way of transporting the bombs to Tientsin, and then out to sea'. I explained that rail would be best; we would load them into a truck at Peking Station (where they would be able to see what was happening), lock it with our own lock, and ask the railway authorities to attach it to an appropriate train. The truck would be unloaded by us and the contents delivered into our depot at the British Concession. We would then bring a small ship right up into our Concession and load the bombs which would have been made ready for sea dumping. If necessary I would be prepared to let my representative accompany the trucks and he too would supervise and accompany the bombs all the way to the dumping site. Even their inscrutable faces slipped a little and they appeared to be relieved at this apparent co-operation. As I bade them goodbye (Sayonara) at the Legation gates they wished me a pleasant stay in Peking, asking when I would be leaving. I explained that I had had a fall yesterday and should remain for the weekend before making my return to Tientsin and Shanghai. I would probably spend a day in the Western Hills and visit the Eunuch's Cemetery!

My ammunition man returned to Tientsin immediately and I got down to solving the 'minor' matters at the Legation Depot and visiting the small detachment of East Surrey Regiment stationed there. So much sightseeing was available and there was so much I should have liked to see in the small amount of time available but friends were able to take me on American tours of the Summer Palace, Coal Hill (reputed to be a huge supply of coal and a vantage point for the best views of Peking), the Temple of Heaven and the Altar of Heaven with their huge white marble terraces, Marco Polo Bridge, and many others. It would take weeks to digest all there was to see in Peking alone. I was getting worried about my family in Shanghai and wanted to get back quickly but I could not go by rail, only by ship, and my return passage was already booked on a sailing from Taku in a couple of days time. I collected presents for my wife and children, a petit point tapestry handbag and embroidery and cloisonné work, all made so beautifully in Peking. I stayed as long as I could in the hope the Japanese would contact me but to no avail. They were obviously in no hurry and I could not appear to be so either. These games of 'wait and see' and pretence, and of long drawn out and unhurried ritual must be understood and the rules abided by. How true I found are the words 'Slowly, slowly, catchy monkey'. Well, we had been waiting a long time and could bide a little longer, impatient though we may be! My return to Tientsin was uneventful but, as usual, I was 'accompanied'. 'Smiler' was, I am sure, glad to see me back! I had a day in the Tientsin Depot and things seemed sufficiently advanced that at least two of the staff were available for posting elsewhere. Good work. There was nothing from the Japanese at Tientsin either, so I briefed my Warrant Officer and Ammunition Specialist as to exactly what my intentions were so far as the Peking ammunition was concerned. If the Japanese agreed to it moving we would empty that Peking Magazine as quickly as possible and bring all of it to Tientsin. This would be the first stage which could be carried out whether I came or not. I covered all the contingencies previously referred to verbally and made sure my aim and purpose were well understood. Nothing must be done 'in anticipation'. My Warrant Officer and I discussed also the stores position at Peking and Shanhaikwan. He would take steps to withdraw anything that was likely to be of use, or required, from the Shanhaikwan Depot. Another trip was nearly completed. I was very satisfied with what others had achieved but of my own successes I was not so sure!

The Political Officer was made aware of the position and the steps which would be taken if the Japanese decision was in our favour. And so, back to Shanghai. The journey to Taku was uneventful but I was aware that I was being closely watched by a Russian who acted as a conductor in our coach on the journey by train. Events had been moving in Shanghai so far as the house was concerned. The question of the key money had been resolved; the place was ours; now all that remained was to get some furniture. My wife had already done a bit of preparatory work and had provisionally selected certain items so we were able to make a deal quickly. The best quotation I could get was for 4,000 dollars (Mex). It was an awful lot of money and more than I could really afford but my wife was sick and tired of hotel life and I could not afford that either so we took the plunge on the understanding that if and when I left Shanghai the seller would make me a reasonable offer for what I had bought. And so, in a couple of days we were installed in our new residence where my wife would be kept busy unpacking our boxes and making another new home as we had done so many times before. Everything seemed to be going our way! We said goodbye to the Palace Hotel. Our Cantonese Amah had returned to Hong Kong and we had engaged two Chinese boys in her place, one as a cook and the other as a handy man. My wife did not like the idea of male servants and I did not exactly 'take to them' either. Still, we now had a home of our own and that would make up for many shortcomings in other directions. The feeling and tensions in Shanghai were growing and on my very first journey by bus from my house in Route Fergusson to my office in Mohawk Road there was an incident with which I was to become familiar. Suddenly the bus stopped, it was surrounded by a contingent of Shanghai Municipal Police who boarded the bus to carry out a search. Everyone stood, hands high above one's head and we were frisked, one by one in a most thorough manner. It did not matter whether we were in uniform, or what our nationality, and there was a rare mixture, as might be expected in an international settlement. Every passenger was 'covered' from the back of the bus while the search went on and each searcher had an escort of two fully armed guards. Just as quickly as they had come, so they left, usually with someone caught with a weapon and no police certificate to cover it. I hardly ever seemed to make a bus journey without this procedure having to be gone through; it took a long time, was discourteous and often alarming when scuffles broke out, and all you could do was to stand perfectly still, looking to your front! All types of transport were subject to these searches so a taxi was not much advantage through for obvious reasons this mode of transport was favoured, particularly if more than one person was travelling. I often came this way from my house with my quartermaster friend from the hospital.

I had reported to my headquarters the results of my visit to the north and the position there, in particular with regard to the ammunition and the evacuation of stores. They were quite satisfied with the progress being made as indeed they had been recipients of many signals giving the day to day position and had already approved the contingency plans. I was soon to hear that the Japanese had agreed to the removal of the Peking mortar bombs to Tientsin and then their onward transit to the dumping area, and had offered any assistance that might be necessary. Excellent! So now my representatives in Tientsin would proceed as planned and signals were sent to them to this effect. I had every confidence in my staff; all I could do now was to hope all would go well; that we should not create an 'incident' (or 'accident') with all the attendant consequences, and wait in patience for a signal to say that the mission had been completed satisfactorily. I did not have long to wait; within a few days came the 'all clear'. Later I got a detailed report. The necessary trucks had been booked and were made available just when asked for; they were placed in a special position in the Peking Railway Yard as far away as possible from everything else. The Railway Authorities gave every assistance, my British staff supervised the loading in the Legation, another escorted each load to the station to which a free passage was given and my Ammunition Specialist loaded the stuff into the railway containers, locked and sealed them. It transpired that the railway people put empty trucks each side of the full ones and my Ammunitions Specialist travelled with the bombs down to Tientsin where he saw them unloaded under precisely similar circumstances into the Tientsin Magazine. I cannot speak too highly of the professional skill and competence shown by those involved in bringing this first part of the operation to such a successful conclusion. They are deserving of much praise and credit and I do so without reservation. Alas, later one was to give his life in the defence of Hong Kong while the Ammunition Specialist died of a brain haemorrhage in a Japanese POW camp. The question now was to get a suitable ship up to Tientsin to take the ammunition on board and the other surplus stores as well and to arrange for the dumping of the suspect and condemned mortar bombs. I waited with interest for approval to charter such a vessel.

Just about this time I received a threatening message written on rice paper and what appeared to be red ink, addressed to my office. The gist of this communication was that the British were not wanted in Shanghai, nor were our families, and if we did not get out immediately 'dire consequences would come our way!' This was a new line in intimidation I had not heard of before. I was about to send it to headquarters when the phone rang and I was instructed to attend a special conference the following day. We were aware that our phones were 'unreliable' so I did not mention the indication of coming evil that I had just received; I would take it with me. I looked a little more carefully when I returned home at the locked wrought iron gates of our dwelling and at the broken glass and barbed wire which surrounded the top of the walls. Yes, the place did look secure, I could not see how it could be made more so. When I got inside my wife handed me another rice paper letter which someone had pushed through the back gate and had been found by our Chinese boys. The children were playing so after a few minutes I was able to get away to our bedroom to change and open and study the contents of the latest epistle. Like the one I had received at my office this one too was written on rice paper and in red ink and contained a couple of gruesome drawings and a message to get my family out of Shanghai before tragedy overtook them. I did not sleep very well and I suspect my wife felt a little unsettled too though she had no knowledge of what the letter contained. I was a little reassured the following day when I arrived at HQ and found the commanding officers of all units were present for the meeting. I passed my communications over to the appropriate staff officer who said 'yes, all other COs had received identical letters and that was what the meeting was about.' Well, at least HQ would know what to do and would do it! They took the threat very seriously, so much so that arrangements were being made to issue to each one of us small calibre pistols to be carried at all times. Police patrols would take care of our houses as well, but we should be on our guard at all times. The children were escorted to and from school and for outside recreation we joined the American Columbia Country Club with its extensive lawns, tennis courts, swimming pool, etc and situated only a short distance by car from our house. The next few days passed without further incident.

On my next visit to HQ I was told that arrangements were being made to get the SS *Lee Sang* to undertake the Tientsin task as soon as present commitments had been completed and I should go to Tientsin to supervise the loading, etc as envisaged in the original plan. The French were being told and invited to take advantage of this opportunity to get their ammunition out at the same time, should they so wish. All they had to do was to move it over into our Concession and we would evacuate it along with our own. The SS *Lee Sang* would take a cargo to Taku and Tientsin, offloading part at Taku to lighten ship and then proceed half empty to Tientsin where the balance would be discharged. I could time my arrival at Tientsin to fit in with these arrangements. Naturally, I did not want to be away from Shanghai any longer than was absolutely necessary but I was satisfied that the arrangements made for taking care of my family were such that my own presence would only add comfort. My wife accepted the position with misgivings, but duty came first. I booked my passage by fast ship to Chinwangtao, then by train, to coincide with the arrival in Tientsin of the SS *Lee Sang*.

As we sailed into Chinwangtao harbour I was amazed to see the whole of the mountains, which previously had been brown and cold and inhospitable looking, were now purple; in fact even the golf course was purple. I could not understand it, it must be a trick of the sun, but when I got ashore I found there were violets, millions and millions of them, as far as the eye could see. It was then I realised how productive the land was and how beautiful the surroundings would be in full summer, a pleasure not to be missed, like the seashore summer bungalows at Peitaho[33] surrounded by flowering shrubs of all kinds and mulberry bushes galore, a summer resort of great charm. Soon I was back again at the Court Hotel with its menu of quail and woodcock and a general Victorian air. The SS *Lee Sang* was berthed quite close to the hotel so I walked round and had a few words with the captain and chief officer to get some idea when they would be ready to load. They were aware of the nature of the task and looking forward to it and to the company of my ammunition specialist who would go with them and assist with the 'dumping' of the now notorious mortar bombs. All was well in the depot, too, with a sizeable cargo of stores all ready to go, along with a large quantity of small arm ammunition and the bombs which would be the last to be loaded. I saw the political officer about the French ammunition but it seemed they did not wish to send it by a British ship and instead wanted it put on one of their own. Perhaps it was a matter of distrust or patriotism but they were hardly going to get a better opportunity than this. However, the decision was final and it was anyhow their affair and henceforward nothing to do with us. There might be advantages in not having it around in the British Concession as it was quite certain the Japanese, or their agents, would be watching just what was being loaded even though they would undoubtedly inspect the ship's manifest a couple of miles down river where they were wont to hold up ships for no apparent reason.

The Japanese were well aware of the reason the SS *Lee Sang* was being brought to Tientsin; it was indeed in accordance with the approval they had given that the bombs would be loaded there together with other ordnance stores, but there was not much they could do while the ship was in the British Concession except to have their spies watch what was going on. The loading commenced with a small military staff deployed on this task. The security forces were of course in the background and giving a helping hand. I did not anticipate any difficulty where stores were concerned though I knew the Japanese spies would be watching every move, so I spent a sizeable amount of time on view and getting rid of unwanted sightseers. The ammunition specialist was there too, for all to see, and he would personally supervise the loading of the ammunition

items including the mortar bombs. We had no objection to
the spies seeing them! Soon everything was aboard without
a hitch worth recording and SS *Lee Sang* was ready to sail.
The testing time would come when she moved down river.
It was not unusual for ships to be held up for interminable lengths of time while the Japanese inspected, looked
through the ship's papers and generally prevaricating for
days before allowing ships to proceed, and of course exer-
cising their 'right' to confiscate any cargo which they took
objection to or just 'caught their fancy'. Need I stress, once
again, that relations were bad and that we were completely
in their hands and could do nothing about it except, perhaps, try to beat them at their own game. Well, away went
the *Lee Sang* with all our hopes and best wishes. It was good
to see it go, the culmination of much hard work by my staff
in Tientsin and Peking over weeks and months, and carrying every bit of cargo that could be got on board. It is quite
surprising how easily and according to plan this facet of the
evacuation had gone. There were no snags at all and looking back it seemed to have been child's play. The stores and
ammunition would be invaluable to the stations to which
they were going. My ammunition specialist would be 'on
view' on deck during daylight hours all the way down the
river until the ship crossed the Taku Bar[34] and safely out to
sea. All I wanted now to know was that 'The Bar Had Been
Crossed'. I was in close touch with the shipping agents and
the political officer for all the latest news. We did not have
long to wait before it was announced that the *Lee Sang*
had been given only a cursory inspection at the first stop-
ping point, having been quickly waved on by the Japanese.
They certainly did not like those mortar bombs and could
not get rid of them quickly enough. Similarly there was
no hold up at Taku either. Now I could get back to my
family in Shanghai so I confirmed my provisional booking
on a ship sailing from Taku the next day. (I could not go by
the *Lee Sang* for the obvious reason that this time she was
not calling at Shanghai). A quick run round the depot with

thanks to those who had contributed to the success of this operation and instructions to my warrant officer on what to do next. I seemed to have been away from Shanghai for such a short time but much had been happening. I gave my latest report to HQ who were pleased to know events had gone so easily and without any friction. They had of course played a major part in all that had been going on, I was really only the front man, plus of course advisor where ordnance services were concerned.

Further threatening letters had been received both by my wife and at my office; they had been collected and sent to headquarters; there was also a message to say that the bombs had been successfully dumped. I was told later that even this operation had been watched. It seemed too that the removal of the East Surrey garrisons at Peking and Tientsin was imminent. Well, I had anticipated these events and action was already in hand. Lastly my chief from Hong Kong was coming up to see me and would make a grand tour of all the installations. It seemed that, as soon as I got back from one trip north, I had to plan for another. I was certainly half separated from my family in what was obviously a rapidly deteriorating situation. I collected my small calibre revolver after having been given a little instruction on its use and firing a few rounds 'just to get used to it'. I did not like the idea of carrying a weapon in Shanghai at all times and I felt I would really much prefer to put my trust in my short stick which had served me so well up to now, particularly up north, but anyhow I would be carrying my stick as well so perhaps I should get the best of both! I wondered how my wife would take it when I told her I should have the revolver with us in the bedroom, probably under my pillow! I learned that the French ammunition had been sent by train from Tientsin to Taku for loading onto a French ship but unfortunately the Japanese had stopped it there and I gather had confiscated it. Well, sometimes you are lucky and sometimes not. I felt sorry for the French but even more so for their troops in Indo-China who could have done with it! My wife was not exactly overjoyed when I explained things to her, the news that the Hong Kong families might be evacuated had got around which in turn had further unsettled the womenfolk in Shanghai. The fact we were in an international settlement was little satisfaction to a woman whose husband never seemed to be there and she was left so frequently 'to hold the fort' in a hostile and foreign land. Her concern was not for herself but for our children, and after them, for me. She could and would cope with adversity from whatever quarter it came. The abusive notes continued to arrive and after a few days so did the ADOS[35] China Command who did a detailed tour of the Shanghai depositions, and by this time a negligible Ordnance Depot. He was bent on seeing the sights and a little of the night life so I found myself having to dine with him and then act as guide. At least I did get home to sleep, but only just! It was common practice amongst the civilian population of Shanghai to leave the office in the early afternoon, have a quick game of squash or tennis, etc and then a few hours sleep before the evening session commenced. The sleeping and waking portions were divided into four distinct periods, two of each. I never became accustomed to this way of life; I much preferred eight hours solid sleep to two stints of four hours each. Getting up when one ought to be going to bed was not to my liking; still that was the way things were done in Shanghai and, if you wanted to keep up with the 'fleshpots of life', that appeared to be the way to do it. Everyone was living on a tightrope and most thought there was an escape in large doses of pleasure whether it was food, women, wine, dancing, cabaret shows or a combination of any of them. The novelty soon wore off and my chief and I were able to recuperate with a couple of nights 'shut eye' on a completely blacked out steamer heading for Taku. I was beginning to be quite well known in these parts, and the faces beamed as we stepped off the boat. They always seemed to think I was going the wrong way and of course wanted to know why. The sight of a very senior ordnance

officer accompanying me undoubtedly set the tongues wag-
ging and the signal apparatus too. This ensured we would
be accompanied and watched even more closely. My boss
was particularly interested in the Japanese army caps which
laced up at the back like shoes and thus could be made to fit
practically any size of head, and he took every opportunity
to get them to remove their head-dress for his inspection.
Why didn't we go in for something like that?

Our arrival at Tientsin too caused a stir; it was not often
that such a senior officer was seen wandering about. Well,
we left cards at Japanese headquarters and my boss was
given a special interview after being kept waiting for a considerable period. He was rapidly revising his ideas on things
Japanese. He had not taken kindly to the spy who travelled with us from Taku to Tientsin. 'Smiler', whose fame
had gone before him was quite another matter. When they
met I thought they might have been long lost brothers!
The inspection of the depot and my staff there did not take
long, for the simple reason that there was not much left to
inspect. The military staff was interviewed one by one; they
appreciated someone coming all that way to see them and
hear their complaints, and to compliment them as well.
And the civilian staff could see their fate staring them in
the face; they needed to be consoled and thanked too! It
was about this time that we heard that all the Hong Kong
families were being sent to Manila en route for Australia
and the colony was being put on a war footing. If anything
happened we certainly were out on a limb in Tientsin. We
debated whether to return immediately to our respective
stations but assumed we should have been ordered to do
so if things were all that bad, so it was decided to proceed
with the tour but shorten it as much as possible. And so
to Peking and the Grand Hotel des Wagon Lits. I showed
my chief the now empty Legation Magazine, and my sergeant there explained just what he did. They got on like a
house on fire, and this was the pattern in Hong Kong when
the sergeant went there. From Peking we went through to

Shanhaikwan via Tientsin and down that narrow gauge railway. On each side of the line corn had been planted and it was then nearly six feet high; as we passed down the line it seemed just like proceeding through a tunnel, so close was the corn to the line. There were no incidents until we arrived at the end of the line and raised the Union Jack on our Flag staff. It was then that I noticed some fifty or more men playing games on our beach below. They were Italians – on our beach! I stood, stick under arm, on the best vantage point I could find and shouted to the intruders to get off our beach, at the same time pointing to the flag. They were loath to go but started hurried consultations. I was standing, high above them, waiting for action when they very reluctantly withdrew to a much inferior beach a little further up the coast. My chief was intrigued at this ironical situation and the way we flew our national flag at every opportunity, even on that small truck pulled by our Mongolian pony. He gave approval for the disposal by sale, burning or dumping of the balance of stock as he had done at Tientsin and Peking. The task completed, we took the train to Taku. Nearing our destination we passed miles and miles of salt pans on our seaward side. Each area was flooded in turn, then allowed to drain away leaving a modicum of salt behind, and so the never-ending process went on as it had done for thousands of years.

Our journey to Shanghai was uneventful. We parted, my chief back to Hong Kong and me, to my family. We consoled ourselves that perhaps this would have been my last visit up north and we should have a chance to get settled down in Shanghai. At least everything that could be done had been accomplished and it was now just a matter of acting on the approvals given. I found I was able to take a more active part in family affairs and felt relieved that my seemingly never-ending trips to the north were over, for the time being at least. The situation in Shanghai was, however, increasingly uneasy but it is surprising what one can become accustomed to and take in one's stride. I did

not take the notes I received at both office and home too
seriously though they arrived with great regularity and in
many kinds of ways and the threats became more dire and
the drawings more vivid. They seemed to be running out
of red ink; some were now in blue, with dollops of red here
and there, probably animal blood. There was practically no
work for me to do (or my staff either for that matter) so
I became a member of a couple of recreation clubs on the
race course just by my office. It was very useful as, apart
from tennis, etc there was always something going on
inside the racecourse perimeter, and it was a safe place for
the children to play and meet their friends; and of course
there were the frequent race meetings. I did not like them
half as well as in Hong Kong where the atmosphere was
leisurely and friendly and the band played amid banks of
flowers. Here the racing was for gambling, sometimes in
a big way, and the social side did not seem to be encouraged in quite the same manner. Most people were strangers
but I did make friends with a couple of the amateur jock-
eys who introduced me to Pelota[36] and dog racing at the
Canidrome. This too was purely a gambling business; it was
not in my line and I did not enjoy it! However, one of
them was a White Russian who had spent his childhood in
Harbin, or thereabouts, and whose parents had left Russia
at the time of the revolution. He and his wife knew all
about the north and had a financial interest in a couple of
holiday homes on the beach somewhere near Inch'on on
the Korean coast. This seemed to be the 'poor man's holiday resort'. It was the custom, during the three hot summer
months, for the civilian Shanghai wives and families and
servants to be transported north where the sea was clear,
the beaches clean, and flowers and fruit grew in abundance. There was a general exodus around July, August and
September. The families stayed as long as they could; the
husbands went up for a few days or weeks as and when they
were able. I had already sounded out the select and fashion-
able holiday resorts with a view to getting my family out of

Shanghai for a week or two but all were either full up or much too expensive for my pocket, so Korea, if the price was right, seemed to be the answer. What is more I could perhaps fit in a few days on my way to Tientsin and again on the way back. Certainly I would not be missed in Shanghai where I was virtually kicking my heels. My children were delighted at the possibility of a few weeks at the seaside; my wife would 'think about it'. The matter of sleeping with a pistol under my pillow had now become routine; the novelty had worn off even though the risks seemed to have increased somewhat. The nights were warm and sleep did not come easily so I did not need much wakening by the sound of gunfire which came from the direction of Avenue Haig, perhaps somewhere near to the Chinese University. There was not much at first, then it steadily grew and grew; a first class machine-gun battle appeared to be going on and it seemed to get nearer and nearer. By now we were all dressed. I was glad there were no windows on the side from which the firing was coming as this was the gable end and there was only a small window looking in that direction downstairs at the back. Just as well because at that moment that end of our house was sprayed with gun fire. I did not think they were after me, or my family; a little more than a few fire crackers would have perhaps been enough to overcome our position, it was not exactly a bastion of defence with our armament one small pistol and half a dozen rounds of ammunition. Gradually the firing drew further and further away and the noise fainter and fainter until at last it was gone, and the first shafts of daylight came instead. We were a bit unsettled and on edge and my wife did not like the idea of our daughter going off to school but the taxi came as usual, together with her school friends, and soon she was away. Our Chinese boys were a bit subdued, too, so I waited a while until things were a little more normal before I went out to inspect the damage. There was a line of bullet holes about four feet from the ground and running the length of our building and beyond. I concluded that someone must have been occupying the open area between the house and the junction of Avenue Haig and Avenue Joffre and was receiving 'the treatment'. The French were responsible for our area; nevertheless I called at headquarters on my way to Mohawk Road. Yes, they had heard of it, a large band of marauding Chinese were undoubtedly responsible. This was not the first time we had heard gunfire, we were quite accustomed to it but this was the first time it had been so close and though it continued nightly (and sometimes by day) this was the only time the whole family was 'under fire'.

The more I thought of the seaside in Korea the keener I got, so I rang my amateur jockey friend at the business house where he worked about that bungalow by the sea. He and his wife would be going and so, too, would a few of the members of the recreation club we both frequented on the racecourse and we agreed tentative dates and a price which was quite reasonable. Furthermore, living in Korea was cheap and the rate of exchange in our favour. The idea grew and grew in its attractiveness and only my wife needed to make up her mind. I had many touches of remorse as I thought about the folk at home and what they might be doing for holidays, and even more about what they were doing for the war effort, and of my friends on the continent fighting what was, so far, a phoney war; and of those on the Western Desert in Africa who had their backs to the wall while we, though so obviously sitting on a powder keg, were nevertheless living in the lap of luxury and even contemplating taking a holiday. It was a sobering thought and helped me to get my own situation in its right perspective. I really wasn't contributing much to the war effort for which I had trained for twenty years, I really did not have a job, or much of one, and I felt sure my sergeant in charge of the Shanghai Depot could have done it just as well. Why was I wasting my time here when my qualifications demanded I should be elsewhere? I had long realised I was caught like a rat in a trap, being fattened up ready for the killing, and there was nothing I could do about it. I needed work but there was so little. I checked every aspect of my minute charge, there was nothing I could improve upon. I went over future plans which I knew off by heart and threw myself once again into a round of visits to units. Were they alright from an ordnance point of view? Had they too much or too little, was it all fit for war? Could I help in any way? I knew the answers before they were given. It seemed the hardest work on hand was throwing dice for drinks before lunch at the Long Bar in the Shanghai Club or in one of the officer's messes. I was worried about my wife and family too. All the Hong Kong families were now in Australia where mine should be as well. That Korean holiday was an escape route out of the tense Shanghai situation. I pondered on what difference it would make if we were caught in Shanghai, Peking or Korea, or for that matter anywhere in East Asia. Yes, they would be better off in Korea, for a short time at least, and when they came back the position might have eased as I had seen it do in North China. I would try to persuade my wife to go to Korea where she would be free from the tenseness and the daily threats, and the now regular bouts of gunfire, robbings, etc and where the only noise would be the lapping of the sea on beaches of silver sand.

Army life is full of planning; it is a constant process of plan, counter plan, contingency plan and then start all over again because the basic assumptions have changed. My life was like that too, except that I needed two sets, sometimes three to cover family and self, and just when I thought that holiday arrangements were complete so there was a change of direction and impetus. The Shanghai situation had been and was rapidly deteriorating, together with that in the whole of East Asia; it did not need a practised eye to see this and I pondered over the consequences and possible moves as I made my way to headquarters for one of the frequent meetings of commanding officers. Obviously something was afoot; we did not have long to wait. All families would

be evacuated to Australia in a few days time; the Eastern &
Australian Steamship Company's SS *Tanda* was on her way
from Japan to pick them up. The North China Garrison and
Legation Guard would be withdrawn and the installations
closed down. The two infantry battalions in Shanghai and
ancillary troops were being withdrawn, and all installations
closed. Appropriate instructions would be issued separately.
That was all! Would I arrange to go to North China as soon
as possible to arrange and supervise the closing there, and
then take similar action at Shanghai. Well, well, well! I did
not know whether to laugh or cry. I had work to do at last,
but I should be losing my wife and family, perhaps for good
and certainly it would be a long, long time before we should
meet again; nevertheless I was glad, very glad, that soon they
would be safe and I hoped out of all possible danger. This
mattered most of all to me. When it was appropriate I told
my wife. I am sure I did not need to do so; she had already
sensed the relief I felt that the tension was now nearly all
over. We talked about where she would stay: Melbourne,
Sydney, Hobart; of the financial provision I would make;
of the children's education; and how we should dispose of
the furniture and where I would stay. Yes, she too had her
planning system capable of adjustment to the vagaries and
sudden changes of Army life, and like the camp followers
of old could alter direction just as quickly and effectively,
but Australia was a long way off, further than she had ever
been from both home, and me. She did not want to leave
me, she would prefer to stay and face the future and problems together, but there was the matter of the children and
the fact that she had no choice but to go and what was
more, I wanted her to go! It seemed a little easier when
put that way, so she got on with the packing and I went to
the Ordnance Depot to initiate arrangements there, deciding what we would evacuate and what we would sell locally.
The days and nights passed so quickly now that we could
see some light and I nearly forgot about the Japanese who
were the cause of our parting and discomfort. My wife and

children embarked on the SS *Tanda* on 23 August 1940 and sailed on the 24th for Hong Kong, Manila, Rabaul, Brisbane, Sydney and Melbourne, arriving there on 23 September. From the passenger list that my wife kept and which I now have, I see there were twenty-eight first saloon passengers, including the wife of my sergeant. Never did I imagine the relief I should feel at the departure of this ship down the Whangpoo River on 24 August or the tremendous sadness and bitterness, it would leave behind. All I knew was they were going away to a safe place, where they would be looked after and cared for by our own kith and kin.

As I returned to my room at the Palace Hotel I could feel nothing but thankfulness they had gone; now I could throw myself into the task in hand of finally closing down my depots at Peking, Tientsin, Shanhaikwan and Shanghai. I was amused recently to find a note in my wife's papers, written by me to her in pencil on Palace Hotel notepaper and dated 26 August 1940, two days after she sailed from Shanghai, and addressed to her in Cabin 21. A friend going to Hong Kong would overtake them there, and he did. The last sentence reads, 'I am missing you, but know it's all for the best', and I was reminded of the Chinese proverb which says, 'Days of sorrow pass slowly; times of joy very quickly'. The two infantry battalions would take with them to Singapore all their vehicles, equipment and ammunition, and would leave behind only those items which were peculiar to the Shanghai task, and of course barrack and training stores. This reduced considerably the work of my small depot; nevertheless all of it had to be gone through to decide what should be sold and what should be sent away. Obviously all warlike and worthwhile stores, including hospital equipment, should go to Hong Kong or Singapore while the very part worn barrack stores, most of which had been locally procured and made, would be sold. In my plans I had listed both categories in some detail, based on what the two theatres had said they wanted. Similar plans were held in Tientsin to be acted on there. Nothing much could

be done until the units had gone so it was decided I should
go north in the first place; my warrant officer there would
be getting on with the job! The only military personnel
left would be the Royal Corps of Signals wireless operators
who would in future form part of the civilian Legation staff
and who were to be 'civilianised' by the withdrawal of their
uniform. (When war broke out later they were, I understand, interned in Manchuria.) Shanhaikwan as it had been
known for so long was now no more. The Union Flag had
been hoisted and lowered for the last time and I would be
the last British officer to stand at the end of the Great Wall
with his stick under his arm and salute the passing of a camp
of 'happy memories' for so many. At Tientsin, sure enough,
'Smiler' was waiting. 'Why have you come?' he asked, 'all
British have gone away'. In as forceful a manner as I could
I told him I was the advance party of the new contingent
and I should be going to Peking tomorrow. I do not know
what he or his headquarters would make of that. Perhaps
I was not very convincing. And so, to the Court Hotel for
the last time.

The work of disposal at Tientsin was proceeding apace,
most of the wanted items were packed, or nearly so, and
sales of the unwanted gear was proceeding. The position at
Peking was even more advanced. A few decisions needed to
be taken at both places; this of course is why I had come!
And so to Peking and the Hotel des Wagon Lits. 'Smiler'
was of course in attendance and for the last time I was to
be escorted, trying to put a brave face on a very sad heart.
I talked to the signals chappies who were in good spirits
and not a bit perturbed or daunted about their role as 'civilians'. Capable men, whether in uniform or civvies! We
relieved them of the former! At Tientsin I discussed all outstanding matters with my representative who, with what
was left of his staff, would be going to Hong Kong in a
few days. I learned the French ammunition was still at Taku.
Well, this was the end of an era. We (the ordnance in all its
progressions) had been present here for many decades; the

corps had become well known and respected. Only the best material had been sent to this outpost of the empire where they had conducted themselves correctly and with dignity, and where we had established for ourselves a name second to none. Down the years many servicemen had given their lives here for their country. They had come because of trade which had flourished to the benefit not only of ourselves but to the inhabitants as well. So often it is said that we battered the natives, took their land and their possessions and gave little in return except cruelty. How distorted these sentiments are, and how grossly we, as a nation, are misrepresented. We had provided stability in all its forms, created an atmosphere of understanding, of fairness, of justice and of safety. Even to the end I had felt secure and respected though armed only with a stick. I, too, was trading on the foundations of respect and trust built up over so many years. It was a sad day for me, for my corps and for Britain and I am sure for the Chinese when I took my leave as the last serving officer to depart from North China.

Back in Shanghai events had been moving swiftly; the battalions had gone and so pretty well had all the stores we wanted to get away. The work of collecting furniture and barrack stores into lots at two dumps, one at the late barracks of the East Surrey Regiment in Great Western Road/Bubbling Well Road and one on the racecourse, was proceeding in accordance with the instructions of the local auctioneer who was our guide as to how we could make most money. We discussed together the final makeup of each 'Lot'. I examined the goods with interest. Many were marked with the date of purchase and it was surprising how many items were still quite serviceable though often well worn; nothing was 'new'. We were even able to say from whom they had been bought, and the price, way back in 1927 when they had been procured locally for the original Shanghai Defence Force of which I had been a member! They were not wanted and had certainly done their duty! Then, the first of the sales commenced. Together with other officers concerned with the sale I took my place armed with my catalogue marked up with prices we hoped each lot might make and a few policemen to keep order and of course the auctioneers and army staff. It was surprising how many people had come, of every nationality, and a large contingent of Britishers who did not usually attend such affairs, according to the auctioneer. The first few lots went for prices above those we had set, much to our satisfaction, and each succeeding lot sold for more and more. The local British press had long been exhorting nationals to 'Help the War Effort' and this was one way of doing it. What is more, they only wanted perhaps one or two of the items from the purchased lot and left the balance for re-sale. The sale was making far more than the goods had originally cost, and we had had their use for years.

This enthusiasm on the part of patriotic Britishers, and others, had disadvantages as, in accordance with the terms of sale, the buyer had some days to remove his purchases and there were (thought to be legal) problems where the whole of the purchased lot was not removed in the time specified, and it was left for re-sale. The effect of these unforeseen developments was to slow down the sales and thus put back the date of our final departure. The auctioneer introduced new tactics to overcome the difficulties but we still found we were selling the same items over and over again and making for the government a very handsome profit on goods which otherwise might have been abandoned or burned! It was hard, tiring work over many days of long hours; time only for food and sleep. Strange how in life the unexpected so often happens and plans and expectations do not materialise. However, we did make headway; as we proceeded, so the number of personnel was progressively reduced, and when I went to my office in Mohawk Road for the last time and collected the remaining papers, only a handful of us remained. A few days operating from my bedroom in the Palace Hotel and it was all over; the evacuation was complete. There were no parties, no jollifications and no goodbyes as I slipped away quietly in my taxi to the ship which would take me to Hong Kong. I had no regrets about leaving Shanghai; it was not my style of life. Money there was, in plenty; most of the larger stores printed their own, each with its daily fluctuating values. I thought of the original corps members of the Shanghai Defence Force who came to keep the peace in 1927 and set up our headquarters in Museum Godown, of Jessfield Park, Mom's Cabaret, the Charleston, of plush living and extreme poverty and gun battles, and of the song which was all the rage when we came out in 1927 and which echoed from each ship as we passed through the Suez Canal 'Bye Bye Blackbird!' and of the parody sung again when troops left for home, the last lines of which were:

Fairest of the fairest Russian beauties,
By the troops you sure have done your duties
Make my bed and light the light, I'll be home late tonight
Shanghai, bye bye!
Shanghai, bye bye!

I was not the last to leave; that questionable honour was for another; I was next to last. My chief, in his official account sent to the War Office, contained the following extract about the closing of ordnance installations in North China:

During the whole of the period our relations with the Japanese were bad. Everything they could do to interfere with our Military Services they did. All movement of stores was extremely difficult and in most cases Japanese permission had to be asked. However, the closing of the RAOC Establishments at Shanghai, Tientsin and Shanhaikwan was effected by Capt. V.S. Ebbage and the work was very well done.

RETURN TO HONG KONG

September 1940

Shortly after my arrival back in Hong Kong I was promoted to captain and given the job of OC Section (which
meant I commanded, and was responsible for, some 130-
odd RAOC, their welfare, training, discipline, feeding,
housing, etc) and as a secondary job that of Officer i/c
Provision and Local Purchase, not at that time a very oner-
ous charge, plus of course the clearing up of the various
depot accounts from North China and sending them to the
auditor. My North China staff was engaged on this work.
I had spoken to my chief about my eventual release and
return to the United Kingdom, where I felt I would be
more use to the war effort instead of doing unfamiliar work
in this subsidiary backwater, and had received the response
I expected. He was even more forthright in his answer
than I am reputed to be: 'No! Not so long as I remain in
Command! Get that idea out of your head! Haven't I told
you that before?' I knew, as others had learned, not to argue.
I was now directly under the 'Eye'. I was living in the
Harbour View Hotel on the mainland while I worked two
rickshaw and a ferry journey away on the island. What was
more, all my club connections, sporting and social, were
over there as well, close to where I had previously lived.
The hotel was frugal and lonely. Others had found it so
and after their wives had been evacuated had formed small
communes of four or more with their own servants where
they lived and entertained more economically. I visited one
or two but they really did not appeal to me, a bit too noisy
and 'fresh'. On the other hand, some like one of my brother
officers (and a friend of my family) and me, were still living
alone in the flat he previously occupied with his wife and
children – 'Keeping it on really, just in case the family come
back'. And so we joined forces, cutting our travelling time
and expenses by hiring a flat in the same block where I had
lived with my own family and furnishing it partly with my

possessions and partly with his whilst putting the balance in store. What is more, our previous family Amah who went with us to Shanghai joined us; she was a mature, reliable and capable person and also a good cook, and had served us well for over two years. My wife thought a lot of her.

My friend was a jovial, happy-go-lucky fellow whose good fortune and exuberant spirits never deserted him; always the life and soul of the party. We had been friends and had served together in stations in England and Scotland and worked in adjoining offices. We both played indifferent golf and tennis and enjoyed going to the races. Now we were only a few hundred yards from all three and football and social clubs as well! I needed someone around who had a bit of luck and hoped some would rub off on me! We settled down easily and quickly and were able to entertain our friends, mostly government employees, home and local, and visited them frequently. Most weeks we had lunch and dinner at the home of my friend, the superintendent of Dockyard Police, or he with us, and we joined forces when out of hours duty visits to naval and military establishments were needed. The resultant car trips round the island were a pleasant interlude and bonus.

Prior to my return to Hong Kong a draft of about thirty militia men had arrived from England; they were completely untrained; they replaced a similar number of highly trained personnel needed in the UK. They were extraordinary, nice, young men, ready and willing to tackle anything but, alas, without the knowledge to do so. My predecessor set in motion various activities designed to rectify this unhappy state. He had borrowed a musketry instructor from the nearest infantry battalion to impart rifle firing instruction to them and simultaneously with my arrival they had all gone to the ranges to fire a course. It had not been a success for the very simple reason that a typhoon developed and this resulted in none of them qualifying. When I reported the results to headquarters

I asked that in view of the adverse conditions obtaining when they fired their course, that they be given some further instruction and an extra allowance of ammunition so they could fire the course again. To my utter surprise this was refused. Apparently all the ammunition available for training purposes was required for those soldiers who would be required to fight in the defence of the colony and that did not include men of the RAOC. I was surprised and astounded; was it the intention that we should not be allowed even to defend our own installations? It seemed quite outrageous and unreasonable to me. What was the point of having soldiers if they were not to be allowed to fight? My mind went quickly back to the days in 1924 when I had been company sergeant major at Burscough, Lanes and the Area GOC[37] had done his annual inspection of the unit and had said of it something like, 'This is a good unit, but the soldierly bearing leaves much to be desired; they are primarily soldiers and secondarily tradesmen; I will inspect them again in three months' time'. And the comments of the GOC of the command who said, 'I do not agree; on my recent inspection of this unit, I found their soldier-like bearing quite satisfactory, they are primarily tradesmen and secondarily soldiers'. Was this argument still going on? It seemed obvious to me that if and when Hong Kong was attacked, everyone would be needed to defend it, not only with rifles but with machine guns and every other kind of weapon that was available to us. Were we still non-combatant troops?

I would ask for an interview at headquarters with the training officer; I felt sure he was a very reasonable and sensible man who perhaps only needed convincing! My immediate commanding officer was the DADOS[38] Hong Kong, a lieutenant colonel and an ex-infantry officer, an extremely nice but efficient man who fitted the caption of being 'primarily a soldier'; he had certainly become highly proficient in martial arts before recently transferring to the RAOC. We would go together to headquarters to argue the case for extra ammunition needed by the militia men in order to re-fire their course. We both agreed this was the minimum acceptable to us; we should have liked them trained on machine guns as well! The headquarters' training officer listened to us with interest and some sympathy but there just was not any ammunition available to us for training: 'As we must well know, the allowance was limited and there were others with higher claims.' In war we would undoubtedly expend ammunition, without training we were ineffective, we would be sitting targets for the Japanese. What about all that small arms ammunition I had extracted from North China under the very eyes of the Japanese and which was surely a bonus? All our pleadings were of no avail and I returned from this, to me most unsatisfactory interview, with deep forebodings. Yes, indeed, we were out on a limb, hostages to fortune in every sense. Everyone knew, as I did, that sooner or later the Japanese would come; were they not only a few miles away now, on the border on the other side of the Shum Chum River,[39] that mere trickle of water that was our frontier.

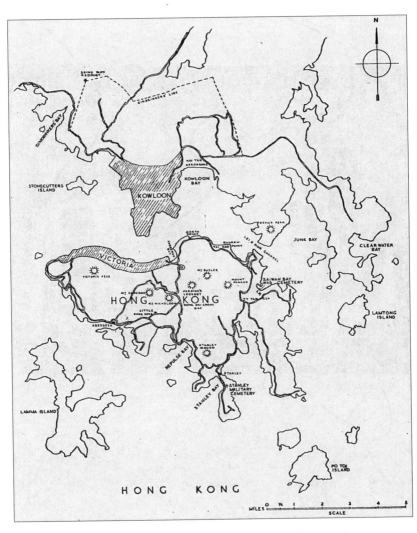

Map of Hong Kong, taken from the Saiwan Bay Memorial leaflet, *c.* 1955. The leaflet was produced by the Commonwealth War Graves Commission to mark the opening of the military cemetery in Hong Kong. (RLC Museum)

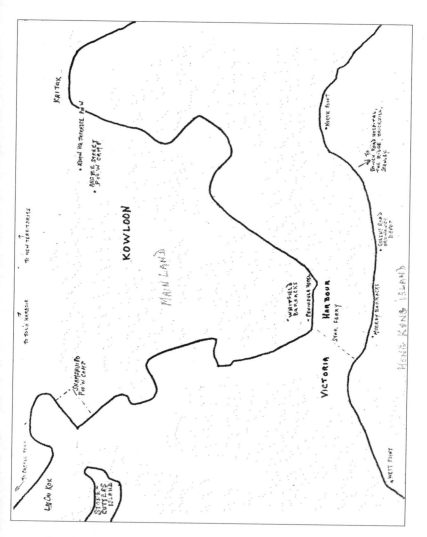

Rough outline map of Kowloon, showing positions of Shamshuipo and Argyle Street POW Camps, hand-drawn by the author. (RLC Museum)

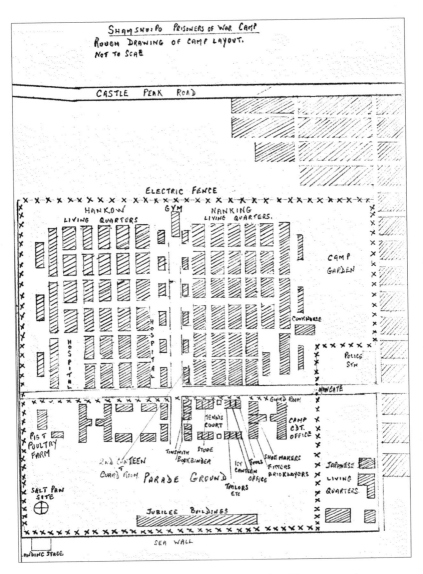

This hand-drawn map of Shamshuipo Camp was produced from memory by the author in the 1980s. (RLC Museum)

1

Chaos

Murray Barracks on the island of Hong Kong was, on 29 December 1941 a hive of activity; I had arrived late on the previous day a weary man, my sole possessions the clothes I stood up in.[1] But, I was amongst friends and they had made me welcome, and I had explained what had happened at the Ridge, and to me afterwards.[2] They had rigged me out, as best they could, from the quartermasters' store of the Royal Scots with blankets, underclothing, towels and money, and now it was suggested I take as much food, cigarettes and anything else that I wanted, because, rumour had it that on the very next day we were being moved out of Murray Barracks to another more permanent camp. I certainly entered into the spirit of a 'free for all' and collected a whole mass of stuff, and this included kit bags, a pack and webbing straps, etc. I expected that, wherever we were to go we should be required to hump our own baggage; the Japanese did not disappoint me in this!

The evening was spent in going through the miscellaneous items I had collected, many were not really what I wanted, and some did not fit, but I was so late in arriving that I had perforce to take what others did not want. Still, I had acquired a hefty lot, far more than I could carry; perhaps the Japanese would provide some form of transport or allow us to pay for it, I could only hope so. Previously,

I had asked my friends to try to get a message out that I was alive and well, and they had done their best to do so, but it was believed that all wireless transmitting sets had been destroyed.[3] My sleeping quarters were in what had been part of the officers' mess of the Royal Scots; an imposing building overlooking a very noisy main road. It was here that I came across one or two items which certainly did not weigh very much, but might be useful in the future, so put them with my accumulation of kit! I had a very good night's sleep, the first for a very long time, aided by a full stomach of good food and a glass or two of whisky and beer; the last to pass my lips for very many months!

On 30 December 1941, sure enough we were herded together in batches, with our gear, and told we were permitted to take only what we could carry. This produced wholesale dumping of all manner of things and provided me with an opportunity to cast out some of my hoard and replace with other more suitable items. My pack was filled with food and underwear items, with, strapped onto it two brand new woolen blankets, while my haversack contained such essential items as a mess tin, knife, fork and spoon, cigarettes, small kit items, and other sundries. I believed I could carry it all, but how far? We made a slow and pitiful procession towards the Star Ferry,[4] watched by many sorrowful looking Chinese and nationals of other countries who gave what practical help they could, or were allowed to give. The ferry journey provided a much needed rest; I was badly out of condition but determined to take what I had got, all the way, whatever that might be.[5] All the items I had were essentials; I did not have boots, just the shoes I was wearing. From the ferry on the Kowloon side (mainland) we made our way slowly up Nathan Road, passed Whitfield Barracks (where many downcast Indians watched our progress) and escorted by hoards of Chinese and other nationals, many giving help freely to those unequal to the strain; meanwhile items were discarded to lighten the load, as walkers tired. The Japanese were doing everything in their power to humiliate us in every possible way, and, unlike the Chinese showed no sympathy, feeling or compassion for their captives. Even so we were still better off than others I had seen in North China, or those unfortunates made captive in so many Chinese cities and towns. I thought of Nanking and the happenings there![6]

So we plodded on, slowly and surely, not knowing where we were going, and many not caring. At each crossroads we speculated on our ultimate destination until, in the end, it seemed that Shamshuipo was a certainty. And so it was, and as we came close to the camp entrance I could see, in my mind's eye, the caption reputedly on many a gaol 'Abandon hope all ye who enter here'. Abandon hope! Never! The one thing never to be abandoned is hope; when there is no hope surely it is the end of life, and I did not intend to pass that way, not yet; and I thought of my wife and children in Australia, and of my mother, and the faith they had in me. I had a duty and a responsibility to them, and even more so to my King and Country 'In pursuance of the trust reposed in me'.[7] Obviously I was feeling the effects of the short sharp campaign, the lack of food, and the forced march carrying my new found possessions over that frightful 3¼ miles (5 miles (8.4km) by circuitous route). The Japanese had done all they could to humble us, lower our self esteem and our physical condition, and abase us in every possible way; and there would be more to come! An infantry friend with a very dry wit summed it up when he said 'we have now reached a very low Ebbage' as we slowly made our way to the nearest unoccupied building and put down our 'Kit'.

Half a dozen of us had chosen a small room, a single officer's quarter in better times. Alas, it had no door, or window, and had been stripped of electrical fittings and everything else that could be readily removed had been looted, but they had left the concrete floor, and the out of reach roof appeared to be intact! It was a night of 'hard lying' and cold as well, so we huddled together, as best we could, for added warmth. Shamshuipo Camp had been, prior to hostilities, the home of the Middlesex Regiment and an Indian Battalion. The Camp was very spacious and well laid out and comprised a number of permanent brick buildings, built on reclaimed ground with the sea on two sides, part open country on the third and a very densely populated area on the fourth. Deep Nullahs[8] ran through the camp to drain off surplus surface water. There was an officers' mess and quarters, a sergeants' mess, barrack rooms, cookhouses, wash-houses, etc in each area, and a very large barrack square. Presumably about 1936 a large block of married quarters had been built on the far side of the parade ground, facing and right up to the sea wall, and known as Jubilee Buildings. Jubilee Buildings comprised four floors of flats, the first, second and third with pleas-ant verandahs, overlooking either the sea or parade ground, and into these flats most of the officers and many others, had taken up residence. They had the advantage of wooden floors which were a little easier on the anatomy than the billet we had chosen.

We were existing on the food we had brought with us, but by now were in need of a drink and a wash, so we explored the possibilities. Water was available at the nearest wash house but unfortunately there were no taps. Only a spout of water coming from a broken pipe, and a queue of people trying to fill mess tins and water bottles from the gushing cascade. Whatever one did there was a soaking in store, so when it came to my turn I quickly filled my mess tin and gave my face and hands a 'lick and a promise'; in any event I had no soap! The day's ablutions completed I made my first tour of the camp in the company of a couple of friends, one of them a major in the Royal Scots. The bar-racks were a sorry sight, every hut had been completely gutted and stripped of everything moveable; in many cases even the window and door frames had gone, as indeed had nearly all the sanitary facilities as well. We were in the posi-tion of 'going' where we could, and where others would let us! Apart from the two sides bordered by the sea there was no fence or other obstacle to keep us in, or other people out, so there was a continuous interchange of people who had homes on the 'Kowloon side' and thus had somewhere to go. Meanwhile, others were doing a reconnaissance of the surrounding hills hoping they might come across gue-rillas who would help them escape, or, perhaps, meet up with that mythical Chinese Army alleged to be coming to our assistance! Surprisingly, morale was quite good at this time in spite of so many trials and tribulations and our cap-tivity had yet to 'bite', while we were carried away on the bright wings of optimism as rumour succeeded rumour.

In my room names were being written on the walls with dates for expected release marked alongside. The most optimistic was 'out in six weeks' with the most pessimistic giving it 'six months'. Reminded me of the days in August 1914 when my friends 'signed on for duration' and eve-ryone was convinced it would be over by Christmas! An ample slice of optimism is a good thing, but an ounce of reality even more so. When invited to add my guess of a date for getting out I refused, asking in return who did they think would want to come and rescue us?

I, too, hoped to get out quickly, by one means or another, but our plans should be based on staying for the rest of our natural lives! I looked at that pencilled list often as the months and years passed by and when the same room was part of the camp store. Tomorrow would be New Year's Day so by then we could claim to have been 'inside' for a year, 1941–1942, and I wondered who would let New Year in? At this time the general[9] was making valiant efforts to establish some form of discipline and get us all back on a unit basis with a proper command structure. Up to this stage it had been a case of everyone fending for themselves.

It was not an easy task to instill a capacity for co-opera-tion and self respect into men who had lost, and who felt a grievance. Becoming a Japanese Prisoner of War is indeed a sorry business bringing no credit to captor or the captured. A man's future is in pawn, all rights are forfeit, including one's own life, and you are the slave of the captor to do with you, as he will!

The general was fully aware of what was needed to put matters right and proceeded to do so, but first there must be some sort of an agreement with the Japanese on such matters as I have described, on food, medical and sanitary arrangements, cooking utensils, clothing, bedsteads, toilet paper, etc all of which were practically non existent. I am sure there were many difficulties, particularly as the Japanese had made it quite clear they did not subscribe, in any way to the Geneva Convention (on the treatment of Prisoners of War) but progress was made.

The Japanese accepted that the general should have full powers over prisoners within the camp, and I am sure, promised to do all they could to help! As a result of all this the Royal Army Ordnance Corps came into being as a unit once more, and I moved from my concrete floor to one of wood in Jubilee Buildings, to join my brother officers there. My isolation was short lived. In Jubilee there were additional compensations in the shape of water closets (the buildings had not been ransacked quite as much as other parts of the barracks presumably because of its more isolated position), electricity, source of power for hidden wireless sets whose operators provided daily BBC News bulletins, and for innumerable immersion heaters which appeared as if by magic. One of my room mates who had a safety razor blade holder, had found a discarded blade in one of the wash houses and with this, after considerable honing we were all able to shave for the next few months. By chance, the holder and blade were in my possession when in April 1942 all the officers were paraded preparatory to being transferred to Argyle Street camp.[10] I used that blade continuously for the next three years, and, at an exhibition in 1946 at Olympia in London, offered it at a stand of the makers of this world renowned blade; to my surprise they were not interested!

So far the Japanese had provided only rice and a few very shallow containers in which to cook it, and some large twisted and knotted tree trunks that defied all means of reducing them to fuel wood, simply because we had no tools with which to chop them up! As the cookhouses had been stripped by looters of practically all fixed equipment and utensils, it was a lucky man who got a portion of his rice in the form known as 'cooked' and even so the wood to cook it came from timber of a dismantled hut! Most men were still living on the food they had brought with them, plus what could be obtained from 'across the fence' either as gifts from friends or relatives, or purchased from itinerant tradesmen. Of the people who daily stood at the camp boundary, many were young Chinese girls from nearby flats, bringing gifts for their boy friends, and known familiarly as 'Dahn Omers';[11] or the wives, children, mothers, brothers, sisters, etc of many members of the Hong Kong Volunteer Defence Corps, who came, almost daily to bring what comfort and sustenance they could muster, to their captive relatives. One cannot speak too highly of the loyalty of these people, in particular of the Chinese girl friends who suffered much abuse and beatings from the Japanese guards, but came back constantly for more![12]

The next day I was sent for by my chief who had decided that all War Diaries would be written up to date and handed in to him. There were practically no facilities at all, but he had contrived to find some suitable paper and ink and got his chief clerk to sit down and make three copies of the Official Account of Ordnance Services in Hong Kong between September 1939 to the end of hostilities in December 1941, in his small and very neat handwriting.

It was realised there might be difficulties in successfully secreting the documents (which comprised three separate accounts covering the activities, during the war, of stores, ammunition and workshops aspects of hostilities; in fact a blow by blow account, plus an overall assessment by the 'Chief' and, if they were found, the penalties of being caught with them. They were enclosed in three home-made envelopes by the chief clerk and distributed by the chief to, as he put it, the three people most likely to survive captivity. I was surprised to find that I was one of them, while the chief would take another and the third would be carried by an armament staff sergeant of the workshops branch. Some three months later the chief was transferred with most of the officers from Shamshuipo to a new camp at Argyle Street, some 2 miles away, and his account which was, I believe, hidden in the false bottom of his kit bag, escaped detection. However, he was not so fortunate when, nearly a year later he was admitted to Bowen Road Hospital. Although he was a very sick man at the time he was most severely beaten up by the Japanese there, I believe on more than one occasion, when they read the contents. As a result of this treatment he sent a verbal message by a medical officer who was moving from Bowen Road Hospital to Shamshuipo instructing me to recover the copy from armament staff sergeant and destroy it at once, together with my own.

It was not possible to comply with this instruction because the staff sergeant had left for Japan in January 1943, with, I think, his copy safely sewn into the lining of his greatcoat.

During the time the staff sergeant was in Shamshuipo there were innumerable searches, including a special one when he was leaving for Japan, but the account was never discovered, and this was obviously the position in Japan as well. My own copy had already survived a number of searches, but it was securely hidden and there seemed no point in destroying it as one copy, that of the chief, was already lost, and so the position remained until after the Japanese surrender when it was taken to England and handed over. The copy safely carried by the armament staff sergeant was also taken back to England four years later, and duly handed over.[13]

2

Some Order out of Chaos

Affairs in camp were looking up, there was a bit more discipline and not so much vandalism; we now had formed units and officers responsible for specific aspects of camp life; one noble Lord volunteered as the head sanitary man so the excreta was now all in one place, one hoped in the trench or tins provided. A so-called hospital had been established and a few iron beds obtained, but there were of course no drugs or any other medical supplies other than those the doctors had brought in with them. Someone had managed to fix up a shower from an old tin can, and as the weather was good, cool and sunny by day and very cool at night, it was tempting to wash off the grime of war and change into clean clothes (if you had any).

The shower was doing good business, but mostly no one had any soap and very few had towels, so, after getting well and truly wet it was a case of running shivering up and down the concrete tennis court to dry with most of the dirt still on. I well remember the commanding officer of the Middlesex Regiment seeing this for the first time commenting 'Zulus my dear fellow, Zulus!!'[1] and I well recall my own words when asked if I was going to join the party and my reply that they would all get pneumonia, and for my part I would sooner be dirty than dead!

I had nothing to do so just stood, with the other officers on parade when the roll was called; afterwards my only task was taking turn with others to guard our belongings in the room against all intruders! And so I spent my time walking round the camp in the company of my friends, while at the same time trying to work out plans for the future. The waterfront was most attractive, the view of the harbour and Stonecutters Island so pleasant. Apart from the food (or lack of it) and the primitive conditions, it hardly felt as if we were in prison. Not many sampans[2] came right up to the sea wall, or landing stage, but one or two did, they discharged their cargo of small packages of food, at the same time exchanging a few hurried words in Cantonese, and were off just as quickly as they had come. It struck me as the easiest way to leave camp if only it could be organised, and then I heard that this was just what was happening and plans were being made to that end. So I rushed off to see my chief and we had a heart to heart talk as we walked up and down the waterfront.[3] I just could not convince him I was fit enough and had the ability to make the arduous journey across mountainous country.[4] The possible opportunity to leave Shamshuipo was therefore lost.

I was surprised when my chief sent for me, perhaps he was relenting, or there was another plan for 'getting out', but I was in for an unpleasant surprise. He told me that the general had been pressing the Japanese, once again, for better food and clothing, blankets, etc; but in addition there had been a visit from some Japanese officers of the Intendant Branch in their army.[5] I was never able to discover the extent of the duties of this unit or department, (my dictionary shows 'Intendant' as manager of public business) but it certainly embraced functions normally carried out by the Royal Army Service Corps, Royal Army Ordnance Corps, etc and they undoubtedly had responsibility for food, clothing and general stores, the items we now stood in most need. I gathered they wanted to know, presumably as part of the surrender agreement, where we kept our stocks, and had demanded (instructed) that a guide be provided to take them to such installations as existed. A Japanese officer and a car would be sent at 9am on the following morning to escort the guide round the various stores. My chief told me I had been chosen for this task and would be accompanied by one of the camp interpreters.[6] There were a few people who could fill the task of interpreter of Japanese, some had been born in the land of the Rising Sun, or had spent many years there. A member of the Hong Kong Volunteer Defence Corps was allocated and would accompany me. He was of Portuguese descent and a fluent Japanese speaker. I did not relish this task and said so, I wanted to keep as far away from anything Japanese that I could. So far as I was concerned they were a cruel, barbarous and diabolical race, and I did not trust them! In addition we should perforce be visiting one of the installations where my commanding officer and many others had been brutally killed.[7] What a bloody assignment! I asked that my terms of reference be made quite clear, just how far I should go in my dealings with them. My instructions were to 'Tell them no more than you have to', or words to that effect.

Next day, promptly at 9am a car drove into camp and a Japanese officer got out and was met by our camp commandant and Japanese camp staff who proceeded to our headquarters, where I was waiting with my interpreter.[8] After cursory introductions we were on our way. To my surprise the Japanese officer of the Intendant Branch seemed to be a pleasant, considerate, and seemingly well educated man who carried out long conversations with the interpreter, so I was only called upon, from time to time, to answer specific questions. All went well until we arrived at the Ridge (a position on the island where we had a small temporary depot) and were met by apparently rough, tough and seasoned troops who appeared to be the ones who had first overcome and subdued the opposition put up from there, and who were probably the very ones who had summarily disposed of, in a most cruel way, my commanding officer and others.[9] There did not seem to be any officers amongst them, but they appeared to be refusing to allow the Japanese captain, or anyone else to enter the premises. From gestures they were making it was obvious they wanted to take me over and mete out to me the same brutal treatment they had given to others. I did not need any interpreter to tell me what was going on, and certainly he dare not speak, but one look at him was sufficient to confirm my worst fears and suspicions. Still the argument went on, from time to time getting more heated; we must have been there for an hour with the Japanese captain reasoning continuously with them. At last some senior characters arrived, probably sergeants, and eventually we were admitted to the houses. Possibly, to show his authority, our captain told us to fill two kit bags of any clothing items we wanted, and this we did. One item that I took was a hair brush which in 1986 I am still using. It is stamped with 1939 as the date of manufacture.

Hardly any conversation passed as our car threaded its way to the ferry for the crossing from Hong Kong Island to the mainland.[10] There was a further surprise in store when our car was driven into the forecourt of the Peninsula Hotel, situated on the Kowloon side and near to the Star Ferry. The hotel was the premier establishment and was now used by the Japanese as their general headquarters and senior officers' mess.[11] The driver of the car was instructed to take the interpreter round to the back of the hotel for refreshment, while I was taken into the main lounge which, at 4pm was full of officers taking tea or other refreshment. After a few minutes a very senior officer arrived, I was given to understand he was head of the Intendant Branch and he spoke perfect English, hence the reason for no interpreter. He offered me tea, while I expect his captain told him of the days' happenings. At the conclusion of tea he asked if there was anything we wanted, so I stated the position inside Shamshuipo, and that we needed clothing, food, and many other items urgently. His lips curled a little as he said 'He would do what he could, certainly some clothing'. This was the signal for our departure back to Shamshuipo. It was some days before I could get from the interpreter a coherent account of what happened that day, and a very long time before I got anything like the whole story, if I ever did! At the Ridge it seemed they wanted to execute us both on the spot, as they had done the others, and they said so very forcefully.

I made my report and hoped that some good might come from this foray. There was great excitement in camp when a couple of three ton lorries arrived and soon there were plenty of eager hands around waiting and willing to unload them, whenever lorries were sighted they provided the event of the day, after food and news. On this occasion the enthusiasm soon wore off when the cargo was found to be old newspapers and rolls of newsprint which weighed two or three hundredweight each. What a difference had the cargo been cigarettes or even something to eat, but the paper was eventually dumped in the road.

This delivery was unexpected, though the general had been pressing for latrine paper. Perhaps those large rolls of newsprint were the Japanese idea of a joke, but more likely they did not understand our requirements. Still, any sort of paper was better than none at all, and, judging by the rate some of it was already disappearing there must be a lot of behinds that needed wiping. But what to do with it? Unless quick action was taken the whole lot would disappear in a few minutes, yes, the law of the jungle still prevailed! A guard was quickly mounted on those old newspapers until a decision could be taken, at the highest level, as to how to hold and distribute them. Yes, we should certainly need a camp store to take care of items that did not come under the heading of rations. The general, and my chief, had decided we must have such a store, buildings were allocated, and staff in the shape of our chief clerk and two or three RAOC storemen were duly appointed to look after it. Eventually the paper was moved under cover and as safe as it could be from marauders in a building without doors or windows! And the storemen found the papers softer and warmer to sleep on than concrete floors.

Of course no such an important store could function without an officer in charge, and the following day, as I was currently without portfolio, I was duly appointed. I certainly did not want or relish this appointment. I should, willy nilly, be in direct contact with the Japanese, and no matter how fair or impartial I tried to be there would be bound to be people who would question what I did and disagree with it. (Many were just like children being given sweets and complaining 'He had two while I got one, or, his was bigger than mine!' It did not take long to learn that in some men, prison life brought out the worst and not the best in them, and shortages of whatever kind only accentuated this position. What a thankless task to be given, whatever one did would be questioned, and in someone's eye would be wrong.

I wondered what sort of accounts I should keep, and who I was responsible to, and if my staff were honest. The life we were living could so easily push an upright man over the brink, and even I did not differ from others. My chief reassured me when he said both he and the general would stand behind me (presumably so long as they agreed with what I did), and all this on account of a load of old copies of the *New York Herald*, about a year old! Still, it was better than food; I certainly pitied the poor devil who had to look after this commodity. It must have been our lucky day for sure enough the ration chappie was now taking in a delivery of meat, the first we had since coming into camp, and it was causing rather a commotion. Being offloaded was a batch of live pigs, which promptly broke loose and ran squealing in every direction. The whole camp watched and laughed, as the pigs ran all over the place, if laughter is as good as food we certainly had our fill; meanwhile urgent conferences were taking place as to what to do with them. If they could not be caught, they could not be killed, and even when they were caught how did you kill them, as the nursery rhyme says 'without any knife'. Eventually, when everyone was tired out (but not the pigs) they were gently coaxed into a building and bedded down for the night, with a guard on the door to sound the alarm in the event of escape. Poor pigs, they were prisoners just like we were, as the search for suitable knives to despatch them proceeded.

The twisted knotted wood I spoke of earlier was still defying attempts to cut it up, and the Japanese had still not provided axes, saws or other tools with which to do so. The few tools it had been possible to get 'over the wire' had also proved ineffective. As a result the head of the RAOC Workshop Branch had been asked to advise, and in turn had consulted his craftsmen. Between them they had decided that, if the springs from an abandoned and derelict bus could be dismantled, and sharpened, they could be made into cutting tools or wedges, and work was proceeding encouraged by an ever changing crowd, and despite the absence of practically any tools. Just off the sea wall, in front of Jubilee Building, and clearly visible at low tide was an abandoned rickshaw with bicycle type wheels. The sea wall was perhaps a sheer drop of some 15 to 20 feet (4.5 to 6 metres) at low tide. There were no steps and scant possibility of getting back up the wall if ever you got down. It was also out of bounds from a Japanese point of view, and their sentries would undoubtedly fire on anyone seen down there. No ropes were available. Even so, one RAOC craftsman decided that some use might be made of the rickshaw if it could be recovered, and spent his days with an improvised grappling iron attached to the end of a length of electric cable 'fishing' for it. I gathered at the time the idea was, if he ever hooked it, to wait for succeeding high tides and then gently ease it in towards the sea wall and over the expanse of jagged rocks, and then, hopefully, lift it up. There is no direct connection between these two events other than the fact that they display the ingenuity, perseverance and determination of these men to succeed. In prison, as in retirement, there is one commodity of which there is no shortage. Time! Eventually, both these projects were successful as the reader will see later.

It had long been evident that there was a requirement for a central place where clothing, footwear and other personal items could be refurbished, and possibly other items manufactured. Many men had no means with which to keep their meager belongings in repair, and would need help to do so if their possessions were not to deteriorate into rags very quickly. So far the Japanese had given no help or assistance or direction, at all. It seemed to be part of their policy to demean their captives, on the other hand they had promised to do all they could for us. This being so they could hardly object if we tried to help ourselves! In this climate it was agreed that I would set up, in the compound a tailor's and shoemaker's shop, and the general would issue an appeal throughout the camp for any tools or sewing materials which individuals might have. No matter what the tools were, or in what condition, they would be welcome, and I would hold them for general camp use. The original appeal did not bring in very much, but it put a price on any such items which existed, so now it was only a matter of finding the currency! It had already been established inside camp that money was of little value and had negligible purchasing power, but cigarettes certainly had. By now they were practically non existent in camp and were much sought after, and their trading value soared accordingly. Cigarettes came to be accepted as currency throughout the camp, and this remained the position right up to the end. A supply of 'fags' was obtained and bargains were struck! The chief engineer of the Kowloon and Canton Railway, and a member of the Hong Kong Volunteer Defence Corps, offered to get his Chinese boy to bring to the 'wire' the next day a portable sewing machine, and as much thread as he could buy, and also a few tools as well. I believe it was from this source that we obtained the immensely valuable 'Stillson' wrench, a tool so beloved of plumbers for dealing with taps and water pipes.

This gesture was a turning, or should I say starting, point in our efforts to provide a service for all who needed it. (Note from the author: I wish to place on record my gratitude and thanks to this particular gentleman for his public spirit in making these initial contributions).[12] The small hand sewing machine and other items were, after some difficulty with the sentries allowed through. Perhaps, too, we were just in time for there was shortly to be a considerable tightening up by the sentries. Possibly, too, the Japanese camp commandant was becoming disturbed by the ease with which supplies were obtained 'over the wire' and the dangers inherent in them! Whatever the cause new rules were applied; there would, in future be no direct contact with outsiders and a party of Japanese camp staff would carry the gifts between donor and receiver, provided they met with Japanese approval.

The camp commandant was of course kept informed by the general of what we were doing to help ourselves and came along to see how men were coping with what was 'women's work'. It had been anticipated that the Japanese would want to see the tools we had collected; they did not trust us any more than we trusted them, so only the innocuous items were put on display for their benefit. For instance, we had acquired just one hacksaw and two blades, a pair of tin snips, a file and other cutting tools which they would obviously regard as escape gear and so confiscate. These tools were kept in suitably high places, and so as to preserve them their use was restricted to only the most essential tasks. The chief clerk and storeman knew where they were hidden and would never let them out without approval, or even admit they existed! Thus far the only tools the Japanese had supplied were I think, half a dozen picks and shovels and a saw, and all these items had to be handed back to them each evening after the projects for which they were required, and they had approved, had been completed. They were only allowed out again at the whim and convenience of the Japanese. So the sanitary men had to wait

Japanese approval each day before they could dig a hole in which to bury the night soil;[13] or the cookhouse staff to saw up wood! This game continued to be played in differing variations all the time we were in Shamshuipo.

At some time, during the early days in camp, my chief handed over to me a small amount of money which was to be used on amenities for the men of No. 6 Section, Royal Army Ordnance Corps, and it is my impression that he made an appeal to all members of the unit to subscribe to this fund, if they were able to do so. I do not know from whence this money came, but the most likely source would be from the paymaster, whose cashier had brought into camp his cash balance in an army safe! He had conveyed it, at the expense of personal items of kit, on a small trolley which he and other members of the Royal Army Pay Corps had towed all the way from Murray Barracks to Shamshuipo. A most noble effort! I understand that two members of the Royal Army Ordnance Corps, who were attached to the Middlesex Regiment, had a hand in this. When the load could not be carried further by others they managed to get a bamboo pole to which they attached their kit, and bundles of money, and finally handed the cash over, on arrival at Shamshuipo, to the rightful custodian.

There was also a private and generous donation from a Royal Army Ordnance Corps ammunition specialist, who became a shoemaker. Until some time in February 1942 all purchases were made 'over the wire' (or by other means), but from early March a canteen was established in part of the compound occupied by our store and workshops.[14] Those with money could of course buy freely of toilet necessaries, cigarettes, etc but there were few in camp who had any money left, so a scheme of 'credit trading' was devised, backed initially by the money brought in by the cashier.[15] I have always thought that the Japanese had a motive for allowing this canteen. Perhaps the scheme was two-fold, from a propaganda point of view to show what facilities they provided, and secondly and far more likely, to drain off surplus cash and thus minimise the possibility of it being used for escape purposes. In any case it was born under difficulties, and if I remember rightly was closed, as a so-called punishment, on a number of occasions. Sometime in March 1942 the Japanese announced that all officers would receive pay (on 1 April with arrears from 1 January 1942) at the rate for equivalent Japanese ranks. There would be nothing for the men, but when work was found for them, they too would be paid. What followed was that a deduction was made at source of Yen 60 per month[16] from the amounts of pay due to officers for the food they ate and for their accommodation. This left the more junior officers with very little money, and in my own case my pay entitlement as a captain was cut by about half. Nevertheless a method was devised and approved, whereby officers of the rank of captain and above would contribute on a sliding scale, to finance the scheme for 'credit trading' at the canteen, for the benefit of other ranks.[17]

'Improvise'

Whenever we asked for anything from the Japanese they told us to 'improvise' (with nothing) and this became their favourite word which we were to hear hundreds of times, so they could hardly take away the meager bits we had got by our own 'initiative'; to them this would have been loss of face. In addition they were, I am sure, also convinced we had many more items we did not disclose. And so we launched out, on our own, all the time pressing them for this or that item! Footwear, or the lack of it was a major problem in camp so the suggestion was put that we make sandals for all those who had no satisfactory footwear, or wished to preserve what they had got. This proposal meant taking down another hut so that the right kind of rafter could be obtained. I gathered that the Royal Engineers had a lot of argument with the Japanese before a small hut near to the perimeter was agreed upon. The hut was not knocked down but taken down, piece by piece by the Royal Engineers. The bitumen and torn felt covering was first removed and taken into store, and then, one by one, the pieces of roof boarding. All the nails were also recovered for further use, then the main beams, etc complete with their nuts and bolts, and lastly the brickwork. There was a requirement for this for the bricking up of windows, and for stoves and boilers in the various cookhouses. Nothing was wasted, nothing destroyed, everything had a use, and a use made of everything, if not today then tomorrow, or the day after! The rafters, beams, etc were cut into suitable lengths and many of these were given out to individuals to shape and cut with their own knives down to size, and then they were finished off in the shoemaker's shop by the addition of a piece of canvas or leather. A record was kept on newsprint, of all those issued with pieces of wood, and ultimately sandals. Similar kinds of footwear were also made from the tyres recovered from the derelict buses already mentioned. Anticipating that the specialist knowledge of members of the RAOC could be put to wrong use, my chief had decided that, where feasible each man should profess to a trade different from his own, thus rendering more difficult future identification by our captors. This process was helped by the fact that easy work should be found for all corps men, as all were better in health and mind if they had something to do.

Thus, from the beginning, armament artificers, armourers, ammunition specialists, etc became bricklayers, boot repairers, tailors and later bookbinders, spectacle repairers, etc.[1] With the facilities at our disposal the arrangements for cooking in each of the cookhouses was not very successful, so the Japanese had been asked to supply some alternative cooking pots. They replied by producing a number of 80 gallon oil drums. Naturally, as might have been expected, they did not cut them in two, or provide tools with which to do so; once again we were reduced to our 'own initiative'. Fortunately the dismantling of springs from the bus already referred to, had been proceeding apace and some were already in the process of being fashioned into cutting tools and chisels, and so the laborious task of cutting the oil drums into two pieces proceeded, with bed legs from a McDonald type of sliding army bedstead being used as hammers. (A small stock of these bed legs had already been acquired). Simultaneously a small party of 'bricklayers' were practising their new found art in the cookhouses building suitable housing for the oil drums, while others tried their hand at bricking up doors and windows. There was of course no cement and so the decomposed granite which had been used for filling in the reclamation on which the camp was built, was sieved through to make mud to hold the brickwork together. It worked, though there were many failures during this trial and error stage, and much rebuilding which gave work and practice and increased the skill! Things were happening, a 3 ton lorry load of clothing arrived, and there was more to come. I went out to view the load before it was taken into store. It was just like the remnants of a United Kingdom jumble sale after all the sought after items had gone, and these were the residue no one would buy. The sort of stuff the local rag and bone men at home were reluctant to accept, even as a gift. My heart sank when I saw the stuff, was this the best the Japanese could do? Now they would be able to say, and justify, that they had given us a large supply of clothing! We took the consignment into store and examined it in more detail. It looked to me as if the Japanese had gone round the various barracks, quarters, and private houses occupied by military and perhaps civilians, and collected all the second-hand clothing they could find; there were dress shirts, tuxedos, tail coats, and a variety of other gear; most, but not all of it seemed to be clean. The next delivery was a little better; while the first had been mainly underclothing, the second comprised mostly outer garments, and we certainly were in need of these. There were a number of greatcoats, and it had been the aim that every man should possess such a garment. The staff sorted out the various items and listed them; we were able to identify, from the markings, the belongings of certain camp inmates, so we were able to re-unite them with what rightfully were their own possessions![2] Our next question was how best to distribute the spoils. After much discussion a plan was evolved which we all hoped would ensure the goods were given to those who really needed them, not to the racketeers and wide boys who abounded, and were after quick profits. One commanding officer said of them 'They were only interested in their bellies...'.

Commanding officers were asked to bring along, half a dozen at a time, men who were in most urgent need, having first verified that this was so, and we would try to bring as many of them as we could up to a minimum standard. Such a system was a bit hit and miss and open to abuse, but in a camp of 3,000 to 4,000, and at least a dozen differing nationalities, was the best we could think of. We did of course keep a record and the men would sign for what they took. This might put a break on the wholesale disposal, usually for cigarettes. It was also a bit heart rending when some poor character came along and we had nothing to give him that he needed, or was too tall or small to fit out. Our hand-operated sewing machine was doing good work but could not cope, so the Japanese camp staff were asked if they could supply us with a treadle machine, and to everyone's surprise, some time later two arrived, but of course without any cotton.[3] Perhaps they expected us to 'Improvise'.

The Japanese camp staff comprised:
>Camp commandant: a captain or lieutenant.
>Sergeants: two or three.
>Privates: do
>Interpreters: do

Plus, of course, a guard who provided the perimeter sentries, and with the camp staff enforced discipline within the camp precincts. The guards also provided escorts for anyone taken out of camp. There was also a higher echelon known as the prison camp's administrative headquarters, situated some 2 miles away at Prince Edward Road, and who were responsible for a number of prisoners of war camps, internment camps, and hospitals.

I never went there, but believe the staff to have been:

> One full colonel
> One senior doctor
> One or two other officers
> One senior interpreter
> A small military staff

Between them they controlled the various camp staffs and dictated the policy to be followed.

All of them were nasty pieces of work, chosen presumably on that account, and were feared by their junior staff at the various camps. The colonel was known as the 'Fat Pig', which was an apt description of a big man around 5ft 9in (in all directions) and in the 15–17 stone bracket.[4] He was the boss, and everyone knew it! The interpreters were drawn from civilian life, given a sword and a uniform and allocated to the various prison camps. One of them at Shamshuipo had spent much of his life in Canada, hated the British from the bottom of his heart, and showed it on every possible occasion. The second had been in Cardiff as a representative of a Japanese shipping company. We nicknamed him 'Cardiff Joe'. I found him to be a kindly and useful person, in outlook more British than Japanese.[5] The interpreters had been 'called home', as were all Japanese nationals, before hostilities commenced. Some of the interpreters, like the last one, were quickly changed. Quite a number came and went during the period of our incarceration at Shamshuipo, one was a Lutheran minister and another a school teacher.[6]

These were the people with whom we had to deal, access to the camp commandant had to be through them, and much depended on how they interpreted your case as to how successful you were in making your point. It was after one of these unsuccessful interviews with the camp commandant that Cardiff Joe said to me 'Life as Prisoner of War,

No bed of roses!' I knew he had sympathy for us and said it in the best way he could, but he did give considerable practical help during his tenure at Shamshuipo and I am very grateful to him!

The RAOC were probably the first unit to suffer an actual death amongst their numbers, and the loss of one of our staff sergeants brought home to everyone the seriousness of our position.[7] The medical officers did all in their power to save him, but despite their efforts, and those of his comrades, who gave freely from what they had, he passed away. The ring he was wearing was taken from his finger after death, and I carried it until my return to England, when it was handed over to the officer in charge of Royal Army Ordnance Corps Records, who subsequently sent it to his next of kin, so that it might be handed over to his boy. I believe the Royal Engineers made a coffin for him from roof boarding, and he was duly buried in an area of open ground near to the camp perimeter, and a headstone bearing his name was erected. He was subsequently re-interred at Stanley Military Cemetery.[8] What meager possessions he had were distributed amongst those of his comrades who needed them.

Two aspects have not been mentioned so far, they are parades, roll calls and searches. The Japanese required daily parade stats and insisted on making checks of their accuracy. Thus, everyone apart from the very sick, had to stand on parade for hours at a time, while they tried to reconcile the numbers they had been given by our own headquarters staff. The Japanese could not count correctly, so there was constant disagreement. Roll calls were held at infrequent intervals, even during the night. A long and slow process. It was not unusual for someone not to hear the alarm; this caused much delay and usually a beating up for the culprit and his officer commanding as well! Nor could they even remember who they themselves had taken out of camp. At this stage the Japanese did not have a nominal roll, so it was possible for someone to slip away and the Japanese be incapable of identifying him.

The counts were therefore interminable and lengthy affairs, often in hot sun, or on a cold wet night, when some dreamy sentry had seen a shadow which he thought might be an escapee. In addition there were genuine escapes as well! The Japanese were convinced and with very good reason, that we had wireless sets in camp, and in addition, possibly arms and escape gear. I was not concerned directly with the wireless sets but naturally, like everyone else, eager to devour the news, whenever it was available. The Japanese idea was to find and eliminate such 'pockets' [of resistance] which were an anathema to them, and so, whenever they detected a better mood in camp, or for any other of a variety of reasons, there was a search. Nothing was respected! For hour after hour while sick men stood, or tried to do so, on parade, they examined every nook and cranny, throwing the contents of kit bags, etc all over the place. Then they retreated with what spoils they had collected and confiscated, and which often comprised minor things they did not understand, like immersion heaters. The remarkable fact was they found just as big a haul at the next search! After such searches followed the usual ritual of interrogation, beatings, punishments by sentries and sergeants, without any regard to the physical condition of the alleged culprit, or other factors. This sort of treatment was meted out, at some time or other, to a large number of people in camp regardless of their guilt of the so-called offence, or otherwise. Yes, there was plenty of 'work' for the camp staff to do, and some of them reveled in it! Both the head of the Hong Kong War Supplies Board and the secretary, were members of the Hong Kong Volunteer Defence Corps, while I was the inspector; and here we were, all three of us together in Shamshuipo. But for how long?

We discussed at great length details of the position on each particular outstanding order or contract, as at the outbreak of hostilities, while they were fresh in our memories, and on many other connected matters as well. The object of our discussions was to establish a record which, if preserved, would form a basis on which claims against the War Supplies Board, could be argued. We hoped that by this means we could all speak with one voice. The absence of any paper on which to keep such records had meant that, having reached agreement we would try to carry the information in our heads. A very unlikely happening!

The arrival of the rolls of newsprint now made this impossible course unnecessary as paper (for this purpose) we now had in abundance. On the other hand, it still might be a useful exercise if any records we made were lost, and assuming we still had good memories and were all alive! The secretary prepared in pencil lists, and so as to minimise the risks if the documents fell into Japanese hands, the contractors' names and addresses were omitted, codes being substituted. Once completed it was the intention that the records be hidden, each of us would have his own copy. I already had a superfluity of documents to keep, and certainly could not carry all of them on my person. So I found a safe hiding place for my copy and recovered it at the time of the surrender. At the conclusion of hostilities in 1945, and in conjunction with the head of the Hong Kong War Supplies Board, we compared notes and lists, and a final document was submitted by him to headquarters, of the Far Eastern Group of the War Supplies Board at New Delhi and the Hong Kong government, setting out the position of each order and contract as we understood it at the outbreak of the war in Hong Kong.

Eventually, the 80 gallon oil drums supplied by the Japanese were cut into two pieces and installed in their brick and mud emplacements in the several cookhouses. For very long periods we had been supplied with only rice as our daily diet, but, after the Japanese got themselves organised there was also a reasonably regular flow of so-called vegetables. Presumably what could be provided from the meager pittance they allocated for this purpose. The cheapest, poorest, in other words items no one else wanted, came to us. The vegetables alternated between unpalatable water chestnuts and hyacinths to lettuce and spinach, all of which had to be boiled as the risks of eating any of them raw were too great. Worms, dysentery, and many other such problems were a certainty unless the strictest rules of hygiene were maintained. All the vegetables provided were foul and many men could not eat or digest them, but I found the boiled lettuce to be the most revolting. The slimy dark green mess looked as objectionable as it tasted, but somehow we got it down. We had to, there was nothing else, and it looked even more repulsive when served in old discarded tin cans, or mess tins! At this stage many men just did not have suitable food containers. On the other hand the cooks were better organised and the rice more skillfully cooked; it was not burned as often now, nor was it always the glutinous mess to which we had become accustomed. Just the same we were, like the camel, living on our 'fat' and with most of us, and certainly with me there was considerable 'slimming down'. The cooks were working under immense difficulties and much credit is due to them for the work they were doing in trying to produce a meal from practically nothing! The doctors, in conjunction with the master baker, were experimenting in the production of yeast, with the object of overcoming some of the disorders resulting from deficiencies in our diet. The master baker had, I gathered, brought into camp with him some army emergency reserves of desiccated yeast, and with sugar, etc eventually a quantity of 'grog' was produced. Everyone paraded most willingly for their doses. This was a particularly good effort on the part of the master baker and pathologist who spearheaded this team. I had hoped that a little yeast might help to keep me more 'regular'. It is understood this yeast or brew was used over the whole period of captivity in the production of the daily type of bread so essential in supplementing our diet. Many of us were suffering from constipation, perhaps helped on by our diet of polished rice, and others, like myself, were finding difficulty in going to toilet more frequently than once every seven or ten days! I was getting a bit concerned as I already had bleeding piles, so spoke to a doctor friend for his advice. He said the longer we kept the food inside us the better; we would continue to get some benefit even when it was 'down below', but if I was having trouble with piles as well, then I should try some vaseline, if I could get any! I scoured the camp and to my surprise was able to purchase a half empty jar for a few cigarettes, and took my capture to see my doctor friend to ask how it should be applied! Long will I remember his reply, 'You don't put it on, you eat it.' So I was able to grease my inside and thus make my next visit to the toilet less of a painful struggle than it had recently been!

Every empty tin can or metal container found in camp was collected so that use could be made of it, in particular as containers for food. Even so there were insufficient to fulfill this requirement. In our small compound tinsmiths were at work trying to fashion mess tins for those who had no other kind of eating utensil. We had acquired a number of sheets of corrugated iron from demolished buildings and, with the aid of a granite roller which had been left on the tennis court, we started to eliminate the wavy ridges. It took a long time, with the granite roller supplemented by the frequent use of iron bed legs, to get a flat enough piece of metal to enable it to be cut into shape with homemade chisels and snips. When this was done each piece could then be folded in such a way that a satisfactory container was provided. As food was our major concern, and there was an amount of room in our compound, in particular on the grass verges which surrounded the tennis curt, and which would provide a certain amount of humus [soil], I decided to try out the interpreter about buying some vegetable seeds from one of the better class departmental stores I knew carried stocks. Cardiff Joe was very willing and he took my small list and money, to see what he could get.

Carrot and tomato seeds were most wanted, so he was asked to concentrate on these. If he could not get tomato

seeds then to bring back a few decent looking ripe tomatoes from which I could extract them. He was as good as his
word, so on his first day off duty went over to the island to
see what he could get. Very few seeds were available; there
were no tomato seeds but plenty of carrot seeds of different
varieties. He was therefore able to select the ones I wanted,
and the ripe tomatoes he brought provided me with both
food and seed.

I sat for a long time just sucking away the pulp and casing
round each seed and putting them out to dry on a piece of
paper. A small plot of ground was dug as a trial area for the
carrots, and a strip down the edge of the tennis court, by
the wire netting for tomatoes. Soon both lots of seeds were
planted and the cause of much comment and interest as
they grew.[9]

Our plea for beds and blankets, particularly for the hospital was partially answered when the Japanese brought in a
few bales of brand new blankets and some extra bedsteads
as well. However, when the blankets were unwrapped they
were found to be of very poor quality cotton type which
were known as 'coolie blankets'. There was no warmth in
them and they would not last very long either, but at least
the patients in hospital now had something to lie on instead
of the old newspapers some of them were using. Even small
happenings, such as this, lifted morale and brought new hope
to many whose faith in the future was running out. Looked
at from another point of view, those who were dying could
now do so in a little more comfort! The Japanese told us
that very shortly they intended to provide Japanese style
(Tatami) beds for all the men and single beds for the hospital
and officers! Our general, the doctors, and nearly everyone
else were concerned about the hospital, so called.

At this stage I ought to say that when a man became
ill, and consequently unfit to stand on parade to answer
roll call, he was moved from his friends, complete with his
few possessions, to this separate area, and was then deemed
to be in 'hospital'. Patients got nothing extra there except

perhaps very slightly better food, plus the personal and constant attention of devoted medical officers who were trying to heal men without drugs, medicines, dressings or any of the usual medical supplies. There were no sheets, pillows, mattresses or any other of the amenities normally associated with a hospital; and it was dirty, as well can be imagined. A hospital in name only.

The general was also very concerned at the lack of soap, up to this point no one had really been able to wash themselves properly and their clothes, hardly at all. He had repeatedly pressed the Japanese for soap, and so had the doctors. Soap was needed in particular for the washing of soiled garments, as well as individuals, but none was forthcoming. In the RAOC we had, as a temporary officer, the late manager of the Kowloon laundry and so had the benefit of his advice where laundry matters were concerned. He had not previously worked without soap, hot water or other aids, but we got down to trying to produce lye, which was reputed to be the answer to our problems. The dictionary describes lye as 'An alkaline solution leached from vegetable ashes'. Well, try as we did success eluded us; we burned bits of everything in sight, and tried this and that, in our efforts to get the items clean, but all we seemed to do was to get them even dirtier! In the compound there was a boiler which was in working order, and a bath, but of course we could not afford any wood as fuel for this, so we tried out the tarred roofing felt we had recovered from the demolished buildings. We created an awful smell, and a lot of smoke, but at least the water became sufficiently warm for us to trail the dirty items through, and we were able to kid ourselves they were cleaner than when they went in! We were not very proud of our efforts, but at least we had tried and found there to be no joy that way! Nevertheless the experience was of value when later it became necessary to wash so many of the blankets. Quite surprisingly, some days after the affair with the boiler, the Japanese did surface with some soap flakes. They were quite insufficient in quantity to distribute to individuals but enough to give each of the cookhouses, including the hospital, a small supply. It was also possible to wash some of the clothing of those in hospital, an unpleasant task willingly undertaken by volunteers.

The question of escape was constantly in everybody's mind and the possibilities were discussed at every opportunity. One or two certainly had got away, but how far, no one knew. What we did know was that, on each and every occasion there were reprisals against those remaining. The reprisals took many forms depending on the whim of the Japanese. They included beatings and interrogation for officers and associates of those who had gone; but always they included a savage cut in the supply of food with consequent suffering for those left behind, and in particular the sick. This was undoubtedly a deliberate move by the Japanese. Furthermore, the now fortnightly parcels' day (for those lucky enough to get them) was cancelled and the women, some of whom had walked miles to bring a small offering or pittance to their loved ones, were turned away mostly without even a sight of them, and often with a beating as well.[10] It was getting grim, very grim. Then, suddenly four got away all in one night and the reprisals were immediate and severe. Hour after hour we stood on parade while the camp was searched from end to end and top to bottom. My chief, who was making a special duty of looking after the unit, was very concerned about the deteriorating situation, and in particular the health, or lack of it, in the RAOC. I had long known it to be his view that many of us would be lucky to get out alive, and he said so in no uncertain terms in an effort to lift morale and put a sense of purpose into those whose spirit appeared to be flagging a little. No one could question his guts, or his intention to lift the RAOC to the highest possible plane. Get out alive they certainly would, if he had anything to do with it!

Exodus to Argyle Street

The 18th day of April 1942 was for me, a very sad day, and I find it difficult to record the sequence of events that took place then, the day when most of the officers were separated from the men and taken off to another camp. It was a crisis for all of us and a turning point in our affairs. For better or for worse? Even now I cannot be sure! Certainly the division was made by the Japanese to suit their own ends and without any consideration whatever for their captives. Most certainly the organisation so laboriously built up by the general was in ruins.

I seem to remember there was an early roll call on 18 April and after this was completed, and while everyone was still on parade, the general was told of the Japanese intention to move all the officers to another camp. All officers and batmen[1] were then dismissed from the parade and told to pack their kits for the move, meanwhile the balance of the men were held incommunicado on parade. I can well remember dashing back hurriedly to my store and quarters to retrieve the RAOC War Records I had been entrusted with, and other important papers, and the frantic efforts to secret them where I hoped the Japanese would not look; and to gather my bits of kit and blankets together, all the while under the supervision of sentries. I was quite ready to get out of this hell of a place, surely our new home could not be worse than this one? But what about the men who were being left behind to fend for themselves? Well, no man is indispensable, necessity being the mother of invention, soon, new leaders would emerge. I felt a sense of relief but also of uncertainty. Yes, in my heart of hearts I was glad to be going! Soon we were back on parade with our belongings, after what seemed an interminable length of time the Japanese camp staff appeared in force and commenced a system of random selection. Like picking out a prize heifer at a cattle market!

Quickly the news spread down the line; they were choosing two or three officers from each unit to stay behind with the men. Two were picked from our general headquarters staff, then three or more from the Royal Artillery, but none from the Royal Engineers (who had a sizeable number of men), three each from Royal Scots and Middlesex Regiments, five or six from Royal Army Service Corps, one from the Hong Kong Mule Corps (who had no troops at all), two from Royal Army Ordnance Corps (myself and the ex-laundry manager), two from the Royal Army Pay Corps and three from the Hong Kong Volunteer Defence Corps (who had I believe in excess of a thousand men), etc. There was no rhyme or reason in the selection, only a very few of those chosen were in any way known to the Japanese camp staff, and all were relatively junior officers. The Japanese certainly knew me, and there seemed to be quite a lot of discussion before the pointer was put on, and I was told to go to my quarters with my kit. The ex-Kowloon laundry manager, also completely unknown to them, followed. My heart was in my boots, what had I done to deserve this?

After a short period of time officers and batmen going to Argyle Street, together with their kits, were assembled on the main road. Only then were the men dismissed and ordered back to their huts, and kept away from the main road by sentries. Soon the 400-odd officers and 100 or so batmen and cooks, after a search, passed through the camp gates heading for Argyle Street camp. They were gone, and we were on our own! The place seemed empty and we all felt a bit lost and overawed. The senior officer of each unit took command of it and dealt with the few rogues and vagabonds who had made hay in the short time the officers were on parade. I found no such problem in the RAOC as the senior warrant officer had taken command of the unit, while the chief clerk had done the same in the small store and workshops. Up to this [time], my charge had been limited to the store and workshops, now I must take responsibility for the unit as well. The whole complexion of my charge had changed; henceforth matters must be looked at in quite a different way. My chief had earlier set the pattern, and I would follow it whenever I could. Clearly there would be sudden and violent changes requiring constant readjustment, but his main theme of 'Getting as many men out alive' would be followed. The first task [was] to talk to all members of the unit and this I did.

All those officers who had been left behind took up quarters, once again, in Jubilee Buildings, and I found myself sharing accommodation with the senior Royal Scots officer and the junior staff officer, who was a solicitor and a member of the Middlesex Regiment.

The other officers were in adjacent rooms. A close association was formed with my new roommates and also with some of the others, in particular the senior representatives of the Middlesex Regiment and the Hong Kong Volunteer Defence Corps. On most days we discussed our problems together and found solutions to them. We at least, were in harmony about what we were doing, but not always so when, nightly, we debated whether General Townsend in the beleaguered Kut-el-Armara in Mesopotamia, should have allowed his favorite polo pony to be killed for food, or how we thought the present war with Japan ought to end.[2] I think the conclusions we reached on this matter were that eventually Russia would have to be dealt with; that Japan could not be contained in their small barren home islands;

that we set one against the other until both were exhausted! These childish discussions at least gave us a laugh and kept us sane; we should certainly need to be balanced so as to meet the trials and tribulations to come!

Gradually, we got ourselves sorted out, and the camp began to run more smoothly. As no Royal Engineer officer had been left in camp by the Japanese it was inevitable that the 'works' side of this unit would devolve upon me. The few tools they had were, in any case, kept in our compound, as was the result of the pulling down of buildings, e.g. timber, bricks, etc. It did not present more than an increase in work, and a few more problems to deal with and solve. Apart from the pulling down of buildings, so that their components could be used for other purposes, the Royal Engineers had been active in fixing up the water supply, lighting, cookhouses, sanitation, coffins, etc. Fortunately they had a number of very efficient warrant officers, quite capable of coping with their own unit and with other jobs as well.

A warrant officer and the engineer staff continued to work with me, as they had done under their own officers, and this element functioned very successfully indeed until their numbers were reduced by illness, death, and the various drafts/working parties which were sent to Japan. These men did very good work indeed for the camp as a whole, and their conduct was impeccable. After the departure of officers and batmen to Argyle Street all units found it necessary to re-orientate themselves and take stock of their positions. For instance, the canteen manager had been left in Shamshuipo and so had the stock, but the whole of the public cash and the canteen cash had been taken to Argyle Street. As a result the whole future of credit trading was in jeopardy and had to be re-examined. It was decided to allow credit trading to continue up to the April limit of MY2.50,[3] but obviously no further credit could be agreed until funds were available to finance such transactions. There was also the matter of getting back cash with which to pay the canteen contractor for supplies already delivered.

Pay of officers for April was issued by the Japanese, with the usual deductions for messing and accommodation, but it was decided that no useful purpose would be served by collecting money from officers in Shamshuipo for canteen credit trading. Any money raised would be insufficient – unless officers at Argyle Street continued the scheme. Canteen trading was by now almost at a standstill.

Meanwhile, the canteen contractor announced a new rate of exchange, HKS4 equaled MY1. (Old rate had been HKS2 to MY1).[4] At the end of June MY6680 was received from Argyle Street for the camp amenities fund, and an advisory committee of unit commanders was formed, and a list of requirements for July was drawn up and submitted to the Japanese camp commandant. Early in August a further conference on amenities was held and requirements for August were drawn up and were presented to the Japanese, who declined to accept them until the July order had been fulfilled! So far nothing had happened. Towards the end of August further enquiries had elicited no information as to the order for amenities. The committee met with the Japanese camp commandant to consider his suggestion for the repair of boots at a flat rate of MY2 a pair. (Presumably in order that men could go out of camp on Japanese working parties, or possibly for other reasons) 2,228 pairs were involved!

The committee could not agree to this, and in turn, asked the camp commandant to assist in the early expenditure of money on the order already sent in. Such are the vagaries in trying to deal with the Japanese! Pay for officers alone naturally caused resentment from those who were to get nothing. The Japanese were quick to say that soon, work would be found for the men, and they would receive pay for any work they did. In other words they would be sent out on working parties. Pay was the only thing officers got and the men did not, this apart, in everything else, all were equal. A portion of the pay of RAOC officers was set aside for unit use, and with this cash essential items were bought.

The first monies were I believe, used to buy soap, razors, hair cutting gear, etc. From my own personal portion Cardiff Joe bought me a pair of shoes, of which I was very much in need. I think it was from 1 April 1942 that the Japanese decided to give pay to officers but not to other ranks.

In a very small way we had a shoemaker's shop, or the nucleus of one; but it did not have the blessing or support of the Japanese. Whenever the general, or anyone else, had asked for help in this direction we were met with their favorite word, 'improvise, improvise'! So far we had concentrated mainly on making sandals from the timbers of demolished huts and buildings, but now the footwear situation was becoming so desperate that it was necessary to follow up the general's repeated requests. This was done, time after time, with negative results.

Meanwhile the need was becoming more urgent than ever. The small and inexperienced staff of shoemakers explored ways and means of prolonging the useful life of footwear in possession of individuals. (Many had only homemade sandals). Tools were of course a major problem, as well as materials, if you have no hammers, lasts[5], nails, pincers, rasps, prickers, thread or leather, just how do you repair boots? Prickers and small screwdrivers were made from the spokes from the rickshaw wheels recovered from the waterfront, and lasts and cutting tools from the remnants of the derelict bus. Steadily, bit by bit, and always by trial and error, some progress was made. Every unserviceable item of footwear, no matter what its condition, was recovered and taken into stores against the day when some use might be found for it, and we 'advertised' for qualified cobblers. Eventually it was found that thread could be made from breaking down unserviceable clothing items, thread by thread, and twisting the threads together, and then dipping it in the bitumen taken from pulled down huts. (A substitute for 'cobblers wax'.) Web equipment too was another source of 'thread'. A machine was later developed from an old gas meter recovered from Jubilee Buildings flats, for the re-winding of the threads. It worked very well and was most useful. Experiments were also in progress as to how best to renovate boots from the unserviceable footwear handed in. A warrant officer whose job normally covered the repair of optical instruments, rangefinders, etc finally came up with the idea of making a kind of protector from hoop iron (taken from the bales of coolie blankets) and taken off cuts from corrugated iron sheets from which mess tins, etc had been manufactured. The boots that were brought for repair were practically finished; no tramp would ever have accepted them. They were worn through, and invariably the welts had gone as well. We were already using recovered uppers for re-soling, but their life in this capacity was short, very short indeed, and so the idea of the protector was born.

The metal was cut into diamond shapes, then these were fitted into recovered leather uppers, with the four points being turned over inside to hold them in position, then the whole was stitched by hand onto the boot, with the thread recovered from garments, the thread having been treated with 'improvised' cobbler's wax! Men who did this kind of work are beyond all possible praise and the camp inmates most grateful to them.

The task of providing mess tins, cooking and eating utensils was going on steadily, and was a never-ending task, so long as materials were available. The doctors had expressed their concern about the lack of operating facilities, and I had been told of their wish to have an operating lamp. As a result of this request the men got down to the job of making one.

The outer shade was made of rolled out corrugated iron, while the reflectors to be fitted inside, 164 of them if I remember correctly, made from diamond shaped snippets of old peanut oil tins and set at different angles to minimise shadow, was nearing completion.

This shadowless operating lamp took ages and ages to make, and required much patience and ingenuity.

The doctors hoped it would soon be ready. Meanwhile, there was an immediate requirement for an instrument. A patient was suffering from internal bleeding, thought to be in the rectum. Could we make an instrument of metal which could be inserted? It should have a small opening all the way up, and a flange to prevent it going in too far. About 8in. long and with a wooden plunger slightly longer, which could be greased to ease the way in and then withdrawn. The metal instrument would then be moved round slowly until it could be seen from where the blood was coming. A rough drawing was provided!

As a large part of the old married quarters in Jubilee Buildings were now empty, the electricians of the Royal Engineers were busy removing the electric wiring from these flats and re-equipping some of the huts used as hospital accommodation, setting up the wiring for a potential operating theatre, and providing light to the various cookhouses and other living accommodation. This was a long, slow and tedious job, accomplished most satisfactorily under the most difficult conditions, with so little in the way of tools, and so much opposition from the Japanese who always suspected some ulterior motive to the most simple of actions.

They always had wireless[es] in mind when anything electrical was involved, perhaps with some justification as receiving sets did spring up in camp, just like mushrooms! Similarly, others were just as busy taking up floor boards from the empty married quarters and bringing them back to store for making into tables for Hospital and cookhouses, doors for huts, coffins, and many other uses. Much gas and water piping was also removed and re-erected in washhouses, hospitals, cookhouses, etc. In fact, everything that could be of use was brought back and stored, if not wanted for immediate use.

affidavit

Towards the middle of May 1942 the camp commandant[1]
let it be known that they would shortly be asking all men
in camp to sign an affidavit not to escape, or try to, and the
consequences if they did, and were caught. It was explained
what would happen to comrades left behind, and the dire
punishments to them, and collective punishment to the
camp in general. The Japanese also hinted that when this
act had been completed then conditions in camp would
improve, and that they did not subscribe to the Geneva
Convention in any way!

This matter was discussed and argued by officers who
were not disposed to accede to this request. The final decision being that we could not freely or willingly, sign such a
document, as it would break our allegiance to the Crown.
This we were not prepared to do. Furthermore, we did not
know what the position was in Argyle Street, or the views
of the general and our superiors there, and we were not prepared to be disloyal to them. Surely the Japanese, with their
supposedly great loyalty to their emperor would not expect,
or extract such humiliation from us? Finally, we would ask
for our general to be brought to Shamshuipo, and certainly
we would not sign any such document voluntarily. We fully
realised that the Japanese could, and probably would try to
force us to sign, but we would only do so when sufficient

duress had been shown, and only after instructions from our general. We did not know what the next Japanese move would be, or who would be called first, or in what order, so we could only wait and see, but at least we were able to tell the men of our decisions and call for their support.

When this matter was put to the RAOC there were no dissenting views. A day or two later the whole camp was formed up on the Barrack Square for the signing to commence. The RAOC were well down the line; the parade being assembled in regimental seniority, after the headquarters staff. My Middlesex Regiment solicitor friend, was I think the first one in. A bad choice by the Japanese as he was tough, stubborn, brave and as loyal as they come, and would stick solidly by any commitment/compact he had made to others. I gathered from him afterwards that he had refused to sign and had asked for the general to be brought from Argyle Street. This was enough for the Japanese who marched him out of camp under a two sentry escort. He was followed into the signing room by others who also refused to sign, and they too, were marched away. I think there were some six or more. These refusals to sign brought matters to a halt and the Japanese into general confusion, so after a while the parade was dismissed, and we were left to await further developments. When some time later, we had reassembled, the camp commandant produced one of the printed affidavits signed by the general, and a direction from him that we should all sign, as the inmates of Argyle Street had already done. I did not see this document myself but other officers did and were quite satisfied with its authenticity. So the sad and sorry business of signing commenced and continued until all had been forced to put their signatures to a document none considered to be binding upon them, and it would make no difference when future escapes were considered.

There were many sad hearted and bitter men in Shamshuipo that day, and few had anything but contempt and loathing towards the Japanese. There were a number of approaches made daily to the camp commandant about the position of those men who had refused to sign on the first occasion, and my solicitor friend in particular. We were smilingly told that he was in Stanley Gaol but would be coming back to camp soon. We were all very worried about him, and the others who had gone with him, but daily enquiries brought the same reply. Some ten or fourteen days later he, and the others, returned to camp. He was just as cheerful, friendly and unyielding as ever. What a man to have as a friend![2]

Shortly after the signing the Japanese delivered some supplies. As far as I can remember this consignment consisted of a bar of washing soap for each man (the first for nearly six months, except that which I had been able to buy from limited funds available), a toothbrush, a packet of tooth powder, a small round box of grease, (supposedly for footwear) a Fandoucis (loin cloth) and a small towel of very inferior quality about 12in. long and 5in. wide. I have also been reminded that our captors also supplied a small packet of toilet paper and three postcards per man. I do not recollect these last two items, perhaps they were not handed over to the ordnance staff. Our captors were pleased with themselves, and the Japanese camp staff came round to witness the distribution of this largesse on a scale of one item per man. Well, they certainly had excelled themselves! The items, and in particular the soap was of very poor quality, it seemed to be full of soda and was very wet, so, within days it had shrunk to half the original size. It was used up in no time! The grease was foul smelling stuff but nevertheless a number of men tried to eat it, or use it to 'make a fry up' with their ration of rice, and consequently became ill. The loin cloths were a novelty but greatly prized by the 'wood choppers', a fatigue party whose daily job was to cut up wood for the cookhouses. It became their official uniform! And the towels were given a variety of names which I leave to the imagination. It was a great day for the Japanese to be quickly followed up by a visit from that most benevolent of hosts, the senior Japanese commandant of all prisoners of war and internment camps in Hong Kong, the 'Fat Pig' in person who would give us a talk. No one was interested, but we were formed up on the Barrack Square where a table and chairs had been assembled to await the arrival of the 'mighty one'. He did not speak English, so everything he said was repeated by that nasty piece of work the senior interpreter from headquarters. The incredible hulk, surely the original one, climbed onto a chair, then onto the table. No one could keep a straight face and everyone hoped he would fall off and so complete the entertainment. I was much too far away to hear what the 'Fat Pig' said, but I did catch the import, Japan was a small country, but a very big land, etc.

The swaggering Japanese were having their day; the Great East Asia Co-Prosperity Scheme was being pushed forward in the rear of the still advancing all conquering Japanese Imperial Army.[3] They could stick their chests out at last and they were making the most of it! Can you imagine the contempt this captive audience had for them, and for the 'Father' who was looking after us!

Recently I had been receiving requests from camp members who had the misfortune to have broken their glasses. Was there anything that we could do for them? Some quite obviously could not see without their accustomed spectacles, while others were so inconvenienced that they were just miseries to themselves and to everyone else. I had seen many of these broken frames and had already taken council with anyone who had knowledge of how best to repair them. Many were tied up with cotton, sticky paper, tape, or anything else which could be found. It was suggested to me that in many cases the tortoiseshell frames had fractured, usually at the bridge, and the only way to repair these would be to find some material which would fuse the two parts together. I was also assured that the best material to do this was 'Amyl Acetate'. So I got in touch with 'Cardiff Joe' and asked him if, when next he had a day off, if he would try to get a small quantity at the chemist's shop in Hong Kong, where I was assured a stock was held. He was shown the state of many of the glasses which had been left in our workshops, and what we were doing to help. He was quite sympathetic, so I gave him money, and waited. A few days later he produced a very small phial with a minute quantity of pineapple smelling liquid in the bottom. Meantime, a small table had been set up in the 'tailor's shop' where 'while you wait' repairs could be carried out. A warrant officer, skilled in the repair of optical instruments took charge. This small section grew until it was like an optician's bench in a large establishment, and we had by now, acquired all kinds of aids and materials with which to carry out the every growing numbers of spectacles which needed attention. I am sure it was a most useful service and a blessing to many! Soon, Cardiff Joe was making further visits to the chemists, and the staff were becoming more adept at concealing that small phial whenever the camp commandant or his staff, came round!

About the end of June 1942 the camp commandant intimated that the officers in Argyle Street would be contributing monthly amounts of money from their pay to a central fund, for the benefit of troops in Shamshuipo. The Royal Navy would set up a similar organisation.

The money for the benefit of the army personnel would be sent to the senior Royal Army Pay Corps[4] [RAPC] officer in Shamshuipo. This aid from the army officers in Argyle Street would be useful, very useful, and would help in saving many lives. On the other hand the Japanese might consider large amounts of cash, outside their control, to be a menace and a danger to them. However, it would minimise the amount of provision they would have to make for the prisoners' welfare, and perhaps they could manipulate or even control the spending of the cash. Obviously all (or nearly all) of the expenditure would have to go through them. It was going to be a difficult assignment for the RAPC officers. From a camp inmate's point of view there could have been no better or sounder choice. This officer had the confidence of everyone in camp that mattered. He had suffered polio, was a highly religious and righteous man, and as straight as a die. Certainly not the kind of man who would 'bend to the wind', though in dealing with the Japanese (and others) he would have to counter much 'persuasion' on their part. Between May 1942 and November 1943 the total amounts of money which came from Argyle Street for army use were, if the documents in my possession are correct, nearly 45,000 Yen! The document I refer to came into my possession in November 1965 at the time some sixty of us made a re-union visit to Hong Kong.

I have been unable to find out who the author was, and hope he will not mind my quoting extracts from a report I assume he made to the general (or senior officer in Argyle Street at that time.) He had obviously just moved there from Shamshuipo.

On the matter of remittances he says:

When the first months' allotment was received a committee was formed consisting of ***** with the R.A.P.C. officer as Chairman. The Navy and the Dockyard Defence Corps had their own organisations. This committee considered the conflicting claims of hospital, cookhouses, sanitation [e.g. soap and disinfectants] and amenities such as cigarettes, and finally allocated money on the following approximate basis: medicines, soap, disinfectants, etc – 50%; hospital amenities – 20%; cookhouses – 20%; general necessities – 10%. Cigarettes were cut out in view of the greater essentials mentioned above, and their relative value [Yen 5,000 would only have given each man about three packets a month].

Little was spent up to September except on small purchases by the hospital and cookhouses from the canteen, the main order for soap and medicines being placed with the Japanese Military Authority as being the only source of supply. [No soap had been received in camp for general use for over 2 months!]

The order, amounting to 3,000–4,000 Yen, was accepted but supplies were never obtained. In this connection the camp commandant was most helpful in spite of the fact that the committee had politely refused to buy boots so that the men could do two hours' work a day, as was suggested by him.

Generally the money has been allocated month by month to the hospital and cookhouse, and a small sum reserved for such items as sun glasses, repairs to dentures, sports gear, musical instruments, scenery and paint.

The above extracts do, I believe, set out the position as known by the author, but obviously, what he did not quote was the undercover activity in the traffic with sentries and others of medicines and other essential supplies.

The committee met as required. Comments on individual activities in which this committee had a hand will come later, but perhaps this general introduction to the Amenities Fund might end by giving details of a certificate in my possession, and provided and signed by that most conscientious RAPC officer.

Camp Fund

According to my records **** has contributed from his advances of pay the sum of MY **** for credit to the camp fund, opened in Shamshuipo Camp, Hong Kong, on 30 June 1942 and operated by me.

I certify that this money was expended for the good of all prisoners of war in the camp, and on items which, in my view, would have been sanctioned as public charges if the circumstances could have been represented to the War Office.

A detailed receipt has been issued.

This certificate receipt has been issued.

This certificate may be used in support of any claim of the officer for refund of the money.

Shamshuipo

24 February 1945, signed ★★★★[5]

According to the original receipts the author contributed a total of 210 Yen to this camp fund between 30 June 1942 and the end of the war.

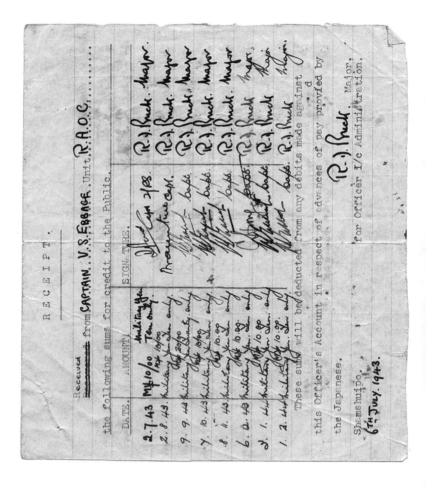

香港俘虜收容所

CAMP FUND.

According to my records, *Capt. V. S. Ebbage. R.A.O.C.*

has contributed from his advances of pay the sum of MY. 210.00

(Mil. Yen. Two hundred & ten only) for credit to the Camp Fund,

opened in Shamshuipo Camp, Hong Kong, on the 30th.June,1942 and

operated by me.

I certify that this money was expended for the good of
all Prisoners-of-War in the Camp, and on items which, in my view,
would have been sanctioned as public charges if the circumstances
could have been represented to the War Office. A detailed receipt
has been issued.

This certificate may be used in support of any claim
of the Officer for refund of the money.

R.J. Rudd.

Major,
Asst.Command Paymaster,
China Command.

Shamshuipo,
24th.February,1945.

Receipt to Captain Ebbage for donations to camp fund with covering letter.
(RLC Museum)

THIS IS THE LAST WILL AND TESTAMENT of me VICTOR STANLEY EBBAGE
No. 118958 a Captain in the Royal Army Ordnance Corps of His
Majesty's Land Forces (at present a Prisoner-of-War of the Imperial
Japanese Army) which I make at Sham Shui Po Hong Kong this
nineteenth day of August One thousand nine hundred and forty-two.
1.   I HEREBY revoke all former wills and testamentary dispositions
heretofore made by me.
2.   SUBJECT to the payment of my debts and funeral and testamentary
expenses (if any) I GIVE devise and bequeath all the real and
personal property of or to which I shall be possessed or entitled
at my death or over which I shall then have a general power of
appointment or disposition by Will UNTO my wife Elsie Ebbage of
6 Scarisbrick Street Ormskirk in the County of Lancaster (at present
residing in Australia) absolutely AND I APPOINT my said wife to be
the sole executrix of this my Will.

SIGNED by the above-named Testator Victor Stanley Ebbage as and for
his last Will and testament in the presence of us both present at
the same time who at his request in his presence and in the presence
of each other have hereunto subscribed our names as witnesses.

No. 103244 Staff Captain
China Command

E.G. Walther Cpt.
No. 99748. 1st Bn. Middlesex Regt.

Last Will and Testament of Captain Ebbage while a POW. (RLC Museum)

6

Letters Home

Earlier in this account I have referred to the ease with which requests to demolish huts for the timber, etc that they contained, and how these requests had been agreed by the Japanese. It had for some time been obvious that the Japanese readiness to accede was because, they wished to clear an area of some 50–100 yards of no mans' land between the perimeter fence and the occupied huts. The Japanese had themselves been busy for some time erecting a new boundary fence. This was to be a formidable deterrent to those who might have a mind to try and escape. Now this fence was being electrified so as to make escape more difficult, and some watchtowers had been erected. We all took a long cool look at these added precautions, trying to spot the weaker points. There seemed to be quite a few that would provide little more than a nuisance to a really determined escaper. We joked about the fence, and wondered if it was really intended to keep us in or the Chinese out! The opinions I got from members of my staff, and their reports to me were reassuring and bore out my own views. In particular the council the electrician gave, and he had more opportunity than most for studying the effects of the 'electric fence' was that 'He knew just how he could put the electric wiring out of action'. Even the perimeter running along the two seaward sides of the camp were 'caged in'. The Japanese seemed very pleased with their efforts!

The arrangements for dealing with the 'night soil' had for some time, been giving cause for concern. Those responsible for buying it were having trouble in getting the picks and shovels from the Japanese each morning. As a result the cookhouses, living accommodation, etc were plagued with flies, and the doctors did not like this state of affairs at all! The health of those in camp was quite bad enough already, with dysentery, diphtheria, deficiency diseases, etc without adding to our problems, but repeated requests to the Japanese for help had brought no improvement. Could I see if some more satisfactory and suitable arrangement could be made with them? The interpreter said he 'would see', but nothing happened. I approached him again later, when he appeared to be in a more receptive mood, without any result. By now the situation was becoming quite desperate so I tackled him again, with a special request to see the camp commandant[1] about this most unsatisfactory problem. In due course the camp commandant sent for me, and his questions were lengthy and varied. It gradually dawned on me that what he was frightened of, but would not admit it, was that we might use these tools for escape purposes. This was the one thing constantly in the Japanese mind (as in ours). The unsatisfactory sanitary situation took very much second place, even though their health, as well as ours, could be affected. He would give the matter further thought, meantime I could take the tools for the rest of the day, but must hand them back by 5pm. Eventually, he took his big decision, sent for me and said: 'He would let me keep the tools permanently if I, in turn, would give him a personal undertaking that they would not be used for any purpose not personally approved by him'. The noose was certainly now round my neck, but we took the tools and the risks involved. My chief clerk took great care to book in, and out, all the tools, and to get signatures for them. It was a worrying and harrowing business, in particular when items became lost or misplaced, which they frequently did! The camp commandant, his staff, and the guards, made repeated visits by day, and often by night, to check the tools were still 'all there'. As a result the chief clerk lost many hours of sleep opening up the store for these random checks, while I, in Jubilee Buildings, some 150 yards away also had some sleepless nights hoping that all was well! The tension eased many months later when the camp commandant, and his boss at headquarters, became interested in our gardening project, and then they provided, quite willingly, a lot of tools to help with this propaganda exercise. The 'Fat Pig' was all for self sufficiency then; words which I thought, ran along nicely with 'improvise'.

An officer had been appointed to take care of 'entertainments' in camp. There certainly was a need to provide distraction from the boredom which we all suffered, something to make us forget, even for a while, the privations, discomfort and utter perplexity of our existence. Entertainment was indeed a step in the right direction, but it meant that inevitably our small workshops, etc would be involved. Concert parties cannot run without 'props' or games and sports without equipment, and somewhere to keep it! There was also in camp a small band of fanatical and enthusiastic visionaries busy enrolling support for their 'keep fit programme'. The belief in physical fitness was unbounded, and of the utmost importance to our getting out alive, or at least not complete wrecks. Good for the mind as well! I did not agree with this idea, nor did I think many of the medical officers supported it either. My unit had already been warned about subjecting themselves to violent physical activities which, in my view, would bring on a state of malnutrition that much more quickly. Anyhow, approaches were made by the 'sports & entertainments' side to the Japanese for sports gear, musical instruments, props, paint, etc. The Japanese were slow to react at first to the needs of entertainments; perhaps as books on escapology so often have their starting point, or cover, in such activities. They did however react with some alacrity to the request for sports gear, and soon quite a variety was brought into camp.

We had every reason to distrust the Japanese motives particularly as the requests for medical supplies by the doctors, food, by the officer i/c of rations, and clothing and footwear by me, had so far met with such negative response. Perhaps we were being unfair to them when the sports gear came in so quickly. Maybe no one outside camp wanted sports gear; while the other commodities were much sought after, (like food) even by the Japanese themselves. But also, at the back of my mind, lingered the thought that perhaps there was an ulterior motive, maybe not quite as diabolical as the leaving open windows on second and third stories of buildings so that prisoners under pressure could quickly dispatch themselves, but nonetheless, an opportunity to commit hara-kiri[2] in a lingering sort of way. This matter was discussed with other officers who took the view that 'It was quite likely'. I resolved to be even more careful where my own unit was concerned, and warned the men, yet again of the effects as I saw them, of too much physical exercise, and considered the matter then closed. I was therefore particularly concerned when a few days later it was announced that a game of soccer had been arranged between England and Scotland, to be played on the decomposed granite pitch used as a parade ground, and that a man of undoubted ability in my unit had been selected to play. I think the names of those taking part had been given to the Japanese, notwithstanding [I] registered my displeasure. This senior NCO I held in the highest regard, someone in whom I had implicit trust, a man who would never dream of doing intentionally, a wrong thing, and here he was, chosen to represent England against the 'Old Enemy'. Intuition said he must not play, but reasoning was that, logically I could not stop him, and he wanted to play! To my everlasting regret I did not prevent him, a flaw perhaps in my judgment which both he and I were to regret. He, alas, for the remainder of his life, and myself because I had not done my duty. It did not matter that no other officer commanding had forbidden his men to play. I knew I ought to have allowed him to play... though in fact he could not be prevented if he wanted to. Part way through the game he was brought down, and left the so-called field with a gravel rash which extended from his knee to his hip bone, and perhaps some 6in. wide. The doctors had nothing with which to help him, and he was told to bathe the wound as often as he could throughout the day. My chief clerk, who was his friend, had the unenviable task of bathing and bandaging as the sore became gradually worse and the inevitable infection set it. I saw the wound often, he was lucky we had facilities to help, and men willing to use them, for everyone had his own problem. Eventually, with a little help and much time and patience, the unnecessary wound started to heal (perhaps the Red Cross food helped). He went to Japan in January 1943. This was I am sure a salutary lesson which he never forgot, and a reminder to me that, whenever I took a decision, be it based on intuition or logic, it should be acted upon without fear or favour. I subsequently heard that he openly expressed his thanks to my chief clerk for saving his leg, and possibly his life. I was blessed with some very good men, albeit some who perhaps did unwise things, with the most noble of intentions. There was no need to address the unit again on this matter; they tried their best to keep fit, without recourse to violent use of body and limb! Others were quick to follow, and to the best of my recollections there were no more 'trials of strength' on the football field; meanwhile, I could console myself with the fact that the men's footwear would last that much longer when it was not subject to 'unfair wear and tear'.

During the months of April, May and June 1942 there was a general deterioration in health of all those in camp and the 'numbers' in hospital became larger and larger. An 'Old Folks Home' was established for the over 60s, on instructions from the Japanese, and then, suddenly, and seemingly without any warning, we were in the thick of a diphtheria epidemic which lasted for some months and carried off a large number of men. It was necessary to form an isolation unit, set apart from the ordinary patients. At first the Japanese did not seem to take this outbreak seriously, though our own medical officers certainly did, and said so to the Japanese. After a while, as the deaths continued to mount, they decided the best thing would be for everyone to wear masks, and would we make masks for everyone in camp? Well, yes, but where was the material and cotton to make them to come from? Couldn't we improvise? This seemed to be a bargaining point, if they would supply the cotton, we could try. (This was always a good line of approach whenever anything was wanted from them, seldom, if ever, did they accede to a direct request), and so they provided some reels of cotton, and we made a dozen or so samples for inspection by the senior Japanese medical officer from headquarters. The profit, from our point of view, a few reels of cotton which could be used for other purposes. Then, as expected, the material did not find favour, and what was more they would want some masks for the Japanese sentries and camp staff as well, and so more cotton, tape and material was forthcoming to make these useless masks which no one wore except when in close contact with the Japanese, i.e. parades, etc. At this point I believe they had not provided any serum despite pleadings from our medical officers who were not sparing themselves, and doing all in their power to help the sick. The Japanese main concern appeared to be to 'find the carrier', so certain were they that one existed in camp. Perhaps we were hiding one on purpose! And so, day by day, everyone in camp had his throat examined by the Japanese medical officer. I do not think they ever found a carrier, goodness knows what would have happened had they been successful! Presumably he would have been 'caged' or eliminated in the interests of those remaining. I wonder? Eventually, the Japanese did bring in a small amount of serum; sufficient to treat a very small percentage of those in need (and our doctors did, I believe, obtain some from 'other sources'). Where there was no serum, it seemed there was little hope. Available serum was I gathered divided up into very small doses for those who had chance of recovery.

My notes show:

> It was about this time that the camp was visited by a
> diphtheria epidemic which lasted some months and
> which carried off a large number of men. A number of
> RAOC were affected, but I am glad to say we lost none,
> though there were two or three who had narrow shaves.

This represented the position from a unit point of view; from
the workshops angle we found it impossible to make coffins
quickly enough, nor did we have the timber and nails with
which to do so. We were thus faced with the problem of
what to do about the growing number of deaths, increasing
daily. Everyone would have liked to have given these poor
chaps the best possible funeral we could, but coffins were
now beyond us; so far as I was concerned it would have to
be blankets only in future! In fairness to the Japanese, once a
man was dead they respected his corpse; never it seemed, his
living body. What a pity they could not, or would not, supply
the serum we needed! The dead, for burial, were taken from
camp daily, and this took place at a vacant plot of ground
which was near, and within sight of the officers' camp at
Argyle Street. The procedure was to load the dead onto a
truck (often the ration truck), and together with a small
funeral party from the man's own unit, (and where possible
complete with headstone made by the Royal Engineers) and
armed with picks and shovels with which to dig the graves,
the procession, complete with parson and guards left camp.
As the cortege departed, (and when allowed by the Japanese)
friends would foregather to pay their last respects. It was a
reverential occasion. The number of deaths during the period
May to December 1942 was probably of the order of 200.[3]

After much delay, and many setbacks the shadowless
operating lamp, so much wanted by the medical officers,
was now ready, and stood in all its glory for all to see! It was
a fine piece of work and a credit to all those who had been
involved in the making. Now came the relatively simple job

of installing it in the allotted place. All those interested were anxious to see if it really worked when the electric lamps were put in and switched on! Well, it did work, and the surgeons and doctors were pleased. If an emergency occurred now, they would be able to do something about it. Surgical instruments, dressings and gut for sewing up the wounds were, it was understood, practically non existent, but at least the surgeons would be able to see what they were doing! So far this was perhaps our most spectacular effort in camp, and all those who had put in so much endeavour, thought and ingenuity, were congratulated. It was a worthwhile job and we hoped someone would benefit. A surprising fact of life is that, when success seems so near, it is just as quickly taken away, and so it was to be in this case. After all the hours of hard work lavished on this project, and in the most difficult of circumstances, I believe it was never used! No, the Japanese did not destroy it, or take it away; they merely cut off, without any notice, the supply of electricity. It is not suggested they deliberately wanted to sabotage this particular plan; on the contrary the cutting off of the electricity was because, they wanted to ensure that no illicit radio could operate, and also make useless the large number of immersion heaters which still abounded at every search. For whatever reason the loss of electricity was a severe blow to us all; no lights after dark, and I am sorry to say, no direct news from home on how the war was proceeding. Nothing to lift morale, only action to dampen it! Slaps in the face so frequently given physically were also given in other ways, but this reverse would never discourage my chaps; every setback was treated by them as just another challenge.

The billet I shared with brother officers from various units was a lively environment in which to live. Together we could at least be free from some of the cares of others, and try to get as much lighthearted and childish enjoyment as was possible under the circumstances in which we existed. There were all kinds of practical jokes, and we devised games to keep ourselves amused, and of course, endless talks on every subject under the sun. It was not unusual, when going to wash ones 'smalls' which had been left soaking in a container of water, to find one or two additions. My solicitor friend was most adept at this and could put over a substantial legal argument as to how it was possible for a handkerchief to fall out of his pocket and be found some yards away in my 'can'; and when we had 'lost' his case, to offer to do the whole of the washing as an act of self mortification. He was also most adept at getting cigarettes out of the Japanese, or extracting them from others who might have acquired the odd one or two, and were looking for a safe place in which to smoke them! And then there were the card games. Somehow we had managed to get a pack of very worn playing cards. A few were missing, and were replaced by homemade substitutes which of course could be easily spotted, and so the dealing we left, unobserved, to the honesty of the dealer, while the other participants turned their backs on the proceedings. This of course produced endless opportunities for argument. We now had to play in daylight and were hard at it one warm afternoon when one of the Japanese interpreters came in unannounced. (They always did!) He sat, most politely for a time watching, and then after a while made a most startling announcement. I think the time was about 2.30pm and what he said ran something like this:

> All prisoners of war will now be allowed to write letter home. Letters to be written on postcards, in ink or typed, and will be limited to 15–20 words. They will be handed in to the camp commandant's office by 4pm.

There was a frantic rush, first by my staff officer, solicitor friend, to make an official announcement to the camp, both officers and men, and by us to our units. Someone would try to get the canteen opened so that those with money could buy ink. As can be imagined everyone was confused, many thought it was a joke and did not bother, while others tried their best to get ink and postcards, or anything that might resemble a postcard. It was not easy, in the heat of the afternoon, when most people were resting, etc to get news round a camp of 3–4,000 men. For practically all the effort would be useless in such a time span as had been given. I did not have any postcards, nor did I have any ink, but a friend had managed to get hold of some cards and was awaiting our return. Quickly, we decided on a wording suitable to the few of us present, and the solicitor staff officer typed out what he could, on perhaps one of the only two typewriters in camp. A standard worded message might make it easier for the Japanese censor, and it could have implications on our own when he saw some were alike! I believe that relatively, only a handful of 'cards' were handed over to the Japanese by the deadline given. After the war I was able to examine this card, which was received by my wife in Australia some months later.[4] It bore the imprint of the Japanese censor and had obviously been held over a candle, or other such flame, to see if it contained any hidden message. It was black nearly all over! I was glad of the opportunity to get any sort of a message to my wife. As previously stated, the colony of Hong Kong surrendered on 25 December 1941, but I had not done so until 26 December. In the meantime the latest casualty details had been given to War Office and all wireless transmitting sets had been destroyed. No one could tell me what report had been given about my position, though it was believed to be that I was 'missing'. So if my card got through then at least my wife would be aware I was still alive. I did not know of any other way that she would find out! This aspect had worried me quite a lot, and over many sleepless nights had turned over in my mind the various permutations that might result. None gave me any comfort or satisfaction. Whether the Japanese would ever deliver that bit of paper I had my doubts, but they might, you never knew, and they would obviously want to look 'humane' in the eyes of the world, so perhaps they would! But two people at least wanted to know what had happened to me, my wife in Australia, and my father-in-law in England, were both making their separate enquiries.

On 27 June 1942 my father-in-law sent a cable to my wife in Melbourne, Australia, retransmitted to her in New South Wales, which reads:

Elsie Ebbage, 73 Queen Victoria Street, New South Wales. 'Red Cross reports Capt. Ebbage, prisoner of war'. Dad Iddon.[5]

and then, on 6 July 1942 my wife received the following:

Australian Red Cross Society
Victorian Division
Red Cross House,
289–293 Swanston Street, Melbourne C.1.

Mrs.V.S. Ebbage,
22 Venice Street,
Mentone S.11.

Dear Mrs. Ebbage,

A cable message dated 29 June 1942, has been received from International Red Cross, Geneva, in answer to our enquiry by cable concerning your husband...

7576720 Capt.V.S. Ebbage,
R.A.O.C. 6th Section, Queens Road, Hong Kong.

We are pleased to inform you that he is safe, though a prisoner of war.

Signed Mrs.T.W.White,
Director, Red Cross Bureau for Wounded,
Missing and Prisoners of War.[6]

I am sure my wife must have felt relieved by the foregoing. I have always held the Red Cross in the highest regard, no matter what the calamity, worldwide, without regard to colour, creed or caste, they are there to help, and they do. Surely a symbol of hope for many in despair!

香港俘虜收容所

Hong Kong Prisoners of War Camp 'S

13th. December, 1942.

My Dearest Elsie,

Am very glad to say that I am quite well and sincerely hope that you and our two children are likewise.

So far I have had no letters from you, but we are all looking forward to the first batch of mail. I am afraid that your letters with news of yourself, Ken and Joyce are what I miss most and I shall be extremely grateful when your first epistle arrives. Somehow I feel that you are alright so do not worry on this score but I often wonder how the bairns are progressing. Hope Joyce is doing well at school and I am sure she will be a great comfort to you. Kenneth must be growing into a big boy. Bet he is a handful, but remember he is a boy and bound to be a bit wild and daring. I should love to see them and you. Hope that our reunion will not be so long now. Was glad to get a Red Cross parcel with sixteen tins of foodstuffs the other day. Very enjoyable! Hope all at home are well and there will be no more vacant places when I get back.

All my love, darling and heaps of kisses to the three of you.

Always your own.

V.S.Ebbage.

香港俘虜收容所

Hong Kong Prisoners of War Camp "S."

My Darling Elsie,

Here we are again all merry and bright, and I am glad to say fit; dont feel a day older in spite of an additional year. Sent you a letter recently thanking you for your cable and was also lucky in being able to send you a broadcast message. Am always thinking of you and the children, and am glad to know you are all contented. I am very interested in Joyce's schooling and to know she is doing so well. I know I shall be proud of my daughter when I see her again as quite a lady. Kenneth will be busy with his lessons, tell him to try hard and grow into a big strong boy. Dad will be coming soon and we will have good games together. Many happy returns of your birthday, the last of the family for this year. Am very happy and proud of you Elsie and glad of all your efforts for the welfare of our children. In you I have implicit trust, in your judgement, dealings and love for us all. There is no one in the world in whom I could have more faith, and I yearn for the day when I can take the load of responsibility from your shoulders. This letter will I believe reach you quickly. It carries all my love and Xmas Greetings. Till we meet again, all my love, may good fortune smile on you all.

I am yours for ever, Your own.

V. S. Ebbage.

Above: Handwritten letter from Captain Ebbage to his wife Elsie. (RLC Museum)

Left: Letter from Captain Ebbage to his wife Elsie, 13 December 1942. Written virtually a year after his capture this is one a few occasions on which the author was able to communicate with his wife. (RLC Museum)

EQUITY CHAMBERS
472 BOURKE STREET
MELBOURNE

TELEPHONE MU 5787

TELEGRAMS ROOTESMOTI

18th. April 1945.

Mrs. E. Ebbage,
22 Venice Street,
MENTONE. S 11

Dear Mrs. Ebbage,

The following message was broadcast from Tokio
on 13th. April at 4.30 p.m. in the "Postman Calling"
session.

"Mrs. Elsie (Abbott or Evatt or Everett), 22 Bennett Street,
Mentone, Victoria.

From: her husband, Captain Victor Stanley (Abbott, Evatt
or Everett) Royal ARmy Ordinance Corps, who is interned
in Hong Kong.

Dearest Elsie: Glad of your many letters (which show)
you are all in good health. Keep me informed of
children's progress and give them both the best education
you can afford. It is all we shall be able to do for
them. Tell them to continue winning prizes for school
work. Hope you have sufficient money for requirements.
You have my authority to draw all pay and allowances
the Paymaster will issue. If you consider it desirable
to return to England, please do so, but as I am
unaware of your circumstances cannot advise, but must
leave decision to you. I know you will act in the
best interests of the family. Am fit and well. Continue
looking after camp workshop and stores and welfare
of my fellow-men to the best of my ability. Fondest
love and kisses to all of you. You are never out of
my thoughts. Vic."

Yours sincerely,

for C. H. HORDERN. Capt.

WELFARE AND ADMINISTRATION
OFFICER
BRITISH SERVICES FAMILIES

Telegraph from Captain Ebbage to his wife Elsie, delivered by Welfare and
Adminstration Office for British Services Families. (RLC Museum)

The Steam Oven

It was not unusual for the Japanese to take out of camp different individuals for questioning, and one of these was an armament staff sergeant of the RAOC (later REME).[1] I remember two Japanese coming into camp to question him and after this unfruitful (for them) interrogation they left say[ing] they would be back later to take him out of camp. When they had gone, and he had recovered his composure I questioned him about what they wanted. They had come about the coast defence guns at Stanley!

With a warrant officer armament artificer, (now the leading 'bricklayer' and advisor on many workshop matters, it was he who masterminded so many of our projects like the shadowless lamp, the steam oven, etc) we discussed the unfortunate position of this armament staff sergeant. We did not know, and could only guess what they wanted, and how much force they would use to obtain their ends, but this NCO had been responsible for the maintenance and repair of the guns at Stanley Port, and obviously knew all about them. Together we tried to build up the courage he was going to need, and gave what help and advice where we could. The following day he was removed from camp, and on subsequent occasions afterwards. I understand he was first asked how to work the guns at Stanley. He claimed he knew nothing about them, and was duly beaten up. Later he was confronted with the Fortress Records of Work Done, which bore his signature. He was again beaten up, severely, and later was I gather knocked unconscious with an iron bar. On each occasion that he returned to camp he was in a sorry condition, and it was necessary to bathe his wounds and reassure him, against further inquisition to follow.

My notes show:

In June 1942 Armament Staff Sergeant **** was taken out of camp by the Japanese in connection with the guns at Stanley. He suffered much at their hands, but gave nothing away. His conduct was exemplary.

Much later, it was possible to get him on a draft for Japan, where at least he was far away from the trials he had undergone, with the possibility of more to come. Unfortunately, while in Japan he lost a hand.

The master baker had been carrying out experiments in the making of rice flour, using one of the rooms in our compound for this purpose. Here we kept the large granite roller found in camp when we arrived. It had already done much excellent work in eliminating the wave ridges in the sheets of corrugated iron, thus making possible the manufacture of many items, mess tins, baking tins, etc. This roller was now tried out on the concrete floor of a small room. Once we got the roller inside the idea was to pull it backwards and forwards through the windows which were exactly opposite each other. The room had been, in better days, occupied as a bedroom by an officer of the Middlesex Regiment. The roller and floor would be washed clean, the rice spread out on the concrete floor, one man in bare feet, in turn, feeding in the grain, and hopefully sweeping up the resultant flour. Meanwhile small gangs of men would be stationed outside the windows, taking it in turn to pull the roller back and forth over the rice! Then we would have a mill! It was all very primitive, but it had possibilities, and from experiments made, seemed to work. So the granite roller was transferred to a new site near to an embryo bakery which had already been started, and I lost interest in the milling of rice grain which, in any event was no concern of mine, and there was already quite enough to do without getting too involved in the responsibilities of others. The master baker was, and still is, a friend. A most pleasant and unobtrusive man with a kindly smile and manner and was liked by everyone. If it was possible to make bread of any kind then he was the man to do it, and he knew he could call on any resources we had, be they ever so meager! The 'bricklayers' had already helped in the making of some sort of an oven, and we had made the baking tins to go into it. So far as I was concerned that was that. However, I was not to get out of the 'bakery business' quite so easily. Some bread, of sorts was made, but my friend the master baker wanted to do better! The existing facilities were neither big nor good enough, but if only we could make him a steam oven then all would be plain sailing. He explained the kind of thing he had in mind, giving size, temperatures, pressures, etc and a general idea of how the thing would work. I do not think he had in his possession an 'army bakery manual, for the use of in the field' or, if they taught 'bakery by steam, prisoner of war style', in the Army School of Bakery at Aldershot, where the 'Aldershot Ovens[2] come from', but he did provide us with a definite notion of what he wanted, which was a help! But where, oh where, were we to get a large enough container to convert into an oven to cook for so many men, or strong enough sheets of metal, angles, rivets, etc to make one ourselves? Then there was the matter of the door, which would need to fit so tightly if it was to prevent the escape of steam under pressure, during the period the bread was cooking. My chaps started to look round. I knew they would accept the challenge, if they possibly could, to make an 'ovens steam, prisoners of war for the use of, patented in Shamshuipo 1942'.

Two or three suggestions were made over the next week or two, but none of them were feasible. However, there were some large galvanised water tanks on the top of Jubilee Buildings which might be suitable, but on measuring them it just was not possible to get them through the doorways to the roof, or down the stairs, nor did we have any ropes with which to lower them down outside. They were heavy and awkward and we would not be able to work on them without the approval of the camp commandant. Even if we could get him to agree we would still need ropes, good long ones to lower the tank from the roof and down the four stories. We thought of making ropes from blankets and electric lighting cable taken from the flats, but this would not have been popular with the camp commandant, and there was no way of hiding what we would be doing. If the sentries saw some twenty or thirty men standing together on the roof, only a few yards from the perimeter fence, the sentries would have shot, and asked questions afterwards. And we would never have got the tank!

In this case honesty just had to be the best policy. [*sic*] But if and when we got the tank down, what did we do about filling in the open top, what were we going to do for a door? Well, my chaps had already taken care of this by removing the door from a gas oven they had found in one of the married quarters, and the parts that went with it. So convinced were they that it would work and they could make an oven, and wanted to, that we decided to make an approach to the camp commandant:

a. for permission to build an oven.
b. to recover a water tank from the roof of Jubilee Buildings.
c. To ask the camp commandant if he would provide a rope!

Now the last item seemed to present the most difficulty. He would not like [to] supply a rope, with all its possible implications, on the other hand if we put the question to him when he was in a good mood, and in the above order, well, you never know! If he gave permission for only a and b we could approach the rope question later. We should need to drum up some support from the doctors and others for the oven project, and the good it would do for the camp as a whole. Anyhow we would and did talk to the camp commandant about it, but first had a long talk to the interpreter on the general idea. The Japanese are unpredictable, when you expect them to say 'yes' they say 'no', and when you expect 'no' you sometimes get 'yes'. When dealing with the Japanese, matters such as this must not be rushed, we had put our faith in the interpreter doing the 'right thing', and so the days passed by. Had we pressed for a decision we would surely have got a quick 'no' and that would have been the end of the matter, slowly, slowly was the best approach, even perhaps an outward show of indifference. In due course I was called to the camp commandant's office to state our case and to outline to him what we should like to do. He was of course well briefed on pretty well every aspect and without doubt had already taken a decision. What we were going through now was the by play leading up to him saying either 'yes' or 'no'.

He expressed himself interested in our proposals and thought it a good idea to build an oven. He, himself, had long wanted us to have bread, it would be good for the camp and he was in favour of anything that would be good for, or help the inmates! And so forth and so on! How did we propose to get the tank down from the roof, what damage would we do, would it be very difficult, etc? He expressed his anxiety that no one should be injured, just concerned for our welfare. What safety precautions would we take? He would send a Japanese sentry to show us how best to do the job.

Yes, we were getting on very nicely! Then there was the matter of the rope; did we have a suitable rope in camp? No, we did not, but were counting on his magnanimity and generosity to get us over this difficulty. We sincerely hoped he had such a rope and would let his sentry bring it with him. Yes, that sounded a good idea, he had been fortunate in procuring a rope, but he had not been able to get one long enough to reach all the way from roof to ground. As a matter of fact he had it by him (and the interpreter brought it for inspection). I said it was a very good rope (though it was obviously only about a quarter of the length we really required and inferior at that) and we would take great care of it, and thanked the almighty for his great and benevolent interest in us. He got up, indicating that the interview was over, and I went to the store to await the arrival of the interpreter who would say when we could start.

Obviously we were not going to be given the rope, so had no means of telling how useful it would be. If it was no good then I would be in a position to go back to the camp commandant and say I was afraid it was hardly long enough, etc. But first we would have to try, and there was always the danger he might tire of the whole idea!

I talked to my advisors, explaining the approximate length, thickness, and tensile qualities of the rope, and we made a reappraisal of our plan for getting the tank down. We thought it would be relatively easy to lower it down from the roof to the top floor balcony, as these were quite open at top and side; the next two would present the difficulty. In particular, on the third floor down it would be necessary to pull the tank over the balustrade and lower it onto the floor of the balcony/verandah.

From there to the ground would be relatively easy! It sounds very simple, but with men who had little strength left, inferior and inadequate gear, only the determination to succeed, it was nearly an impossible task. In the event stage one proved fairly easy and that effort had to suffice for day one. Day two proved much more difficult, and if I remember rightly the tank was suspended for some hours before it was finally resting safely. Day three was very similar, but each stage produced new problems, but all were made to be overcome. And day four or five saw the tank safely on the ground. I am sure the chaps now realised just how the Egyptian slaves must have felt when the last stone was placed on the pyramids! The sentry duly took the rope away; escorted would perhaps be a better term. We had no further use for it that we could think of that would have met with the approval of the camp commandant! The tank was lugged to our compound and the slow task of changing it into a steam oven commenced, with fitters, tinsmiths, plumbers and all and sundry taking a hand, and the camp commandant periodically showing (or so he said) a benevolent and fatherly interest in what was happening. Many weeks afterwards the task was completed and the oven installed in a hut of the master baker, bricked round and secure. The tale of the making of the bread is, I know, a long one, fraught too with untold difficulties, but bread, and under the circumstances good bread, was produced, I am sure the master baker's thoughts were then on cakes and puddings, pies and Cornish pasties, but our task, maintenance apart, was now complete. I wish to place on record my appreciation to all those, and there were very many of them, who helped bring this project to a successful conclusion. Their ingenuity, perseverance, with only such pathetic facilities available was quite remarkable. The steam oven was one of the very best of our many efforts!

Soon, the Japanese started daily inspections of the camp, ordering this or that item to be removed and put out of sight; a spate of tidiness, sweeping up of roads, and the general appearance of accommodation and inmates now became a matter of concern.

This unusual activity on the part of the Japanese could only be a prelude to some kind of visit. Then we knew, the Japanese announced that the camp would be visited by a Red Cross Society representative who would carry out an inspection. Everyone would carry on normally, but no one would be allowed to speak to the representative, who turned out to be Swiss. He toured the camp in silence, but it was quite obvious that he was taking it all in, and realised he was being shown only what the Japanese wanted him to see. One or two people tried to get in his way, and a couple were actually called upon to speak, including I think, the officer commanding the Middlesex Regiment, but all were whisked away even before they could say anything that mattered, or was detrimental to our hosts. The visit was so obviously stage-managed, and the shortcomings impossible to conceal, that I am sure the Swiss representative was not bluffed by what he saw, and his reports could have even painted a picture worse than it actually was! One or two people were in trouble afterwards, but nothing really untoward occurred!

8

The Party System

In the main the camp guards were either Koreans or Formosans, but they were commanded by Japanese NCOs, and up to this point I had got on reasonably well with them. They were more tolerant than their masters and seemed to have a sense of humour, but at times they could become most difficult. One day, one of them on patrol heard me humming snatches from songs I knew, and at that particular time it was Dinah Lou. The words were something like this 'Dinah, there is nobody finer, in the state of Carolina, than my little Dinah Lou', etc. He appeared to like the catchy tune and laughed, then put down his rifle, slapped his sides and joined in. We were not practising a double act, but I quickly found out that all the guards knew this tune, which was a favourite with them, and they sang it often, just as well as they could.[1]

I found that it eased the situation, when relations were tense, to try and hum this tune, and in particular when stopped as I so often was, at the guard room, or when passing. Most people, whose duty it was to pass the guard room, had to run the gauntlet, not of sticks but of rifle butts or any other weapon that was at hand. Always depending on the whim! What was more, many of the guards had now got into the habit, (or had been ordered to) of making regular inspections of our compound and workshops while on their rounds just to see what was going on, and presumably reporting to the guard commander, and then to the camp commandant. They had also found out that we could do many little jobs, the sort of 'stitch in time' tasks that need immediate attention. It was therefore inevitable, when they wanted something done, to stop at the appropriate point and ask whoever was around for help, and would pay for the service with a packet or a few cigarettes. Neither my chief clerk nor I liked this idea one little bit, but there were obvious compensations, and we could not stop it short of going direct to the camp commandant. We could see the possibility of a racket being set up by the guards. It says much for the force of character of this warrant officer that he was able to control this new facet just as well as he had done all the others. The Japanese were still very worried about escapes from camp which had continued, and so they decided to introduce what they called the 'party system'. This system was in effect, that each man should at all times know what his neighbour was doing, and they would be subject to collective responsibility, one for another. A party consisted of an officer and 100 men, a group under say a sergeant was twenty-five, and the smallest element was a sub-section under a corporal or lance corporal which comprised five men.

The underlying dangers need no amplification by me! Furthermore, to assist in controlling this scheme everyone in camp was given a camp number to be worn on his outer garment, or shirt, if he had one. It was required to be displayed in a prominent position and be on view at all times. The Japanese brought in the numbered pieces of material and the cotton with which to sew them on the garment, and if I remember rightly stood by as each man produced his garment and had his camp number sewn on! This enabled every man to be readily identified by the camp staff and guards. To be without one's number cost at least a slapping. For a while great attention was paid to this matter, but, like everything else they produced it became a five days' wonder, and then gradually shrank back into obscurity. To make sure the scheme worked properly, all men were required to sleep together, by sub-section, group or party. They had also decided we should all adopt the Japanese way of life, where possible, and sleep on Tatami beds. A Tatami bed is matting placed on a raised platform which ran down the whole length of one side of a hut. Made of wood and about 18in. from the floor, it was open on one side so that items of kit could be stored there. As can well be imagined this cavity became filthy and quite impossible to keep clean, and very soon the boards themselves became bug infested and stank. But at least the Japanese had now provided the beds they had promised, and in fairness to them, this was the way they themselves slept. It was not very long before this novelty too wore off and soon the men were deserting their Tatami beds, preferring the hard concrete floor with all its shortcomings! The introduction of Tatami beds had the effect of releasing a number of other types, of miscellaneous kinds and descriptions, which could now be given to the hospital where there were additional requirements. The health of everyone in camp was deteriorating rapidly.

The notes I have on this read:

During the period May to October 42 the health of those in camp was frightful and alarmed all officers commanding and medical officers alike. The ones who were able to assimilate the diet of rice and vegetables were able to struggle along, but those who could not soon became in a very bad way. All became very thin and worn looking and there was considerable apathy among everyone. A visit to the hospital, (so called) was a most depressing experience, but the medical officers who were doing their best were helpless without medicines and dressings, which were no[n] existent. We were now at the height of the diphtheria epidemic which showed no signs of abating, while at the same time more and more men were suffering from dysentery, malaria, and deficiency diseases associated with malnutrition, pellagra, beriberi, aching (or electric) feet, and of course eye troubles and sores of various kinds. On the lighter side I remember our unit medical officer telling me that 'If ever I have a daughter, I intend to call her Pellagra'. Many years afterwards when I met him again at his house, I found he had two lovely daughters, but I heard them called by much more conventional names!

The complaints from which we suffered were devastating. No one escaped them, everyone had his own problem. The least bearable of all were those suffering from 'aching feet'. These poor chaps just could not sleep at all, and remained awake every night, hour after hour. The symptoms were that the feet 'ached' while at the same time there was an unbearable 'pins and needles' and practically no other feeling, even when placed in the hottest water. My chief clerk, a tall lean man, suffered untold agony from this affliction and we became very concerned about him, but the doctors could not help. I think the condition was new to them and they just did not have any answers. Better food would put it right, so they said. But from where did we get better food? I took careful stock of the unit, as we stood on parade waiting to be 'counted', everyone had become emaciated and looked so ill and thin that I became very concerned about them. We should not be able to go on much longer; if one was to succumb it seemed that others would follow swiftly. Nevertheless the RAOC turned out on parade daily, looking as clean, smart and properly shaven, as was possible under the circumstances, and in good spirits! They did not intend to give in to adversity. Their spirit could not be bettered! The officers had endless discussions about what we could do. Could the amenities fund be stretched a little further? Was there any way we could help ourselves?

I looked carefully at them too, they looked in no better shape than the men, and then at myself. I must have lost about 5 stone in weight since coming into camp. Certainly

I now had no 'rear elevation' (my friends had already christened me 'The Bottomless Wonder'). I had malaria and knew that my eyesight was deteriorating. But I was better than most. I thought again of my mother and my wife, and the good food they had given me, perhaps against the day when I should need all the fat they had put on my bones! We all made regular visits to the hospital; as a unit we had done very well so far; only one death early in January! There was one basic essential which all must have if we were to get out, hope. Depression was the worst possible master to have around, so we tried, all of us, to instill a spirit of cheerfulness and expectancy... courage if you like! And the parsons did their job too, with the sick, while the doctors were working perhaps up to 18 hours a day, ministering, as best they could, without medicines, to all in need of help. The carrots and tomatoes I was growing were doing very well, and soon it seemed likely that there would be benefit from my investment, all seemed to be coming along nicely! Others too had taken up gardening as a means of improving the standard of living, and it was interesting to see how they were progressing with their sweet potatoes, tomatoes, etc. Perhaps it was the gardening idea so generally adopted, which prompted the start of the camp garden. This communal project, which was started in a very small way, but gradually expanded into being one of the best of the camp ventures. Human manure we had in plenty, and this provided the humus necessary to mix with the decomposed granite and make a fertile bed!

On 24 July 1942, there was considerable excitement in camp. The Japanese had discovered that an excavation had been made, (which presumably they associated with an attempt to escape). I was quickly informed that two members of the RAOC were involved, and had been arrested by the Japanese along with a number of others. The kits and bedding of these two men were searched and certain items were removed and hidden, prior to the expected investigation of the kits by the Japanese. The other officers commanding did the same. Our two men, with the others, were taken out of camp on 5 August 1942 and did not return. In due course the Japanese came and took away their kits. (One recently on transfer from 1st Bn, Middlesex Regiment).

The RAOC did not have very many men in hospital. Most men did not want to go there anyway, as they would be separated from their friends who were a valuable stimulus. Only when they were too weak to stand on parade to be 'counted' did many of them opt for a stay in 'hospital'. One such man had been admitted into hospital with dysentery and was, alas, sinking fast. He was so weak that it was not surprising when he finally gave up the unequal struggle, and died. Many of these men, who were close to death, and beset with all their trials and tribulations, seemed always to be more cheerful than those who were visiting them. Always hopeful; surely for then it could not get any worse, and must improve, though for many this was a forlorn hope.

It seemed unbelievable that our last loss had been seven months ago, and we wondered who might be 'next'.

So many people leave making a will until it is too late. In the nightly discussions we officers had together, this question was given a good airing. I was surprised to find how few of us had, in fact, made a will. For some reason soldiers seem to have an aversion to doing so; perhaps it is because of the life they lead. Sort of feeling that it cannot happen to them, at least, not just yet, and so few of the married ones had even discussed with their wives what the effect would be should they ever become widows!

Most young wives do not want to look so far into the future, or find it disagreeable or unpleasant to do so, while their husbands, aware of the desirability, just 'leave it till tomorrow'. It must be admitted that I was in this category! None of us thought that our 'passing' was imminent, but commonsense demanded that we do something about it, and do it now! My staff officer, solicitor friend, knew all the jargon and was quite prepared to forego any legal costs, so

I, and some others, talked him into producing our 'Last Will
& Testament'. He needed a little convincing that we were
of sound mind, and if he did not agree then we would take
our business elsewhere!

In front of me now is a very much worn piece of paper
which says:[2]

> THIS IS THE LAST WILL AND TESTAMENT of me
> VICTOR STANLEY EBBAGE, No. 118958 a Captain
> in the Royal Army Ordnance Corps of His Majesty's
> Land Forces (at present a Prisoner of War of the Imperial
> Japanese Army) which I make at Sham Shui Po, Hong
> Kong, this nineteenth day of August One thousand nine
> hundred and forty-two.
> etc.

and my signature is witnessed by him and my close friend
the officer commanding, 1st Bn, Middlesex Regiment (in
Shamshuipo).[3]

What a time and place to be considering such action
as this, and as we laughed and joked none of us realised
that in only a few more days our solicitor friend would be
on his way to Japan. When the officers had left for Argyle
Street, the discipline in camp showed some improvement,
there was no longer a superfluity of officers without jobs,
and more responsibility fell upon the warrant officers and
senior NCOs who were left. Now they had a job to do,
including those in my own unit, and they were doing it
very well indeed. Nevertheless there was a very small element of individuals who had no intention of sticking to any
code of conduct that did not suit them. Men who would
not obey any order unless it had the power of enforce-
ment behind it, and only the Japanese had such power.
Naturally too these same men were anti-Japanese, as they
were anti anything! There really were not so very many
of them, and most had already fallen foul of the Japanese.
They had earned the name of 'Bad Hats' which they most

certainly were. Quite suddenly and without warning the Japanese ordered that the ground floor of Jubilee was to be cleared and the occupants moved to other accommodation. We tried to guess the reason for this sudden move, and then, just as unexpectedly my solicitor friend was sent for and told he would be going to Japan and taking with him a draft of about 600 men for work there. All the 'Bad Hats' and any others who the Japanese considered to be 'Undesirables' or troublemakers, accompanying him. The imminent departure of my friend was a considerable blow to me. I had come to regard him as a pillar of strength... someone who could be relied upon... come what may, and a counsellor who could apply a legal mind to a problem and find the right answer. The men the Japanese did not like, 'Bad Hats' apart, were the ones we could least afford to lose, and so the draft was chosen and took up residence in the ground floor of Jubilee Buildings. Maybe they would be known as the 'gallant six hundred'. There was no doubt they would give a good account of themselves in Japan, and they were fortunate in being led by an officer of such outstanding qualities. Personal observation had taught me that there were often a lot of extraordinary good men amongst those who, in time of peace, did not always conform to the required pattern. My own experiences in Basrah[4] in 1920 and the Isle of Man in 1925 confirmed this. They had all the qualities needed to win through, courage, fortitude, resilience, etc. Pioneers!

They departed for their new destination early in September and carried the good wishes of the camp with them, for we were sorry to see them go. Perhaps the food and conditions would be better in Japan! I was not to see my friend again for nearly 10 years when, by chance, we were both working in London. We found an awful lot to talk about! Up to this time the camp commandant had given no indication as to what had happened as to the order for amenities. He was asked to assist in the early expenditure of the money on the order already sent in, and the canteen contractor to be asked to supply a list of stocks available. The camp commandant was still pressing for MY2 to be spent from the amenities fund on the repairs to some 2,228 pairs of boots, but the committee could not agree to this. On the departure of the draft for Japan, the sum of MY1,000 was given to the solicitor staff officer from the amenities fund, representing roughly their pro rata share of the balance. With the help of the Japanese officer conducting the draft, part of this money was used to buy foodstuffs prior to departure. After the draft had gone, the Japanese required parties for work out of camp at Kai Tak Aerodrome, some 500/700 being called for daily. They were paid a daily rate of 25 sen for a warrant officer, 15 sen for an NCO and 10 sen for men. (Very small amounts).[5] The reason for the pressure to have the boots repaired out of amenity fund monies was now obvious, and what the committee had feared all along. Now it was agreed that no charges for boot repairs would be met without prior reference to Argyle Street who, in any event, provided the funds in the first place. There was a substantial balance held in the amenities fund because it had not been possible to spend it on the items for which it was intended!

9

Parsons & Books

In camp there were a handful of parsons, known to the troops as 'sky pilots', and amongst these was a quiet, reserved, and not very strong looking man, a priest of the Roman Catholic Church. I got on very well with him, right from the start. (though from a religious point of view I was a non-conformist) and we became very friendly.

He had won the Military Medal in the First World War, and was a likeable chap trying to do the best he could for his flock, which was quite large because there were many Portuguese members of the Hong Kong Volunteer Defence Corps now in camp.

The padre had managed to get the Japanese to allocate to him a building for use as a church, and now he was concerning himself with getting the necessary trappings and regalia. In pursuit of this aim, he came to [see] if we could make him a tabernacle. He would get a couple of his flock to do the work, if we would allow them the use of tools and material we had in the compound. Well, we had already tried our hands at many things, so perhaps church furnishings should be a comparatively simple matter, but was that all he wanted? Yes, there were other items, but he was doubtful if we could make them. He was proposing to ask the camp commandant to approach the head of the Roman Catholic Church in Hong Kong, (who was an Italian, and not interned) to see if vestments, etc could be provided, but he also had a more pressing need, which was bothering him quite a lot, to confess his sins! The Japanese paymaster had informed our own, some days earlier that the Pope had sent a sum of money, unspecified, for the purchase of amenities for the prisoners of war, and he required a list of items desired, but food was not to be included. The list was duly handed over and comprised drugs and invalid foods. In his interview with the camp commandant, I gathered the priest also reminded him about the Pope's gift, and asked what had happened to it? When he returned it seemed that he, and his requests, had not met with the approval of the camp commandant, and he was given a beating!

The poor chap was hurt physically and mentally, and was very badly shaken. It was some time before he recovered his composure, but he was never the same man again; the beating he received left a permanent mark on this quite innocent man, who had no harm in him at all. Eventually, his written application for vestments was approved and they were brought into camp and given to him. Even more important another priest came in to listen to his confession, but I believe it had to be done in the presence of the Japanese! This parson was much respected by his flock, and by many outside it, and getting larger and larger attendances at his church as a result!

The Entertainment Committee had been trying to obtain additional reading material, and had no doubt taken council on possible sources of supply of suitable books. I have been unable to establish from where the additional books eventually came; if they were bought, and if so, who paid for them, etc. Perhaps the Red Cross had a hand in the transaction, for it is believed many of them were acquired from the few book shops in Hong Kong. Whatever the background, a substantial number of volumes did arrive at the camp commandant's office, and the interpreters were busy ensuring they were fit material for 'prisoners', and at the same time looking for hidden messages.

The arrival of these books would make a welcome addition, and augment those already in camp. One of my roommates, the officer commanding the Royal Scots in camp, and a linguist of some distinction, wanted to add another language to his lengthy list. The question was, should he learn Russian or Japanese? After much consideration he decided on the former, and submitted an application to the camp commandant for some 'Russian books'. There was also a demand for instructional literature from other quarters as well. My roommate figured out he could learn Russian in two years; and there were at least half a dozen men of Russian nationality in camp who were prepared to help him! When the books were handed over it was found that they were mostly novels, or other harmless types of literature. The Japanese were not being caught out supplying books of an 'instructional type', such as 'how to build a wireless set' or 'dig a tunnel', etc which was a pity because we could do with any information which told the reader how to sew without thread, or repair boots without leather, rubber, etc! Otherwise I really had very little interest in reading, and my eyes were not up to it, unless the print was fairly large. In any case, it seemed that within hardly any time at all, the books had disappeared deep into kit bags, only to be brought out for the occasional read, or as we were later to find, when the holder needed to go to the toilet! Then, as many pages as were required were removed. The books too quickly became a kind of barter, passing in exchange, one to another.

The entertainments side certainly had a job getting them back, but this they eventually did, and a system of borrowing was devised which kept a tighter hand on them, which would enable everyone in camp to get a turn! As can be imagined the turnover eventually became very rapid amongst too many avaricious readers, and the consequent wear and tear enormous! The libraries surveyed a mounting pile of pages which had come away from their bindings and covers without leafs. Obviously something would have to be done quickly if the volumes we had were to be saved; so after a while someone who knew about bookbinding was found and with a small team tried to carry out repairs, but they had no materials and little in the way of facilities either. Inevitably eyes were turned towards the 'ordnance' compound, where the remnants of the books, and the men trying to repair them, were removed.

There they were set up in business! The man in charge of this project was a member of the Hong Kong Volunteer Defence Corps who had an interest in a printing and book selling business in Hong Kong called 'Ye Olde Printerie'. He was a dour but pleasant character who was now about to find his forte in camp. We had been opponents at bowls during the piping days of peace! After the Japanese surrender, and before the relieving force arrived, he gave me an account of the activities of the bookbinder's shop from the time of taking over responsibility for this kind of work. I can do no better than to give some extracts from this report, which are self explanatory:

A suitable hut was found for this work in the Ordnance Yard and was run by a staff of 'C' men (unfit for work from a Japanese angle) varying from 6 to 8 in number.

Sewing frames and benches were made by the carpenters, presses were conceived from all manner of scrap metal and piping by the plumbers, glue and paste pots came from the tinsmiths.

Odd scraps of cloth and drill were utilised for coverings and a few reels of thread were supplied by ordnance as long as it was available.

Thread was almost impossible to obtain and old bits of canvas, kit bags and web equipment were unravelled and made use of.

Old mosquito nets, sugar bags, linings and disused bandages served as material for backing purposes.

In spite of all these handicaps, makeshifts and improvisations, some very presentable work was turned out. During the period from May 1943 to August 1945, no less than 3,579 volumes were turned out.

Of these, 80 per cent were major repairs, viz. the books had to be completely stripped, sections reinforced and re-sewn, and torn pages patched with transparent paper which was obtained from cigarette packets etc.

In addition to the above mentioned work, this department was called on to do all manner of other jobs, such as making record books for the camp, files, scribbling pads and theatrical properties, whilst reams of newsprint was taken from the reel and cut into convenient sizes by hand. The whole camp benefited considerably from the efforts of these dedicated men, sick, though most of them were! The occupation of time, by means of useful pursuits was, I am sure, of great benefit to them as well!

The bookbinders made a name for themselves, and a good one at that. From my point of view the shop was 'clean' and the staff worked diligently, without any thought of personal gain! A few people had offered to 'unearth' a library book for me if I would say what kind was preferred. I was offered *Gone with the Wind* by my Royal Engineers warrant officer, but when looking at the small print and the hundreds of pages, was sure I would not be able to read it, and such was the case. I had always wanted to read again, Pearl Buck's *The Good Earth* and there was a copy in camp but no one that I knew could find it. However, someone suggested a book by a Yorkshire woman, Phyllis Bentley, called *Take Courage*. Well the title was most appropriate, for courage, in its broadest sense, all of us needed. A most noble word!

Of all the qualities to be admired in man, courage of the right kind is possibly the greatest. It brings out the best in all types of men, the pure, the good, kindness, humility, unselfishness, self sacrifice. It fortifies the weak in time of need.

Yes, perhaps a book which inspired courage would be right for me! My eyesight was very poor and deteriorating. I found that standing out on parade in the very bright sunshine, a trial, and could not bear any bright light shining into my eyes, and had to shade them constantly, my vision was blurred, and there was an amount of pain behind both eyes. The doctors told me there was nothing they could do except to console me with the fact that my sight would improve with better food! They were however, able to provide me with a pair of spectacles, which helped. With these aids a start was made on the book *Take Courage* reading one or two pages at a time, and others [including] my roommate read to me, a page or two as well. For some reason the book impressed and took a hold on me, and I could not keep away from it. I seemed to be applying what I read to my own situation, and am sure, reading more into the book than what was really there. Just the same it did me good to read of the trials endured by others, even though partly fictional. The book ended with the following:

> The strife is sore while it lasts, yes, it is very sharp and bitter, and wearying to the spirit, for it seems as if it will never come to any end, but if we keep a good heart and cease not to care for justice and truth, someday the storm will pass, and the nations rejoice in the sweet air of peace.

So far as I can recollect this was the only book read by me in camp, perhaps that is why it made such an impression!

Our workshops, and in particular the shoemaker's shop was going through a very thin time, practically no materials having been provided by the Japanese, and we were just struggling along, giving a stitch in time service and cannibalising where ever we could. A watchmaker's shop had now been added, and was doing good work with improvised tools, and parts from other watches which 'would not go'. The Japanese had been pressed constantly for resources, but to no avail, apart that is from some cotton which they brought for the tailor's shop. I was reminded of this by the storeman assistant, and repeat what he wrote:

> The Japanese supplied us with 20x100 yard bobbins of thread to repair clothing, as the thread (cotton) was in a tangled mess, the chief clerk sat for hours over a period of a month untangling the mess, and if I remember rightly he only snapped the cotton on two occasions, he had the patience of a saint, he sat for many nights on end unravelling this cotton and doing our guard duty, as he could not sleep because of 'happy feet!'

And the end result of this unremitting application to the job in hand, was that someone was able to have his rags repaired, and thus be 'respectable' for a little while longer! Yes, at the moment we seemed to be in the doldrums, certainly so far as materials for repair of boots and clothing were concerned, but we could, and did follow the Japanese adage to improvise. There was however, one small matter which gave both my chief clerk and I concern, it was the periodic visits to the tailor's shop of one of the interpreters, by repute a Lutheran minister. The interpreter came apparently to visit one of the members of the staff and who was, perhaps the best of our 'tailors'. This man belonged to the Hong Kong Volunteer Defence Corps, and his father-in-law, who so far as I am aware, did not belong to any unit, worked alongside him. The latter had come from Shanghai where he was employed. It was not unusual for the Japanese camp staff and the guards to walk through the workshops unannounced, we could not prevent them, and indeed it was to be expected that they would want to know what was going on there! But this case seemed a bit different from the usual run. The interpreter knew quite well that it was customary to speak to the chief clerk first, and obviously chose to ignore him by walking straight into the tailor's shop where he proceeded, in hushed tones, to carry out conversations with the Hong Kong Volunteer Defence Corps tailor. It was the rule that no one went into any of the workshops until receiving permission to do so at the office, and the chief clerk was assiduous in applying this rule without fear or favour. A rule which of course could be applied only to camp inmates. The Japanese did as they liked! The visits to the tailor's shop by this particular inter- preter were becoming more frequent and protracted, so the chief clerk or I made a point of being present at these meetings whenever we could. The interpreter was always friendly, which only tended to increase our doubts about him. Even more so when he started to bring in food parcels for the tailor and his father-in-law. So we tackled these two men to find out what these visits were about (after first discussing the matter with the senior officer of the Hong Kong Volunteer Defence Corps). The interview was most illuminating. Apparently the wife of the younger one had managed to get in touch with the interpreter. She desper- ately wanted to help her husband and father, and he was the means to the end.

There seemed to be no more to it than that. The cir- cumstances in which we existed demanded that a careful watch was kept at all times. On a number of occasions this interpreter (like all the others) was asked for material help, either from the camp commandant or by purchase outside. He was always 'correct' in his dealings with our requests, invariably replying 'I will put your request to the camp commandant'. We got nothing! Not long afterwards he left camp, well that was that. An enigma, if ever there was one!

10

SS Lisbon Maru

About the middle of September 1942 I was sent for by the camp commandant. On the short walk round to his office I thought over what the reason might be for this sudden and unexpected call; perhaps the Japanese had relented and were going to make an announcement about giving us soap, repair materials, etc. The interpreters, never communicative, told me to sit down and wait. This was the regular procedure for keeping visitors in suspense while awaiting audience, and could last for an hour or more, and was, I am sure, designed to place the visitor in a state of uncertainty, even in a quandary. At last I was ushered into the presence, and he said something like this:

> A further selected party will be going to Japan, and you, Captain Ebbage, will be in charge of this party. You will like Japan; it is a very beautiful country. All men will take with them warm clothing. End of interview.

It is always difficult to know what to make of such a meeting; for some time I had been aware I was unpopular, perhaps this was a way of 'moving me on'. Whatever the reasons I was not unhappy to be leaving Shamshuipo, had tried my best to do what was possible for the camp, maybe my successor would be able to improve on the foundations already laid. At least he would be assured of a true and loyal staff in his constant battles with the Japanese. These and many other thoughts passed through my mind on the short walk back to our office. I did not want to look pleased or sad; perhaps a show of indifference might be the right attitude to take. My chief clerk and my sergeant major would be disturbed, but in any event our plans had been laid for just such an eventuality as this. All we could do now was to accept the inevitable, with good grace, and get on with the job. Discussions took place with as to who would most likely take my place; we were all thinking of the RAOC officer who shared my room, and who had, at the outbreak of war, been recruited as a temporary officer for laundry duties, he having been a laundry manager. He had not military or ordnance experience, but in our present situation this could be an advantage. One thing he did have was a very good knowledge of Cantonese, which he could read and speak. I was sure he would give a good account of himself! Then we got down to discussing the unit which was, despite all the illness and setbacks, in good heart. We discussed the possibility of taking half of them with me; the idea behind this was that, if we divided more or less equally between Japan and Hong Kong, then there were hopes that some of us might get out alive, which seemed very doubtful when currently discussing the position in Shamshuipo. We spoke of the warm clothing which would be wanted, and the camp commandant had spoken about, and which was practically non existent. Hardly anyone had an overcoat and the Japanese view had always been that this garment was for officers and warrant officers only. Perhaps the Japanese would bring in a few tunics and trousers, as had been done for the earlier draft; or issue the warm clothing when the draft got to Japan. Certainly we had none in store to offer, the method by which they could be obtained inside Shamshuipo, was to take from one man and give to another. This we all agreed, and were prepared, we must now await the will of our masters! One thought worried me; there would be no hope of escape from Japan! I had expected this draft to be similar in size to that taken by my solicitor friend such a short time ago, but it quickly became apparent that the new draft would be much larger.

Accommodation was being cleared for what appeared to be in the order of 2,000 men, and as the selection proceeded they were moved to new locations where they were segregated pending medical, etc inspections. Quickly the draft took shape, and down came the 'Fat Pig' with his retinue from headquarters to inspect. I had been detailed to be in the offing with an interpreter. There was much waving of arms and it was apparent the big man was not pleased with the arrangements, and I was ordered off the site and back to my room. When all the tumult had died down, it transpired that a smaller number of men would be involved than had first been estimated, and they would be formed into two separate drafts, and there would be a large officer compliment of fifty to sixty who had already been selected, and would be coming from Argyle Street. No one could, or would, tell me whether I was going or not, so I should just have to wait and see; and of course this fitted in which the usual Japanese flair for organisation. A day or so later the commanding officer of the Middlesex Regiment, a lieutenant colonel, arrived from Argyle Street with some fifty or more other officers from majors downwards and the whole thing was reorganised afresh. It now seemed unlikely that I should go, but no one told me so, apart from the commanding officer of the Middlesex Regiment, who had a list of all the officers who had come with him from Argyle Street and who would be going, and I was not on the list.

I never found out why I had been 'dropped', no one told me, but why should they? Nevertheless there was profit to be drawn from most circumstances; the RAOC had experienced a trial run of our plans, while I had access to the commanding officer, the Middlesex Regiment, for information, advice and council. Must get down to this facet as quickly as possible, before he was whisked away. There was much to impart to a sympathetic ear of the right rank and calibre, something akin perhaps to the Roman Catholic priest, who needed to 'get it off his chest'. Nevertheless, the first concern of the commanding officer of the Middlesex Regiment was for his own unit, and the man who was in charge of it, here in Shamshuipo, and they had long discussions on all matters of relevance to unit and camp, so it was some time before I was able to take my turn. When I did, I was able to give a general appreciation of the position in camp, and in particular so far as matters normally of ordnance responsibility were concerned, and he looked round our store and workshops. He was impressed, and indicated we had made much more progress than they had so far done in Argyle Street. In turn, I was given a general run down of the position in Argyle Street, and verbal messages from my chief there, and the official views on the matter of individual escapes, and the damage they could do commensurate with the possible gains, which of course we were only too well aware. We heard about the signing of the 'Affidavits' by the officers in Argyle Street, and we gave a resume of the position here, including those who had taken the brunt of the Japanese displeasure when refusing; and in particular of the solicitor staff officer, (also of the Middlesex Regiment) who had led the way. He expressed agreement with what we were doing, and was astounded at the poor state of health in Shamshuipo, which distressed him very much. I came away from this interview with reassurance that we were 'on the right lines', and had his approval and support. A forthright and likeable man, but I shall always remember him for his quick repartee. (Zulus, my dear fellow) and when we first came into camp, seeing him resplendent in highly polished Sam Browne and immaculate service dress. Yes, a typical pre-war commanding officer! It was a very pleasant interlude, having all these officers amongst us, and the talking never stopped until well into the night, we drank in the news of our friends, and came back for more. Then, seemingly ever so quickly, they were gone, and the camp appeared empty.

There is a Chinese saying 'Days of sorrow pass slowly, times of joy very quickly'. Over 1,500 officers and men had departed, taking our very best wishes, (and their share of the amenities fund), all eager and hopeful of a better place in Japan, and our future Japanese camp commandant, accompanying them. Alas, the SS *Lisbon Maru*, in which they were being transported, was torpedoed some 4 miles off Shanghai on 4 October 1942 and over half of them were drowned. Most had to swim for it and were fired on while doing so, others clung to whatever they could, until rescued. I gather it was a sorry business! The commanding officer of the Middlesex Regiment I was told had made the shore in an exhausted condition and required hospital treatment for some malady he picked up, subsequently, I am sorry to say, dying in Japan.[1] How easily it could have been me, I did not have the advantage of being able to swim! With the reduced numbers the camp seemed empty and dead, and occupied chiefly by folk who were sick. It would be easier to deal with the lesser numbers, resources would go further, with fewer men there would be fewer problems, and less available to die... the diphtheria epidemic showed no signs of abating... and some forty had died during the month of September. Perhaps the worst was over, now there were fewer mouths to feed, everyone might do better. Even the Japanese might now be able to cope. It was always part of my philosophy that events never stood still, they improved or deteriorated. Maybe we were coming to the end of the downward cycle!

Just when we were getting into a new rhythm of events, and had got used to the empty spaces, another unexpected occurrence took place. The two battalions of Canadians (or what was left of them) arrived from North Point. This camp was situated on the north side of the island, and it was in this area that the Japanese made their initial landings on the island. The camp had originally housed Chinese refugees from the mainland, later it was occupied by the Royal Navy, and then subsequently by the Canadians. Now it was being evacuated and all would be joining us. We had often wondered how our Canadian friends were faring; if their lot was any better than ours, now we should soon be able to find out. There would be a new lot of people to talk to, and new faces to see, and undoubtedly, new problems as well! The 'Imperial' (British Army) troops so-called were re-housed closer together.

The original Japanese intention had been to keep us, and the Canadians, apart, and said so. The Canadians had their own living accommodation, cookhouse, hospital, etc but no physical barrier was erected; only an imaginary Japanese one, which quickly became non existent as the two elements began to associate, one with another. I became very friendly with a number of Canadian officers and enjoyed many interesting hours finding out all about life in Canada. So far as we were concerned, there was to be further reorganisation, as the Japanese had decreed that Jubilee Buildings would be evacuated. They had never been 'comfortable' about our occupying this accommodation. Now there was to be a grand clear out. Most of the officers were moved into the small huts which were situated on either side of the main road which divided Nanking from Hankow Barracks, while for some unknown reason I, the other RAOC officer (laundry manager) and the officer commanding, the Royal Scots, took up residence in one of the rooms in our compound, which in palmier days had been the Middlesex Regiment officers' mess and quarters.[2]

The removal from camp of such a large number of men on the two drafts, plus other casualties, had the effect of reducing the number of workers available to me. For instance, the plumber and electrician, both members of the Royal Engineers had gone, and replacements were urgently needed, in particular for the former. It is a surprising fact of life that 'as one door closes, another opens', and so it was to be.

Along came a jovial, red-faced, middle-aged, grey-haired man with the broadest Cornish accent I had ever heard, and accompanied by his far less loquacious mate of roughly the same age. Did we want a couple of plumbers? They were looking for a job! They looked such an odd pair that I could not help but laugh. Both belonged to a unit called the 'Dockyard Defence Corps' which had been raided from civilian dockyard workers for, as the name implies, defending the Admiralty Yard. To use the common parlance they were 'Dockyard Mateys'. The Cornishman's laugh was as infectious as his geniality, and he did not seem to have a union card, but was a plumber of some distinction, prepared to do anything. Well, if he and his pal were good enough for the Royal Navy they were certainly good enough for me, so they were told to get permission from their officer commanding, and report for duty when they had done so. As was the custom, when taking on new men I had a few words with their officer commanding as well. Courtesy demanded no less.

What it was necessary to know was if they were 'reliable' in every sense, I needed assuring that they were 'with us' and not 'agin us'.

One of the first jobs they were required to do was to rearrange the layout of the water supply in the cookhouses. With the departure for Japan of the two drafts, some of the cookhouses had been closed down and others amalgamated, which meant a redistribution of the cooking facilities. New boilers to be re-sited and others cooking appliances rearranged. It was not possible to comply wholly with the Japanese wishes to 'close up' until this had been done. We were short of piping, and even more so of taps and there were none in camp that we knew of. The Japanese were anxious to see progress. The new plumbers explained their difficulties, if only they could get more pipes, of the right lengths, and taps, elbows, etc it would be child's play to finish the job. Just the right lengths of piping were necessary, as we had no facilities for cutting, or putting threads on the pipes. As we wanted the supply of water over the boilers, this work was done first, and then the boilers were sited accordingly. The opposite of the usual practice! It was not very long before the Japanese were taking these two plumbers out of camp to raid empty premises, and bring back the pieces we wanted. These two men did extraordinary good work in cookhouses, wash places, hospital, and in connection with the building of the steam oven spoken of earlier. This oven had to be built, and located, in accordance with the lengths of piping at our disposal. Both plumbers worked from our compound until the surrender, helped by the son of the Cornishman. They were renowned throughout the camp, liked and respected, and 'on terms' with the Japanese in just the right way. All were a great asset and help, and I am most grateful to them. The Cornishman wrote to me some time ago, when he was eighty-seven, and I cannot do better than give extracts of what he had to say:

> When we were captured and then interned in Shamshuipo, I made up my mind that if I was to survive I should have to work; having always been active pre war. Until things were more settled in camp, with nothing to do, I can feel myself weakening and going down hill. When the first batch of prisoners were sent to Japan, and I was able to turn to your command and became the camp plumber I was very happy, because now my time was more or less fully occupied, and so kept my mind working, and was really hopeful of release, especially with my son in camp as well.

Their tools comprised three items, an iron bed leg for a hammer, a shifting spanner and Stillson wrench. Afterwards they purchased a hammer, one 8in. half round file ([for] four cigarettes), etc.

As well as the moves already indicated, the effect of the two large drafts resulted in the Japanese changing the locations of pretty well everything in camp, with resultant disorganisation. The isolation hospital, diphtheria, malnutrition centres, sanatorium, old men's home, etc moved. These fancy titles, given by the Japanese, were often just empty huts, frequently only shells of buildings, with no windows or doors, all of which needed to be made good before they could be used. Yes, my chaps had plenty of work! My gardening activities were about to pay dividends, the tomatoes were ripening and the carrots looked good; they really had roots on them and seemed to be swelling daily. They were the envy of most people who saw them, and a great temptation to starving men. I could hardly keep my fingers off them myself, and certainly they were now hardly ever out of my sight. Perhaps not the best carrots ever grown, but never were carrots so welcome! When we tasted them, they were just as good as they looked, and provided a few very welcome feeds, fry ups! I was able to save the seeds of the tomatoes right away, and spent hours just sucking the fleshy bits that contained the seed, and then 'popping them out' onto a piece of paper to dry. Four or five of the better carrots were allowed to run to seed, and after a few months' time, [I] was also able to reap this harvest as well. The ripening and quantity exceeded all expectations. The other gardens looked good too! Then, suddenly, about this time, parcels were allowed in again, from relatives and friends, and this even caused such excitement. Those who brought them now had to stand a couple of hundred yards away from the camp gates, where tables had been arranged for their inspection and acceptance. The interpreters examined each gift closely, cross questioning those who brought them, presumably about details of their backgrounds, relationship, etc.

Only items acceptable to the Japanese were passed through, the others being pushed back. Many of these gifts were pitiful objects; perhaps a couple of bananas and one or two sweets, but even so humble offerings were like manna to those suffering acutely from lack of food. The parcels did even more good to those lucky enough to receive them, as the recipient had some tangible evidence of their loved ones; and their morale soared accordingly.

11

Working Parties

The Japanese now required from camp daily working parties. At first men were glad to go as they had been promised pay for the work they did, and from their point of view it would be an outing. Most of them considered that any trip outside camp as a welcome change, and some would, perhaps, be able to see friends or relatives. The latter held considerable attractions for those who lived locally. Unfortunately many men were quite unfit to go, and those who were had, in the main, either none or very inadequate footwear. Reference has already been made to the repeated suggestions made by the camp commandant, that monies from the amenities fund be used for the repair of footwear, and that this had been resisted. Now the Japanese put pressure on me, and other officers, to withdraw serviceable footwear from those who had it, and give to those who had not. (Provided of course they were working party material). We resisted this pressure as well. The next ploy was to suggest that boots be 'borrowed', i.e. loaned to others for working party purposes. However, most individuals were not prepared to lend their boots to others (even if they would fit) and coupled with the fact that the footwear position was so grim, this suggestion produced negative results.

Suitable footwear just was not available in Shamshuipo. Thus the Japanese were thrown back on 'their own resources'. They could not very well take men out of camp with unsatisfactory clothing and bare feet; it would be too much loss of face! I had constantly approached them on the footwear question, and my repeated requests had all fallen on deaf ears. Now it was up to them! Sure enough they responded by producing a quantity of locally manu-factured rubber shoes. The difficulties were resolved. They would have a pool of shoes solely for the use of working parties, the items being issued to the men before they left camp, and while on parade, (if in the view of the Japanese their existing footwear was not considered adequate), and withdrawn on their return from work. The Japanese did not bother over much about sizes; so far as they were concerned, a shoe was a shoe. We, the RAOC, were not involved in this episode.

These working parties assembled in the early hours of the morning, when the light was none too good, and often returned to camp at dusk, or even when it was quite dark. It had the advantage, from a Japanese point of view, that prisoners could not be seen very well by outsiders as the journeys to and from work was made by lorry.

The first day all went well until the party arrived back in camp and the Japanese tried to withdraw the plimsolls. The Japanese had no list of names of those who had been given shoes so could not pin down any particular man, and the lads held them wherever they could, so it was ages before they could be dismissed from the parade, and the Japanese could count their losses which, I believe, were considerable. The following day they tried again with no better results, but accompanied by 'slappings' before the famished workers were dismissed. The men ate before they left camp and again when they got back; for midday break, well, a little water and anything else they had taken or could lay their hands on, and they were searched before leaving and on return. Soon the Japanese gave up the unequal struggle of trying to control a pool of shoes, they seldom fitted the different men who appeared on succeeding days, and consequently fell behind with 'numbers' they were supposed to be producing. In future men who were fit enough to go out on working parties (not others) would be issued with shoes, and charged with taking care of them! Well, from my point of view we had advanced a little! These working parties (mostly for work on the runways at Kai Tak Aerodrome) provided a source of news, rumour and gossip. The prisoners were working alongside Chinese, and many of them and in particular the Portuguese element, could speak Cantonese fluently, so many tit bits of information came back to camp. What was more, they were a medium for getting notes and local newspapers in at first, and then later other items were brought back as well. Anything useful which came to hand, found a quick hiding place, and in some way, a journey back to camp despite the many beatings up as a result of the purloined goods having been found by the guards during the search, on return to camp. Soon there was a regular newspaper service through this medium, Chinese language papers, eagerly transcribed and avidly read came in at regular intervals. Dropped by Chinese and picked up casually by working party members. We were starved of news and welcomed these papers like manna from heaven. When things were going particularly well for the Japanese they would, on occasion, leave an English language paper behind, after one of their visits.

This benefaction had however long ceased, and because of it we had drawn our own conclusions. Receipt of Chinese language papers, although undoubtedly heavily censored, provided a rosy picture so good for morale. The translators were busy, but whatever they produced had to be kept 'close' and circulation to a minimum.

We were better able to judge the mood of the Japanese camp staff in our approach to them. Like looking up your fortune in the morning daily at home, to find out whether the omens were good or bad. This access to the outside world was our life blood and a turning point in our existence. The good it did is impossible to assess, its potential immense, and its dangers obvious. We should have to take care. Our elation muted.

Providence now seemed to be on our side, strange things were happening at the ration store where the truck was being offloaded. This procedure was one of the regular highlights in camp, everyone being interested in what the Japanese brought in to eat.

Never did we imagine they would be feeding us on turkey, grouse and pheasants, but there they were, frozen solid, and just out of cold store. Perhaps the birds we had ordered for Christmas Day Dinner 1941 were amongst them, and there seemed so many. My Royal Scots room-mate was quickly on the scene as he was responsible for our cookhouse, and I awaited with interest his return, and to have explained the reasons for this sudden windfall. It transpired that the refrigeration plant at the Cold Storage Company had broken down and could not be repaired, (or the electricity supply had failed) so the whole contents were being distributed for immediate consumption. A once only effort, and no plum pudding! Appetites were sharpened with hopes of a 'slice off the breast', but the cooks had other ideas and turned out a most delectable stew instead. The birds were eaten with much greater relish than they would have been, had they followed their accustomed journey to the dining table of our over-fed peace time society. All however was not good news from an RAOC point of view, as one more member of our unit had just died from dysentery and enteritis. Like so many others, he had no chance without the necessary medicines.

It was sad to have to consider, in our elation, just how close to the borderline we all were. The diphtheria, pellagra, beriberi, blindness, 'aching feet', dysentery and skin complaints showed no sign of abating yet. Many, like our man, were so weak and emaciated that only a miracle could save them! Then rumours started to spread that Red Cross supplies were on the way. No one seemed to have any idea from whence these statements of doubtful accuracy emanated, they buzzed round camp like wildfire, and mostly died out just as quickly as they had started. But this one persisted, gaining credibility hour by hour, and none of us could find out the source from which the information came. If it were found to be incorrect, false hopes would be raised, only to be dashed when reality overtook optimism. And those in hospital, and the sick, would be just that bit worse off, for it is only human nature to cling to any straw when near to despair! A few days later however, it seemed clear there was some foundation to this persistent rumour, as the Japanese had been inspecting the size of our ration store, and letting slip that supplies from England were expected, and a working party would be needed to help unload the goods. I think the whole camp would have volunteered, and even the infirm would attempt to stand again!

12

Red Cross Supplies

Very shortly after all the speculation had died down, Red Cross supplies started arriving in camp. So far as can be recalled, all the goods were put first into a Japanese store which was situated in the centre of the camp. This store also kept supplies for the Japanese staff, Argyle Street camp, Shamshuipo camp, etc. They were issued to the camp ration store periodically. Only when all the goods were safely stowed away would a distribution be made, even when the Japanese mind moved ever so slowly, and their actions even more slowly still! During the checks, counter checks and re-checks, the ration officer found the consignment consisted of bales of clothing as well as food, quite a lot of them in fact. The Japanese wanted him to accept responsibility for these, and he had great difficulty in convincing them that ordnance should take them over. Eventually the matter was put to arbitration, to the camp commandant himself. At that point I was summoned to the presence and told to remove the clothing items to our store, report quantities taken over, and await his instructions about distribution. My chief clerk and a small but eager working party transferred the bales of clothing, etc (not food) to our store. Perhaps this made the handling of the food items a little easier, and thus speeded the ultimate distribution.

The following are extracts from a report (already referred to earlier) which was made at Argyle Street by someone who had moved there from Shamshuipo:

Food

Red Cross supplies arrived on November, 29, 1942 when every man in camp received one parcel.

Bully beef was issued at a scale of 4 per tin, three times a week.

Meat and Vegetable (M&V) at 4 per tin twice a week, Cocoa at 1/4lb per man per week and Sugar at 1lb per man per month. Ghee was issued direct to cookhouses. In January this scale was reduced to 6 to a tin of bully beef three times a week, and 6 to a tin of M&V once a week. Cocoa was reduced to a very small quantity and issued to troops from the cookhouse at two mugs per man per week. Sugar remained the same.

From 1 July 1943 a new scale was put in to force, amounting to slightly less than one ounce per head per day of combined bully beef and M&V, which was issued through the cookhouse. The scale was fixed up to the end of September and when the draft left in August a small increase in the ration was consequently made. The exact scale of Atta issued is not known, but Atta porridge was issued daily at breakfast and 4 ounce Atta loaves twice a week. Dried fruit was issued about once in ten days.

Every man received a second Red Cross parcel on 13 January and a third on 19 April 1943. When fresh meat and large flour issues were being made, the cookhouses vied with each other to produce the best results and if one established a baking oven another immediately countered by making a communal frying pan! The best effort perhaps, was a Cornish pasty produced by the Dockyard Defence Corps.

As the numbers in camp diminished so the cook-houses were amalgamated and in September last there were only two in addition to the Canadian Cookhouse, i.e. Imperial Cookhouse, Hospital Cookhouse, Canadian Cookhouse.

The above report is undated but was probably made in November 1943.

I have had some difficulty in making an approximate judgement of the numbers and items of clothing, etc that were received from Red Cross (in spite of research into this question). The main areas of doubt are footwear, towels and underwear. However, my assessment is as follows:

Summer Trousers & Shorts	6,000
Shirts	3,000/4,000
Hats	3,000/4/000
Windcheaters	Quantity quite unknown but certainly over 8,000/10,000
Socks	6,000 plus
Footwear	???
Shoemakers repair kits	10
Leather soles and heels	Quantity
Cotton, needles, etc	Quantity
Towels	???
Underwear, vests	12,000

This consignment was quite unbalanced, in sizes and in every other way. The Red Cross would have access to such things as standard range of sizes, etc and I am quite sure the fault lay with the Japanese. Faulty administration probably sums up the position! The allocation of these items posed something of a problem. All officer commanding units were consulted and an agreed plan was made for their distribution, and submitted to the camp commandant. Where there were insufficient items to go round they were issued proportionately, and where there was there was not, need was the criterion used.

The Japanese concern was that men who went out on working parties should be 'best looked after', but in the end did not press this point and agreed with our suggestions. Every man got, if he wanted them:

2 pairs of trousers or shorts
1 shirt
1 hat
2 windcheaters
2 pairs [of] socks
Underwear, towels, footwear

When this distribution had been completed we were left with a few thousand windcheaters which no one wanted. We could have done with warm jackets and trousers, as many men, in particular those who were inactive, felt the cold during the winter months. The windcheaters were made from Khaki Serge material, without sleeves, and were mostly of very large size. The tailors experimented trying to modify them into some kind of jacket, but this was not very successful, while another couple were busy making sample trousers, for which there was an even greater need.

Eventually, after much trial and error, a suitable nether garment was produced. It did not have the Saville Row cut, zip fastener, or fly complete with buttons, but followed and was 'cut' on austere Shamshuipo lines. Charlie Chaplin would have been delighted with them! The specification was simply 'to keep a man warm', which it certainly would! The finished article looked more like pyjamas than anything else, with a 'slit' in the front and fastened by a narrow belt made from oddments of the same material. We all rocked with laughter as the 'mannequin' paraded up and down for inspection. It took three or four (depending on size) of the windcheaters to make one pair of trousers, and there was much waste; but many windcheaters nobody wanted!

There were of course one or two snags. We were finding it increasingly difficult to get sewing machine needles. Cardiff

Joe had bought the last lot, and had reported great difficulty in locating them, so they were becoming scarce and precious.

We should need quite a lot of needles, because our old fashioned and decrepit sewing machine played havoc with them, and needles quickly became broken.

There was also the matter of cotton. Some cotton had been received from Red Cross, but would be quite insufficient for a manufacturing task of the magnitude we had in mind. The camp commandant had expressed his concern that 'All men have warm clothing', so perhaps he would give some practical support to this project! On the next suitable occasion this matter was taken up, reminding the camp commandant of his own wishes and of our desire to bring them to fruition, would he care to see some sample garments we had prepared? If so I would bring along my mannequins.

Mannequins!!! He nearly had a fit. Possibly the interpreter, (and all our conversations had to be through an interpreter) must have said something about 'women' and we had got a couple in camp. (Probably 'improvised' as I had so often been told)! Well, when we had got over that little problem by telling him our mannequins were men, he laughed, and was in a receptive mood once again. Yes, he would see them, bring them round.

With the Japanese there is no point in waiting, strike while the iron is hot, so I took round my two 'models'. I knew he would laugh, and he did not disappoint me, in fact he nearly went into convulsions, slapping his thighs, and, as was the custom, so did everyone else! Bring in the sergeant of the guard, so he could enjoy the spectacle!

When he had simmered down, and put his seal of approval on the better of the two samples and I had explained, in some detail, that we had far too many windcheaters, and this was not a scheme willfully to destroy them, I introduced the matter of needles and cotton. Ah so, he replied, here was the catch. Without further ado I offered to buy a few needles, if he would allow me to do so, so that we could make a start on this project. Yes, he would allow purchase of a small quantity, to make a few more samples, say ten or twenty. This gesture was not much use, but his offer was graciously accepted, and I withdrew. I talked over details of this interview with my chief clerk, and some of my brother officers. Our requirements had been estimated to be in the order of 500 plus pairs of trousers (in the event the final number we made was over 600) and could not understand why he had stuck at ten to twenty pairs only. Slowly it dawned upon me; he might want approval from his 'Superior Authority'. Shortly I might be singing a different tune if the 'Fat Pig' did not approve! A small number of needles and some cotton were brought in the very next day (a record) and when, within 48 hours the camp commandant came into the tailor's shop to see progress, I was more certain than ever we had made the right deduction. This lot of garments was quite passable, or perhaps we were getting used to the sight of baggy trousers, and the skeletons inside them; and the tailors more adept at making them! Some days later the 'Colonel' arrived in camp, and an interpreter came to collect samples, worn by models, and take them round to the camp office. Soon, they came back smiling, and complete with cigarettes. I knew then that the 'Fat Pig' had given his approval, and the camp commandant was taking the credit. Well, we should need a lot of needles, and literally miles of cotton before we completed this assignment, and it would take a very long time indeed. Mass production was not our forte, from us everything was 'tailor made'.

I wondered if further drafts for Japan were the reason for the concealed enthusiasm of the camp commandant? By now, I hoped, the reader of this account will have acquired some idea of our captors, (as seen by me) and of their mentality and idiosyncrasies, and of their ability to confound, of their unpredictability, and lack of humanity. For me they never ceased to amaze, bewilder and beguile!

We had pressed the Japanese frequently on the matter of writing letters home, but there had been no response. As a result we had come to the conclusion that they must be awaiting instructions from Japan! Now suddenly they were supplying special headed paper and envelopes, and the items could be purchased by those who had the necessary money. In the main, only officers and those fit enough to have been out on working parties had money, the sick, infirm and the weak had none. There was also a limitation on how much, and what could be said, and the implements which could used for saying it! Whether from the amenities fund, officers, or working party monies, paper and envelopes and writing facilities were made available to all who wanted them. Those unable to write themselves were given help. We assumed that the Japanese in Hong Kong and Japan would pick and choose which letters they were prepared to let through; it was essential therefore that the contents be innocuous, guarded and as circumspect as it was possible to make them, at the same time, trying to get over on paper what one would really like to say. This advice I gave to members of my unit, and sat down to draft my own. I found it difficult, very difficult indeed to say what I wanted and what our masters would accept, and to convey some idea of my position, and how I felt. Eventually, it was finished, and to help get it through I had it typed, as had been done on the previous post card. What a pity it had not been printed in ink, or even written in ink, both of which were now equally acceptable. When my wife received the second typed communication she assumed I was unable to write myself, and had to get another to type my letter for me! My letter was not even signed; even the 'signature' was typed. You can never win! This letter is in front of me now, with the Japanese characters in the top right hand corner and two holes, where it had been filed by the Japanese along with all the others, and evidence of how it had been torn away from the clip. I am sure this censoring and selecting was done in Japan!

The letter, dated 13 December 1942 and of some 200 simple words, was mainly on family matters apart from the following sentence:

Was glad to get a Red Cross parcel with sixteen tins of foodstuffs the other day. Very enjoyable.

I cannot now remember what the sixteen different tins contained, but they were exceedingly well chosen items for men in our position, and the good they did was incalculable. They represented just one parcel, and we received three in all from this consignment, plus of course, our share in the bulk supplies. Indeed, we are all so deeply indebted to the Red Cross that no action by us can ever repay. The following statistics (taken from the report made at Argyle Street by someone who had moved there from Shamshuipo), on deaths in Shamshuipo illustrates the effect of the receipt of Red Cross Supplies far better than I could ever do:

Deaths

1942

	April	1
	May	3
	June	2
	July	21
	August	28
	September	38
	October	52
	November	26
	(Point of receipt of Red Cross Supplies)	
	December	19

1943

	January	7
	February	1
	March	1
	April 1	
	May	nil
	June	1
	July	nil
	August	4
	September	1

13

Pig & Poultry Farm

Some weeks prior to the receipt of Red Cross Supplies, I had spoken to the interpreter (Cardiff Joe) about my wish to give a few small Christmas presents, and he had promised to assist in any way he could. It was impossible, at that time, to imagine the change that would have taken place by Christmas Day. My first in captivity! Or of the celebration we would be able to have on the great day, by the opening of a tin of meat, followed by pears! (Shared of course, with others). The gifts I had been contemplating now seemed so puny and inconsequential… of no account, lost in the comparable abundance which had now descended upon us. To a hungry man the difference between poverty and affluence is small indeed, no more perhaps, than a bite or two of bread! Cardiff Joe had no intention of forgetting my request, so I gave him my money, and some from my colleague, and he made the meager purchases we wanted, and brought them back to us. Whether with the knowledge of the camp commandant I do not know. On Christmas Day, he too was not to be outdone and came to our room with a gift for the occupants. This and other generous gestures set this man apart from all the others, perhaps he too wanted to show the spirit of Christmas, and provide a little comfort for deprived men! Japanese who did not lift his hand to smite, but to help! He was the best Japanese I knew,

This photograph of the author's family shows Stanley with his father Tom, mother Rose, and sister Phyllis Ebbage. It was taken on 3 September 1910, just two years before his father's premature death from tuberculosis. (Collection of Miss Ebbage)

This identity card, which identifies Ebbage as a Captain, was carried by the author throughout his captivity in Hong Kong. (RLC Museum)

A postcard of the ship M.V. *Dilwara* (M.V. = Motor Vessel, H.T. His Majesty's Transport) on which the author travelled with his wife and daughter to Hong Kong in 1938. (Collection of Miss Ebbage)

A souvenir postcard of SS *Tanda*, the ship that took Mrs Ebbage and her two children from Shanghai to Australia. (Collection of Miss Ebbage)

EASTERN AND AUSTRALIAN STEAMSHIP CO. LTD.

T. S. S. "TANDA"

M. B. Skinner, Commander

Sailing from Miike for Shanghai, Hong Kong, Manila,

Rabaul, Brisbane, Sydney and Melbourne, 20th August, 1940.

LIST OF FIRST SALOON PASSENGERS

Mrs. M. H. Ashmore & Child	Mrs. E. A. Hennessy & Child
Mrs. V. N. Andrews	Mrs. D. C. Levis & Child
Mrs. M. L. Bryan & Child	Mrs. D. A. Macfarlane
Mrs. T. F. Burton	Mrs. J. E. Marsh & 3 Children
Miss. J. M. Burton	Mrs. F. A. Magee & Child
Mrs. M. D. Cornelius	Mrs. D. F. Orme
Mrs. K. B. Crew & Child	Mrs. I. A. Rogers
Mrs. M. I. Campbell & 2 Children	Mrs. I. E. Stone
Mrs. M. Chidson	Mrs. E. Simmons & 3 Children
Mrs. E. Ebbage & 2 Children	Mrs. N. E. Smyth
Mrs. F. E. Eynon	Miss. M. K. Thomson
Miss. M. F. Eynon	Dr. T. K. Abbott
Mrs. D. F. Fleming & 2 Children	Miss. M. Linklater
Mrs. I. Hoskin & 2 Children	Miss. W. M. Jackson

--SHIP'S OFFICERS--

B. W. Dun	Chief Officer	W. Steven	Chief Engineer
K. L. Dawson	Second „	H. Hukin	Second „
J. D. Richmond	Third „	T. H. Bryce	Third „
R. N. Lindeman	Fourth „	K. H. Krummel	Fourth „
D. N. Devonport	Apprentice	J. Gillies	Fifth „
A. W. Robinson	„	T. Sawyer	Sixth „
R. J. Funnell	Purser	W. J. Mcguire	Seventh „
G. L. Morton	Asst. „	J. Walklett	Refrig. „
J. N. R. Stephen	Surgeon	A. W. Hooper	Radio Officer.
W. Gilson	Steward-in-Charge	J. L. Carrel	Asst. „
J. S. Campbell	2nd-Steward	Miss. C. Casserly	Stewardess

This printed list of passengers aboard the SS *Tanda* was kept by Mrs Ebbage as a souvenir of their voyage to safety. (Collection of Miss Ebbage)

This telegram informing Mrs Ebbage that Captain Ebbage was alive and a prisoner of war, was sent by his father-in-law, and did not arrive in Australia until 27 June 1942, seven months after the surrender of Hong Kong. (RLC Museum)

COMMONWEALTH OF AUSTRALIA—POSTMASTER-GENERAL'S DEPARTMENT. Office Date Stamp.

Funds may be quickly, safely and economically transferred by **MONEY ORDER TELEGRAM** (PLEASE TURN OVER)

RECEIVED TELEGRAM.

This message has been received subject to the Post and Telegraph Act and Regulations. The time received at this office is shown at the end of the message. The first line of this Telegram contains the following particulars in the order named.

Office of Origin.   Words.   Time Lodged.   No.

3

69 VIA CABLE 89 ORMSKIRK 27 TH 8-55 P RETRANSMITTED

FROM MENTONE 5-45 P 29 TH

1/8 COLLECT GLT ELSIE EBBAGE
73 QUEEN VICTORIA ST BEXLEY NSW

REDCORSS REPORTS CPT EBBAGE PRISONER OF WAR

... DAD IDDON

(EBBAGE 73 CPT EBBAGE DAD IDDON)

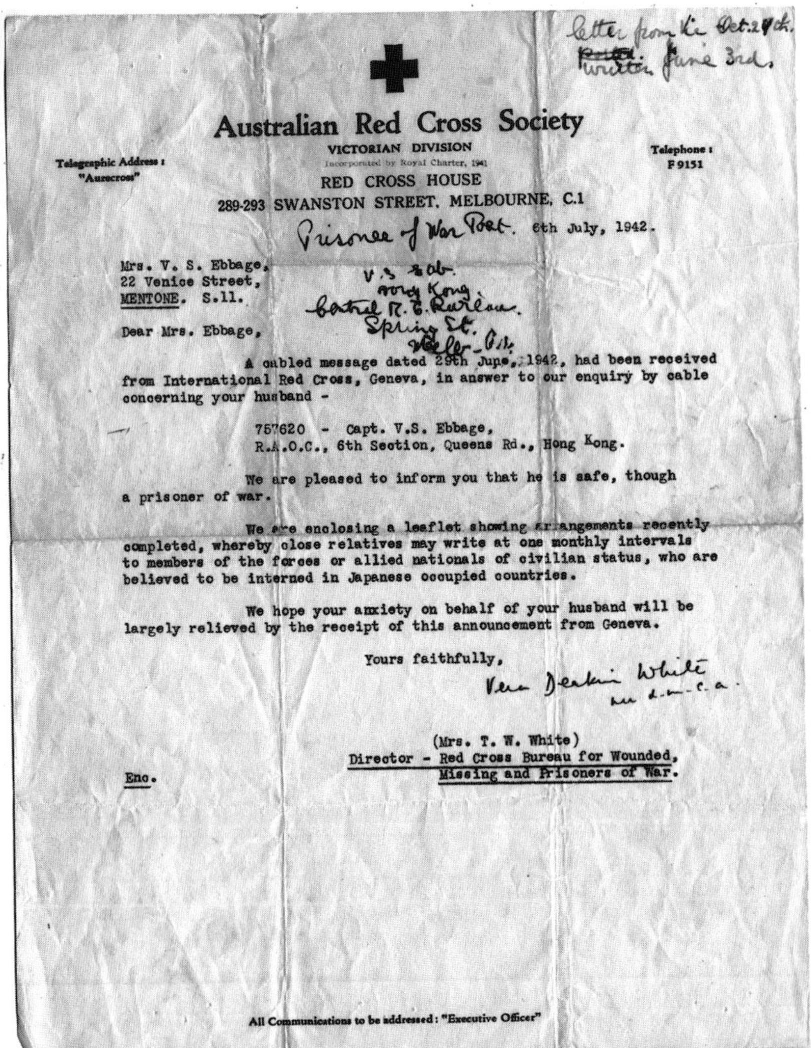

(handwritten, top right) letter from the Oct 29th.
Rectified June 3rd.

Australian Red Cross Society

VICTORIAN DIVISION
Incorporated by Royal Charter, 1941

RED CROSS HOUSE
289-293 SWANSTON STREET, MELBOURNE, C.1

x

Telegraphic Address:
"Aurecross"

Telephone:
F 9151

(handwritten) Prisoner of War Post. **6th July, 1942.**

Mrs. V.S. Ebbage,
22 Venice Street,
MENTONE. S.11.

(handwritten) V.S. Ebb.
Hong Kong
Central R.C. Bureau.
Spring St.
Melb. Vic.

Dear Mrs. Ebbage,

      A cabled message dated 29th June, 1942, had been received from International Red Cross, Geneva, in answer to our enquiry by cable concerning your husband -

           757620 - Capt. V.S. Ebbage,
           R.A.O.C., 6th Section, Queens Rd., Hong Kong.

      We are pleased to inform you that he is safe, though a prisoner of war.

      We are enclosing a leaflet showing arrangements recently completed, whereby close relatives may write at one monthly intervals to members of the forces or allied nationals of civilian status, who are believed to be interned in Japanese occupied countries.

      We hope your anxiety on behalf of your husband will be largely relieved by the receipt of this announcement from Geneva.

      Yours faithfully,

      Vera Deakin White

          (Mrs. T. W. White)
     Director - Red Cross Bureau for Wounded,
         Missing and Prisoners of War.

Enc.

All Communications to be addressed: "Executive Officer"

The International Red Cross followed the first message with one received by Mrs Ebbage on 6 July informing her that he was a prisoner of war and 'safe'. (RLC Museum)

HONG KONG PRISONERS OF WAR CAMP "S"
VICTOR STANLEY EBBAGE.

DEAREST KENNETH,
                DAD IS WELL, HOPE
YOU ARE GROWING BIG. WANT TO
SEE YOU SOON WITH JOYCE
AND MUM. BOTH BE GOOD.
ALL LOVE
                DAD

This card from Captain Ebbage was sent to his son Kenneth from Camp 'S', Shamshuipo. Note how the author has self censored the information in order to avoid the card form being destroyed by the prison authorities. (Collection of Miss Ebbage)

Photograph of parcels being delivered to Shamshuipo Police Station. (RLC Museum)

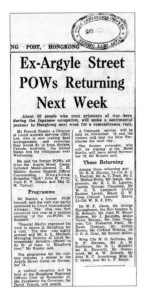

Photograph of the hut Captain Ebbage occupied while a prisoner of war, this was taken during his return visit to Hong Kong in 1966. By that time it had been repaired and looked nothing like its war-time appearance. (Collection of Miss Ebbage)

Ex-Argyle Street POWs Returning Next Week

About 60 people who were prisoners of war here during the Japanese occupation, will make a sentimental journey to Hongkong next week for a remembrance visit.

Mr Francis Rossini, a Director of Lloyd Aircraft Services (HK) Ltd, who is now making final arrangements, said yesterday they would fly in from Britain, Canada, Australia, the United States and the Philippines next Wednesday.

He said the former POWs, all from the Argyle Street Camp, included Major-General C. M. Maltby, former General Officer Commanding, Hongkong, Brigadier "Jack" John H. Price, Capt F. V. Dennis and Maj G. H. Calvert.

Programme

Mr Rossini, a former POW himself, said the visit was partly sponsored by Lloyd International Airways. The idea was first conceived last year at a reunion meeting of the ex-POWs in England.

"General Maltby expressed his wish to return to Hongkong for a visit. The idea was highly praised and Mr A. L. Macleod, Managing Director of Lloyd International Airways, offered to fly 25 of them to Hongkong free," Mr Rossini said.

The programme for the visitors includes a dinner at the Argyle Street Camp on November 12.

A cocktail reception will be held at the Hongkong Regiment Officers Club on November 15. His Excellency the Governor, Sir David Trench, will attend.

A Cenotaph service will be held on November 14 and the visitors will tour the New Territories the next day.

The former prisoners, who will be staying at the Hotel Merlin, will leave about November 18, Mr Rossini said.

Those Returning

Among those returning are: Mr B. E. Simson, Lt-Col R. J. L. Penfold, Mr A. C. Ford, Mr J. V. Hutton-Potts, Mr Ralph Stephenson, Mr R. I. D. Lamble, Captain Duncan Campbell, Mr W. C. T. Lampard, Lt-Col Eustace Levett, Major G. W. Cross, Colonel Leonard Hayes, Lt-Col W. N. J. Pitt.

Mr W. F. Davis, Mr George Keraghgaren, the Rev Gordon S. M. Bennett, Mr John H. Stuart Hudson, Mr J. Sutcliffe, Major Victor Ebbage, Mr John Trapman, Col Frederick Field, Mr Evan Graham, Mr Arthur Brown, Mr Clifford Webber, Dr J. D. A. Gray, Mr Robert Millar.

Wing Cdr W. G. Sullivan, Mr E. P. Stevens, Mr A. M. Buchanan, Mr D. L. Streillett, Mr E. Elsworth, Mr Greenwood, Mr A. W. Roberts, Mr John R. C. Armstrong, Miss D. Green, and Mr L. P. Ralph.

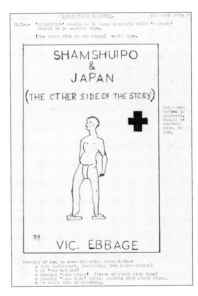

Left: Newspaper article in the *South China Morning Post, Hong Kong* on the return of the Prisoners of War for a visit in 1966. (RLC Museum)

Right: This is author's original hand-drawn design for the cover of his memoirs. He felt it was critical that it should show the true appearance of the prisoners and feature the Red Cross emblem. (RLC Museum)

A photograph of Captain Ebbage playing bowls taken in Hong Kong in happier times. The author was a keen sportsman throughout his career. (Collection of Miss Ebbage)

This envelope was entrusted to the care of No 7566331 Armament Staff Sergeant W R Peters RAOC (subsequently transferred to REME and promoted Major) by Colonel G R Hopkins, OBE Assistant Director of Ordnance Services, China Command, for safe transit to the Director of Ordnance Services, War Office.

It was carried by SSgt Peters safe and sound throughout his captivity, first in Hong Kong and then in Japan, at much personal risk and in spite of many searches by his captors, and safely delivered to it's destination some four years later.

On 30 December 1941 most of the RAOC survivors of the Hong Kong Garrison were taken to Shamshuipo Prisoners of War Camp by the Japanese.

The RAOC War Diaries were written up and three copies of the official account prepared by Sub Cdr J C Haskins (subsequently Lt Col) in his small and very neat handwriting, on paper and ink Col G R Hopkins found. Facilities were nil.

The difficulties in secreting these documents were overcome and the penalties for having them realised; Sub Cdr J C Haskins enclosed them in three home made envelopes and they were distributed to Col G R Hopkins, Capt V S Ebbage and Asst SSgt W R Peters.

Col Hopkins copy was sewn into the false bottom of his kit bag, and when he was transferred to a new Camp at Argyle Street some two miles away it went with him. It survived numerous searches, but was found by the Japanese when he was admitted to Bowen Road Hospital a year later. Though sick he was most severely beaten up. This brutal treatment caused him to send a verbal message by a Medical Officer to Capt Ebbage, to destroy his and SSgt Peters copy.

SSgt Peters went to Japan in January 1943 his copy believed safely sewn into his Greatcoat; so Col Hopkin's orders could not be complied with. It had already survived innumerable searches in Shamshuipo including a special one on his departure for Japan, but the account was never discovered. Much credit is due to SSgt Peters for carrying his copy safe and sound throughout his captivity, at some personal risk, and many searches, amply justifying the trust placed in him. Four years later, in England, the documents were handed over.

Capt Ebbage remained in Shamshuipo, his copy safely hidden. The constantly changing locations were also known to Sub Cdr Haskins who would take over if events made this course necessary. Both were in Shamshuipo when the Japanese surrendered. On returning to England this copy was handed over to Col Hopkins.

NOTE

Brigadier A H Fernyhough CBE MC used the account when writing the History of the Royal Army Ordnance Corps 1920-45; and Colonel J A Tatman REME also used this and some additional material on the Prisoners of War period in Craftsmen of the Army, The Story of the Royal Electrical & Mechanical Engineers.

Envelope which carried the official RAOC account of the fall of Hong Kong. This was hidden from the Japanese guards by Staff Sergeant Peters and was the only copy that survived to be returned to the United Kingdom. Now exhibited at the Royal Logistic Corps Museum. (RLC Museum)

yes, they were not all bad![1] In previous conversations he
had indicated that he was loyal [to the] Japanese, but did
not approve of the methods they used. A man who, by our
standards did the right things. No fraternising, but plenty
of fair dealing. I was only to see him once again, as he left
Shamshuipo for another appointment, possibly because he
was too humane. On that particular occasion my chief clerk
saw him in the company of a sentry, standing inside our
camp. His 'superiors' were nearby, and the chief clerk had
spoken to him but got no recognition or reply, and I was
told he looked ill and apprehensive. I think of him kindly,
for he was a man who did his duty as a Japanese, and by us!

About this time there was an intimation that the Imperial
Japanese government had made available the sum of
MY 3,000 for the purpose of forming a camp band, and for
sports in the camp, and a list of requirements was asked for.
I am unaware if we got anything, but there may be some
connection with the propaganda shown opposite page.[2] A
friend told me there were also other musical instruments
in camp, and some were used for jazz sessions in the huts,
etc. Up to this point there had been three different camp
commandants of Shamshuipo, the original lieutenant, then
a captain, then a further lieutenant. All appeared to be
men who did not want the job and had no interest in it.
Maybe they were fighting men temporarily detached from
their units, or recuperating from some ailment. Whatever
their problems none were very suitable for the job in hand.
Definitely not from our point of view. So far as I was concerned none of them had been helpful or even tried to be.
Perhaps they were following a set policy, which gave little
cognisance to the prisoners, or welfare of the prisoners.
There is no doubt at all in my mind that they were responsible for the parlous state we were in by the end of 1942. They
did not care, showed it, and on occasion said so. Now along
came number four, also a Lieutenant, with glasses and small
in stature. He became known to us as 'The Little Man'. He
had the ability to smile and wanted to be friendly, but was in

fear of the 'Fat Pig'. That at least was my summing up after he had been with us for a short time. My task might be a little easier with him, but there was another factor, which put a damper on these possibilities, the ability of the Japanese to provide us with anything (apart from basic food). It was quite apparent from their appearance, and little things they let drop, that they were feeling the pinch.

The time had gone when they were able to live on the fat of a prosperous and well stocked colony, whose resources had, in the main, been shipped to Japan. They too were having to tighten their belts and, although accustomed to austerity in the past, they did not like it. The impression they gave was that we were better off than they were; now we had Red Cross supplies. This jealousy was not hidden by at least one of the interpreters who showed his resentment by more frequent slappings over even the most trivial of offences. They were losing the war. The news that we had been getting showed that now the tide had turned against them. There would be no room for the arrogant, domineering and tyrannical attitude so far shown. A more moderate role would perhaps be a better line. Perhaps these factors could be the reason for the arrival of 'The Little Man'. The new camp commandant was not very long in command before deciding to carry out a full and detailed inspection of the facilities we had in our compound. With his arrival, we had been expecting such a visit, and had taken steps to see we did not show ourselves off 'to the best advantage'.

The Amyl Acetate[3] was not on view, nor was any work being performed which might have 'upset' him, we had 'set out the stall' very well indeed. The things we did not want him to see were kept well out of sight. Of course the camp commandant's staff had constant access to the store and workshops, and in the main knew, and approved of, what was happening there.

'The Little Man', however, seemed surprised and amazed at what was going on, I could nearly see the wheels going round in his head. He was undoubtedly thinking of the risks the workshops had for him, and the misuse to which, from his point of view, the facilities could be put. By this time we had a store, tool room, tailors, shoemakers, carpenters, plumbers, tinsmiths, watchmakers, fitters, bookbinders, etc all 'shops of sorts'. All were born in adversity, started from pathetic initial resources, but all were doing very well, despite efforts to strangle them by depriving them of tools and materials. 'The Little Man' was shown how short we were in the tailor's shop of sewing machine needles and cotton, and of the complete lack of materials for the repair of footwear and shortage of tools in the shoemakers, of the need for Amyl Acetate, or some similar substance in the spectacle shop, of empty tin cans and corrugated iron in the tinsmiths, of taps and piping wanted by the plumbers, of bricks, of timber, etc. We told him what garments we had received from the Red Cross, and all those windcheaters waiting to be converted into warm trousers, of the shortage of soap to wash garments and blankets of the dead! Now he had seen for himself, I would be better able to press that something be done about these shortages, at subsequent meetings. I introduced him to the word 'improvise' and he seemed to squirm at the very thought, and at the possibilities.

He expressed himself as wanting to help, and would do what he could, so I asked now for Amyl Acetate and offered money with which to purchase it, or similar material. This would be his first test of good intent! A few days later 'The Little Man' sent for me, and there, on his desk was a minute phial of Amyl Acetate. I smiled and was about to thank him when he said 'Did I want this stuff for making explosives'. I was flabbergasted, but quickly said 'No', it was wanted for the repair of the frames of spectacles. It seemed he had taken council with Japanese chemists who had checked on the uses to which Amyl Acetate could be put. He would come round and see just how it was going to be used, and gave it to the spectacle repairer for a demonstration. Eventually he was satisfied, but would not allow the bottle to be retained by us. It had to be kept in the camp commandant's office, collected, signed for when required, and returned the same day by our chief clerk who, with myself, and the spectacle repairer, would be held responsible for any misuse. Well, you live and learn!

I am not very sure of the background before the start of the pig and poultry farms in Shamshuipo, because it was no concern of mine. As far as I can recollect, the first I heard of the proposal to establish such farms came from the chairman of the Amenities Committee, when the members were called together by him. This committee had met regularly and a lot of useful work had been done to improve conditions in camp, and in particular for those in hospitals. It had been working very quietly and efficiently, in various ways. It seemed the chairman had been summoned to the camp office to hear of a proposal to spend the fund's money on the purchase of livestock. I gathered that the idea had come from the 'Fat Pig' and was being conveyed to us by his local representative, the Japanese camp commandant.

So the committee got down to considering the desirability or otherwise of obeying this edict. When all is said and done it was our money the rascal intended to spend. The first reactions were I think, to say 'NO' as the Japanese had, up till now, shown really very little interest in our welfare. The outlay would undoubtedly be considerable and the risks great, and possible losses through mortality even greater. Was there sufficient food? Where would they be kept? Who would be in charge of them? Would they be safe, etc? Finally, I believe it was agreed to finance a trial scheme for the benefit of hospital patients. Well, that seemed to be the end of that, and the poor chairman was left with the unpleasant task of telling the camp commandant of our views (and possibly of our fears?), which I am sure he did! Once the Japanese had the ball at their feet they were away, and it seemed only a very short time before I was sent for. I had not anticipated a call so was somewhat taken aback when 'The Little Man' asked if we could build a 'home for poultry'. There were to be hens and ducks, and later pigs, and in a very short time the whole place would be swarming with them, and the hospital patients would soon get well on all those eggs, (and then, presumably, be fit for working parties). The site for the project was indicated to me, and was in fact, the old sergeants' mess in Hankow Barracks.[4] Would we please make nesting boxes for the birds so they would be happy and comfortable in their task of laying? Windows and doors would need to be provided, and wire put round the whole place to make it secure from thieves, whether by guards or inmates was not stated. Oh! and the ducks would require a pond on which to disport themselves and preen their lovely coloured feathers. I could nearly picture the place as 'The Little Man' saw it; artist is sitting painting the rural scene under non existent trees, while the feathered friends created a farmyard display of peace and tranquility. All that was needed to complete the picture was a buxom farmer's wife with a basket full of eggs!

Instead, the person who would be in charge would be a Portuguese lance corporal of the Hong Kong Defence Corps. Apparently there were to be no limits on furnishing the place, if we would make an assessment of the requirements, and tell him, and he 'would see what could be done'. Well, we might be able to make some capital out of this. Could I come back and see him tomorrow morning with my proposals? Meantime could I have permission, with my men, to visit the site and calculate the requirements? The buildings were just a shell; they always were when we vacated them. No windows, doors, water pipes. Nothing but roof, walls and concrete floors, and a sandy bit of decomposed granite where the poor things would scratch! We made our list, floorboards from Jubilee buildings for nesting boxes, we had two doors on hand which might do, bricks would be needed, and wire, and nails, and water pipes and taps. The pond would pose problems. Making one that would hold water was the difficulty. 'The

Little Man' had indicated [that] they made very good ones in Japan, while I tried to remember something I had once read about dew ponds. But these needed straw, and clay, and solid ground (not reclamations), and the all important dew, none of which we had. Still, we would try 'The Little Man' out, and if he could not oblige, then we would settle for more bricks and piping! The latter would be laid with a tap, which would be kept running permanently, and turned on just sufficiently to keep up the level and replenish wastage, oh, and an overflow, just in case! The list was presented, but before he took fright invited him to select the site of the pond, which was to be the focal point of the whole thing. On this, and the size he wanted, depended how much clay, straw, bricks, etc we should need. Yes, he would come right away, and so we proceeded, in procession, to the Hankow sergeants' mess where my men were waiting.

They had already marked out a proposed site for the pond, in quite the wrong place, and at the furthest point away from the water supply. No, he said, that would hardly do, it would require too much pipe, now if we put the pond here, you would only need half as much pipe! What a blessing we had such a helpful camp commandant! He looked carefully at our list, he did not think he could get clay, couldn't we improvise, and straw, perhaps some grass would do instead; bricks, he had found a building we could pull down, nails, he would see, wire, yes, that should not be difficult, piping, he had found a place, a private house on the Castle Peak Road which had been abandoned. This afternoon we would go out on the ration lorry and take what we wanted, taps, could we not 'borrow' one from the cookhouse? Would the premises be ready by Friday? Perhaps the men would work harder if he sent them a few cigarettes! What a game it all was! The raid on the house at Castle Peak Road was very productive, the plumbers had a field day, there was piping galore. Lengths and lengths of it all down the sloping garden were quickly disconnected and removed to the truck, while others found a door and lots of other items which would be useful to us, not only for the poultry farm, currently in hand. I found a second door on an outhouse, but when it was opened, there, lying on a concrete bench was a dead Chinese woman dressed in coolie clothes. We did not take that door but closed it reverently, after paying our respects.

On my way down the hill to join the others I found a passion flower, so dug it up, and replanted it outside my hut where it gave such pleasure to others, and was a constant reminder of the effects of war on poor and innocent people. This particular foray provided an afternoon out of camp for a few of the workshop staff, who enjoyed the change and it did them a world of good, and the supplies obtained were of value to us quite apart from those needed for the 'farm'. Work on the 'nesting boxes', etc was going on apace, but the pool was giving a bit of trouble until eventually 'The Little Man' produced some cement. (Only a small quantity was eventually used, the balance was kept for use elsewhere.) Eventually the stage was set for the arrival of the poultry, a few Chinese hens and ducks that would live with us (we hoped) and share our food, and provide eggs and progeny. The 'Fat Pig' was delighted, and so was 'The Little Man' who, I believe, suggested that the first batch of eggs be given as a present to our benefactor, but that is a tale I am not competent to tell!

The following is an extract from a report made by an officer from Shamshuipo, on his arrival at Argyle Street:

The Pig and Poultry Farm
The Poultry Farm was started at the beginning of 1943. The sergeants' mess (Hankow Area) was prepared for this purpose, the rooms being used as hutches. Chinese birds only were purchased. The project had a bad start with most of the birds dying, but health was regained under Lance Corporal **** of the Hong Kong Volunteer Defence Corps. A farm of 300 birds was going strong in September last.

There had been one batch of fifteen birds for the table. These were raffled to the amenities fund, through which the finances of the pig and poultry are controlled.

Pigs were purchased about April (forty-three) and the kitchen of the sergeants' mess was turned into sties.

The pigs did well, and by September last they were eighteen including two boards.

Three sows were in fallow and litters were shortly expected. Pigs weighing 18lbs when purchased were, by September weighing 75–100lbs.

Four pigs off colour were slaughtered and made into stew for the camp.

Permission to kill a pig for the draft before it sailed was refused.

(The draft referred to left in August 1943.)

14

Propaganda Draft

We greeted the New Year of 1943 in better spirit, perhaps it would herald our release, whatever was to come we were in better shape to 'take it'. Hardly had we settled down from previous upheavals when it was announced there was to be a further draft for Japan. No ordinary draft this one, but a 'Propaganda Draft' which would sail on a 'luxury ship' and everyone conjured up thoughts of comfortable palatial liners threading their way to the various ports on the inland sea of Japan! This cruise would take 1,200 men and no officers.

The Japanese painted the whole thing in the most glowing colours. With this party went forty-five men of our unit, the Royal Army Ordnance Corps, and were led by the warrant officer who had been acting as my sergeant major, and had done the job very well! They would be in good hands. In many ways I was glad this party was going together, we certainly did not know what the future would hold in store for those left in Shamshuipo, and so far I was concerned this meant we were divided into two more or less equal parties. Alas, this excellent warrant officer died in Japan. My chief clerk then took on the task of acting as sergeant major in addition to his other duties.

A member of No. 6 Section, Royal Army Ordnance Corps who went on this draft said in his narrative, written afterwards:

The camp commandant gave a short speech in which he said that we would be going to a land where everyone would be treated fairly, but where each man would have to work hard. Everyone received a Japanese banknote to the value of 10 Military Yen.

Military Yen was the currency in use in occupied China which was of no value in mainland Japan. The commandant said that the money was a present from the Pope.

As each succeeding draft left for Japan there followed immediately a complete reorganisation. It seemed that, no sooner did we get one cookhouse working satisfactorily than the whole lot had to be pulled apart and rebuilt in some other place. It sounds very easy, but the rebuilding of boilers and cooking appliances, plumbing, doors and windows took time, ingenuity and a lot of hard work. The staff we had was, by now, highly practised in this kind of job. Just the same, we were becoming short of materials such as bricks, piping, taps, boilers, etc, even taking into account the amounts recovered as a result of lessening numbers.

I would have to put this point forward to the camp commandant at an early opportunity. The very large numbers of men required for work at the aerodrome at Kai Tak and the docks were diminished, while the variety of tasks increased. For instance, a further party was now wanted to go over to the island of Hong Kong by launch, to work in the Godowns[1] there. My friend the officer commanding the Middlesex Regiment was allocated to this job.

Naturally I was eager to hear all about this special excursion when they returned, as I knew the premises at West Point. They were used as storehouses by the army when I came out with the Shanghai Defence Force in 1927, and for a time, I had worked there.[2]

The task was to move drums of high octane fuel; empty those that were leaking, and fill up others. My friend was enthusiastic about this task and would, I think, have liked to have set fire to the whole place, so keen was he to sabotage the Japanese war effort. Unfortunately he did not have matches, and in any case the party was searched! However, he and his men had decided to take with them, the very next day, their ration of sugar, and place a couple of ounces or so in each drum of fuel they opened. Well, that should 'gum up the works' a bit!

He was, however, even more enthusiastic about a destroyer which was anchored in the harbour and which they passed very close, on both outward and inward voyages from the landing stage at Shamshuipo.

His main topic of conversation had always been that of escape and had suggested to me, on so many occasions, ways and means of accomplishing a getaway. An escape enthusiast if ever there was one, unfortunately so many of his proposed schemes had practical disadvantages and all had, up till now, been abandoned. But this one was different.

He had noted that the gangway of the destroyer was always down when they passed early in the morning, and he had seen only one watch keeper on deck. It would be a relatively simple matter to overpower the two sentries who accompanied the working party as guards, take over their arms, run alongside the destroyer and board her, dispose of the watch keeper and take over the ship. Tomorrow, he was taking with him some officers of the Merchant Navy, navigators and engineers, plus some naval ratings who knew all about such ships, in order to get professional advice. Once the destroyer had been taken over, the launch would be used to run a shuttle service between the camp landing stage and ship, until all who wanted to go were safely on board, then they would up anchor and away. It all sounded too simple and cut and dried, in fact a 'fait accompli'. I warmed to the idea, just the kind of deeds of daring reminiscent of schoolboy newspapers of my early youth; they were never known to fail. But this was reality, a bit different! Had they tried to find out why the destroyer had been lying at anchor in the harbour for the last month? Was she sea-worthy? Bunkers full? Boilers working? Ammunition, etc? Did anyone have a plan of the minefield we had laid at that end of the harbour? Perhaps she was immobile, waiting to go into the dockyard for repairs, in which case surely the fuel and ammunition, etc would have been taken off? This might be the reason for there being only a watchman on board. We would wait with interest the views of the naval specialists on the feasibility of the proposed operation, and even more so on the state of the ship. Their opinion was that she appeared to be a very old ship, waiting her place in the dockyard for overhaul and repair. My friend kept a very close eye on this vessel for some days, he just could not bring himself to believe this was not a heaven sent opportunity to, figuratively, hoist the skull and crossbones, and sail away to rejoin our friends and fight the war with added vigour. He did not take kindly or easily to imprisonment. Some days later we witnessed a tug being put alongside the destroyer, and the slow business of moving her from the anchorage near to Stonecutters Island, and to the dockyard commenced. Just one more morale boosting escape plan had come to an end.

This and so many other similar incidents did not lessen but even strengthened my regard for this particular officer. He was a product of the Honourable Artillery Company, and had been commissioned and joined the Middlesex Regiment in Hong Kong at the start of the war. He rebelled at being sent on this plum assignment, and at the smug feeling of security which seemed to pervade the colony. The fleshpots of life here did not interest him, and I gather it was his wish to go out and fight Germans – not Japanese. Recently married before coming to Hong Kong, and eager to get back to his wife. I heard so much about her that I felt we were already old friends. In camp, when his duties allowed, and he was not planning further escapes, he got down to designing and planning his future home. A most courageous and loyal man, bubbling over with ideas, enthusiasm and ebullience. If and when the time came, I knew he was someone I could trust, implicitly. We consulted daily on many matters, on the state of the camp, and what we could do about it! Mention has already been made of my own gardening activities, and that others so minded were also active, primarily on their own behalf, so that 'cook ups' had become the fashion, and 'small fires' a daily occurrence. The Hong Kong Volunteer Defence Corps had however pioneered a much larger scheme, and had started cultivation of vacant ground to the east of the camp buildings. As yet, this garden had not been very productive, though it had solved the problem of what to do with the 'night soil' apart from just burying it! The Japanese had not shown very much interest in these activities, they were a bit too near the perimeter fence for their liking. So they tolerated the originators of this enterprise, grudgingly loaning the tools (picks and shovels) for the prime purpose of burying the night soil, and not for gardening, and keeping a close watch on the return of the tools each evening. The man in charge of this undertaking was a warrant officer of the Hong Kong Volunteer Defence Corps who was doing his best to make certain it did not fall further into the doldrums.

With the arrival of the new camp commandant there was a new interest and 'work recommenced in earnest', and I quote from a report:

There are twelve permanent gardeners and ten fatigue men allocated daily for work in the garden and for trimming the grass around the paths and roads in camp.

The parsons too found an outlet here for any surplus energy, as there were fewer sick and burials! There is no doubt that the garden was undergoing a new lease of life, based on the second foundations laid by the Hong Kong Volunteer Defence Corps warrant officer. By now it was becoming, or had become, very difficult to obtain seeds, and this aspect defeated 'The Little Man' just as much as it did those that wanted them. I was able to hand over a few from those obtained originally through the good offices of Cardiff Joe, and some saved from my 1942 crop. Tomatoes, sweet potatoes, carrots and green vegetables were grown in reasonable quantities and allocated to cookhouses, where they were a very welcome addition to the diet. The Canadians also had a section of this garden for their special use. The actual quantities of vegetables supplied from this source are not known, but they were substantial, and much credit must go to the Volunteer warrant officer and his team. Even the smallest contribution to the basic diet was of help, as the Red Cross supplies had already shown.

This garden did I believe, continue producing right to the very end! The general improvement in health by March 1943 was apparent, and it was possible to close down the diphtheria and isolation hospitals for good! Three months after the receipt of Red Cross supplies the good they had done was plain to be seen, and the general health of the RAOC had markedly improved. Most had shaken off the lethargy and there was a better spirit pervading amongst all sections of the camp.

My eyesight had not improved very much, and of course I was still having bouts of malaria, but was much better than I was, and we were all thankful for the upturn in our fortunes. The entertainments side had taken rather a long time to get going, but this was to be expected, as like all of us they had no facilities initially and had to start from scratch.

Now that everyone was better fed, in better health, clothed, and we were into the warm sunny weather; now was their opportunity. Entertainments had been low in the priority. From my point of view the men's clothing and footwear came first. The staff of the workshops had been, and were, involved in providing facilities, props, etc and much work had gone on 'behind the scenes'. A stage had been made, the plumbers had, from unserviceable piping provided means of hanging drapes and scenery, and the tailors had made costumes from unserviceable mosquito curtains, etc. One or two people had got together to write a 'musical' and had composed both words and music. The selected artists had put in much practice, and now we were getting near to 'opening night'. (Perhaps day would be more accurate). The show had been given a big write up, the 'Fat Pig' and 'The Little Man' had said they would be coming. (I believe this called for some modification of the words). The music was very catchy, the words apt, and the title 'Where there's a will, there's always a way', most appropriate. Star of the show was a popular Portuguese member of the Hong Kong Volunteer Defence Corps, known then, and possibly still amongst the Portuguese community of Hong Kong as 'Carmen Miranda'. A pseudonym by which I fear he will always carry. I was not present at the opening performance, but thoroughly enjoyed the repeats, and on occasion still find myself humming the easily caught up tunes, and recall the great pleasure many people got from this and similar entertainments. All concerned earned, and deserve our thanks and congratulations for a very excellent entertainment, well written and performed.

15

Term Report or Salt Pans

My main responsibility in Shamshuipo was the welfare of men of my own unit, No. 6 Section, Royal Army Ordnance Corps, and secondly for the store and workshops which were for the benefit of the camp as a whole. So at this stage, approximately mid-1943, it is an appropriate time to review the position of both. There is no doubt at all that the receipt of Red Cross supplies, in particular food, had a great beneficial effect on every one of us. We were certainly much better in health and spirits and the prospect of an early demise had receded into the background. Right from the start I had always thought that we should go through a bad patch, as the weaker ones amongst us went to the wall. It now seemed we were over this phase! Those who could not assimilate the diet had gone, and those who remained had adjusted to the slightly better circumstances, but this improvement was relative.

The Royal Army Ordnance Corps had been fortunate as, up to this stage we had lost only three men from illness.[1] My chief's policy of 'getting out alive as many as we can' seemed to be working, but I was not over sanguine about the future. We were very close to the borderline beyond which the descent could be very quick indeed. Confidence and self respect were high, and so long as it was kept that way, the unit would give a good account of themselves.

Perhaps they had taken to heart the words it was customary to repeat, parrot fashion, when as recruits they received their grounding at the regiment depot. It started with 'The first duty of a soldier is obedience', etc and ended with a bit about 'honesty, sobriety and self respect'. They could not be faulted here under any of those headings! Our numbers in hospital was also small when compared with those of other units. We were a compact little body of men who helped one another in difficulties. Yes, they were 'gentlemen of ordnance'. Most were now employed in one capacity or other inside camp, most of them in our small store and workshops. The store and workshops were controlled by the chief clerk who issued items to individuals in accordance with need, and authorised the repair of goods in possession on a stitch in time basis. All issued and jobs done were recorded. It worked!

Perhaps, in fairness to the Japanese and in particular the camp commandant, ('The Little Man') it ought to be stated that there had been some improvement in the general supply position. This man showed some interest, (more than the others had done) and listened to requests, and pursuing them whenever he could. (The Japanese were short of nearly everything themselves). The tailor's shop was busy, roughly half on repair work and the other half on manufacturing trousers from Red Cross windcheaters, etc. This bulk manufacturing job was coming along nicely and I was hoping that, by the time the cooler weather arrived, that everyone who needed them would be in possession of a pair of warm trousers. The Japanese had provided some cotton and had promised more, but the position on sewing machine needles was acute. We had already, on occasion, been reduced to hand sewing so as to limit the machines to straight run jobs, like making trousers. I could see that if we did not get machine needles soon then produce would practically come to a halt. Because of this possibility I asked my experts, (highly qualified instrument artificers) if it was feasible to 'make' needles, just in case the Japanese supply broke down. They were not optimistic, but would certainly try, if we could get some wire. We decided that Dannert wire[2] might do and as we were surrounded by the stuff, it seemed appropriate to 'knock a bit off'. This we did, and then four of them spent several weeks in an attempt to make a sewing machine needle from Dannert. Many were the 'near misses' and time and time again success seemed very near, so that I became quite confident that, in the end, we would not fail.

Imagine trying to make this kind of item with practically no tools and facilities, and only a bit of rusty Dannert wire for material. Comparable perhaps to trying to get a camel through the eye of a needle! The 'eye', yes, that was our difficulty too! Then suddenly, the Japanese produced lots of needles and the immediate problem in this respect was over. I am getting a little in advance of myself in recounting this enterprise in its entirety now. However, before moving to other matters tribute must be paid to the men who, by diligence and perseverance, came so near to success. They were of course the elite of the Royal Electrical and Mechanical Engineers tradesmen to which they had unknowingly been transferred in 1942, but at that time they still wore the Cap Badge of the Royal Army Ordnance Corps![3]

Although the shoemaker's shop had been in existence for more than a year, it was only recently that the Japanese recognised its existence and had agreed to supply materials. This was a bit like locking the stable door after the horse had gone, for the footwear was by then in very poor condition. Had we received adequate assistance earlier many pairs of boots might have been saved, still, one never looks a gift horse in the mouth; we could find a use for everything.

Below is a report made to me on the subject:

They sent in five hammers, rasps, and awls and a supply of leather. From then on they sent, at various times, materials which were absolutely insufficient for our requirements, as will be seen from the following scale for each quarter.

Items Received from Japanese	Actual Military Authority	Requirements
Soles pairs	225	700
Heels pieces	900	2,500
Nails lbs	15	45
Protectors	15	35
Studs lbs	21	55
Thread Balls	3	6

Consequently through lack of these materials, footwear was being made unserviceable, and the only men receiving repairs were those who were doing outside work which was extremely heavy on footwear. The result of this was that supplies were usually drained in the first fortnight, and until the next quarter's supplies were received, time was spent in stripping down old boots for materials once again. The leather from these boots was mostly used for making laces, straps for wooden clogs (sandals were the main footwear of the camp) and patching other boots. The activities in bookbinders, spectacle repairers, carpenters, plumbers, watch repairers, tinsmiths, etc shops were proceeding normally, and much good work, for the benefit of the camp was done. The plumbers were on occasion taken out of camp whenever we had new requirements of piping, etc. The Cornish plumber had added his son to this gang.

The back had been broken of the number of spectacles awaiting repair, and the bookbinders are covered in my previous report about them. Bricklayers were in constant demand by cookhouses, bakery, etc and for bricking up windows, etc. By now they had become extremely skilful and efficient in the re-building of boilers and other cooking apparatus, and in particular in the use of mud, made from decomposed granite. The carpenters were still fashioning sandals, re-fitting doors, etc while the tinsmiths were still busy recovering empty tins from Red Cross parcels, and converting them into eating utensils, and many other uses, while the watch repairers continued to tackle any repair within their capacity.

The Japanese had at least shown a willingness to help, but of course this was to suit their own ends, if the camp as a whole benefited, then this was fortuitous! From a store point of view the situation was improving. The Japanese had been making monthly issues of certain items and these were distributed proportionately to the men. Where there was sufficient to make a distribution 'per man' this was done. Soap was one item which came in periodically, but was withheld, like everything else, when the camp was under punishment. The soap was of very inferior quality, while the quantity received quite inadequate. There was never enough for the men to wash themselves and their clothes, and mostly it ran out long before the next issue was due. Regular and repeated requests for a larger issue to be made fell on deaf ears. I was told bluntly, on one occasion, that we were now receiving the same ration of this item as the Japanese themselves and that the men should 'make it last'. Small hand towels were issued in a similar way, they were, like soap, regarded as expendable. They were so small and thin, and of little practical value, being approximately twice the size of a face flannel customary in England. There were ample toothbrushes, tooth powder and talcum to meet our requirements, but up till now there had been no issue at all of boot preservative since May 1942, about a year ago. Most men had no underpants, but the Japanese issued loin cloths (Fandoucis) in lieu. We certainly were better off than we were some months ago, when we got nothing at all, and there were heaps of things we could do with. For instance, there was no material for darning socks, few men had eating utensils, and were making do with empty cans which had contained Red Cross items from individual parcels, in place of mugs. They fed from these, and improvised mess tins we had made in the tinsmith's shop from corrugated iron.

Whenever the camp commandant wanted to see me, or I was waiting for an interview with him, the meetings were invariably held in the afternoon. By that time, I assume, he had got over the ordinary business of the day, and was perhaps in a more amenable frame of mind than first thing in the morning! I had just got down to my afternoon siesta when an urgent message came from 'The Little Man' to come and see him at once. No call had been expected, so, as I took my seat in his office, braced myself for the unexpected. Then the interpreter said something like this:

> 'The camp commandant is very worried about the health of the men in camp' (so were we all).
>
> 'He thinks they are short of salt. In Japan we eat a lot of salt which keeps us fit. We make our own salt by getting it from the sea.'
>
> (By this time my mind had done a series of mental somersaults, but was beginning to see the direction in which we were proceeding).
>
> The interpreter continued, 'Why do you not make your own salt? It would be better for your health'.
>
> (Quickly I wondered if it was the intention to cut our present salt ration, in which case he should be talking to the ration officer and not to me)
>
> 'Captain Ebbage, you made very good pond for ducks, if you could make much larger one, and get some water from the sea, soon you would have all the salt needed. The men would soon become quite fit again, like Japanese soldiers were. Did I think it was a good idea?'

Experience in dealing with the Japanese had taught me to go along with this kind of proposition. My mind went quickly back to one of his predecessors, and the matter of the rope to get the tank, to make the oven, that ordnance built! Inwardly I thought of the seashore at Scarborough when, as a child, I carried buckets of sea water to fill the moat made round my sand castle, and remembered how quickly the water disappeared when I poured it on the sand! Surely the decomposed granite would act similarly. Then I thought of the brackish and sewage polluted water available to us. (We were in the estuary of the Pearl River). How did we get the water up to the pond which would be well above the high water mark? I did not imagine pumps would be made available. In North China and other places, I had seen the crude but simple methods to obtain salt by evaporation from the sea. Certainly we could do with salt, my roommate (who was in charge of the cookhouse) and I had already had long debates on this matter, but the futility of this particular operation for the production of salt seemed doomed to failure! However, there could be gain in everything, and if we were to get water we should require access to the harbour. My experts could then advise on the best methods to immobilise that electric fence, should we ever need to do so! There might be other bonuses as well. So I asked, had the commandant got a site in view? Yes, he had, and we would go and look at it now, with the sergeant of the guard! The area selected was to the northern end of Jubilee Buildings, now 'out of bounds' to us, and wired off to make it so. It was as near as possible to the jetty (which was the place we used to empty and rinse the latrine buckets used by dysentery patients in hospital) which would be opened to allow access to the sea, and very close to the electric fence which formed the outer camp boundary. We should certainly welcome a sentry or two if we were to be engaged on digging a hole so close to the fence, and within sight of the watch towers! Work would start at 8am tomorrow and it would be supervised by 'The Little Man' himself, and the sentries. My presence would not be required. Well, that let me out, and did not want responsibility for something I had no faith in! The interview was over; all I was apparently required to do was to supply some of my men, complete with tools. I discussed the camp commandant's proposals with my advisers who were even more skeptical of success than I had been. Still it was something to do; a change of scenery from which there might be some profit, though not of the kind envisaged by 'The Little Man'! My men were not very long in digging the hole the required few inches deep, but there was nothing to line it with, as we had done in the case of the duck pond. I was able to watch the operation from the compound and absorb the latest information brought back by my stalwarts. The camp was very short of containers, and in particular of the larger sizes. The Japanese had provided practically none at all, and most of what were available in the cookhouses had been made in the tinsmith's shop from sheets of corrugated iron. There was consequently much consternation in camp when, a few days later 'The Little Man' called for a party of some 200 men (not from me, thank goodness) to parade with buckets or suitable containers, to form a human chain from the jetty to the embryo salt pan. This 'party' (and the men regarded it as such) turned up in carnival spirit with all kinds of containers, but mostly small empty tins of about 15oz size. Some were their own food containers which they were loath to let out of their sight. The whole thing I gathered, took on a comical look as the containers were passed, hand to hand, until finally what water was left in them was duly cast into the prepared hollow. Amidst all this jollification the 'Fat Pig' arrived, but the scene caused him little amusement. His presence effectively put a damper on the merrymaking, and in the subdued atmosphere the 'party' was over and the men returned behind the barbed wire. I assume the 'Fat Pig' did not approve of what was happening, for as far as can be remembered, this was the last heard of 'Operation Salt'. Still, 'The Little Man' deserved full marks for trying; he at least did have some initiative!

'Albert' or Intelligence Tests

It was never safe to predict what next might emanate from the camp commandant's office, so many strange and varied things came from there and they fell, like balloons at a children's party, from above. We had just heard of the latest effort! All fit men, who might be going to Japan, were to be tested. A special team of Japanese psychologists and educationalists would be coming tomorrow to carry out these tests, which might continue for some days. A programme had been drawn up by units and we were required to submit names of all men who were fit, so they could be tested. Only the best were good enough for Japan! Officers would not be required to attend, as I assume we were regarded either in the category of 'Honours material' or perhaps as unteachable idiots… No-one said. Yes, this was to be a test of ability and potential, and we gathered that, dependant upon the results, decisions would be taken on fitness for work either on the docks at say Osaka or the coal mines in Hokkaido. (Both in Japan). Apparently it was to be a psychology test based on visual perception and discrimination. Just the sort of thing the boys welcomed and were good at!

Mostly they expected to come away with, at least, a certificate of merit. A party spirit pervaded the whole place as the first contingent were taken inside the gymnasium and were handed their examination papers. It was a very serious business, and one or two of the candidates had to be slapped before order was restored, and the pupils sat down (at their desks, sic) cross legged on the floor with their exam papers in front of them. I was told that the basis of the examination was a series of coloured charts with circles, squares, objects, etc. Some were shaded rainbow fashion, while others were just plain colours, while many had horizontal and perpendicular lines. The men had I gathered, to say what the different colours were, going through the shading in a given amount of time. Then the examination papers were marked up by the examiners. Apparently there was another game which entailed counting up the number of horizontal lines on each page, and try to beat the other men in your team who had to count about half as many perpendicular lines. The lads just lapped it up, they loved it, and when the first break came, and the party broke for the tuck shop and their rice and veg; and the nearest latrine, the laughter was deafening. Even at this stage the Japanese examiners had not raised one single trace of a smile. I understood that about half of those tested so far had proved to be colour blind, which was; I guess, a bit more than the national average for servicemen. Perhaps this is what the doctors would have called 'acquired colour blindness' or something like that. Everyone was in carnival spirit and waiting round two which think turned out to be finding the answers to simple sums like eight plus nine, and thirty seven divided by four. Naturally the lads suffering from malnutrition had difficulties with these, and few had completed their papers when the bell rang for time.

Will Hay[1] would have loved it, and on any English stage it would have brought the house down. Hands frequently went up for 'Benjo' (toilet) and when the absent one returned to class found that another had completed the papers for him. After about the third day sterner and swifter measures were used, so that those who qualified or failed, emerged with a rapidity known only to those who have experienced the Japanese ire. The men of No. 6 section,

RAOC must have done very badly, which did not surprise me. As a result none of them were selected for the Fourth Draft of 500 men due to leave for Japan in August 1943.

Perhaps their tests and the colour of their hair and eyes had denoted they were rated high in the intelligence field, or of course, they might have come out of the examination as 'delinquents'.

Some time after the departure of the August draft for Japan there had been a further reorganisation of the whole camp. So far these periodical upheavals had not affected me personally very much. However, the Japanese had now built a new barbed wire fence between our small compound and the main camp. There was a gateway between the compound and guard room which was open during the day, but closed and locked at night.

The effect was to segregate the two parts. I have previously described that I occupied, with two other officers, a room at the end of the complex of buildings in the compound with our batman in a small one adjoining, while the chief clerk and his assistant, lived in a room next to the office. It was a most strange situation, for when darkness came and the gate was locked, then the six of us were isolated.

The Japanese intention may have been four fold:

a. To shorten the perimeter.
b. To deny, during hours of darkness (or at any other time) access to the workshops and store, and the tools that were there.
c. To provide an additional obstacle at that side of the camp.
d. To isolate the camp from the parade ground.

It had been apparent for some time that the Japanese doubted the integrity of some of their Korean and Formosan[2] guards who were, from a Japanese point of view, getting, on occasion, a little too friendly with the prisoners.

On the other hand, these guards had developed a habit of helping themselves to whatever they wanted. Perhaps the camp commandant feared the store might be raided! So, for a while we were left in situ, but realised that this peculiar state would not continue for very long. The fact that we should shortly be parted from the stores and workshops meant that new hiding places would have to be found for some of the items that had been concealed there. Others would need to be duplicated (where possible) and went to new homes from whence they could be quickly recovered, when required. The cookhouse which my Royal Scots roommate ran was an obvious choice, but so it was by the Japanese whenever they made their periodic searches.

Friends in other parts of the camp helped provide other resting places. After a month or two, the odd state in which we were living was brought to an end. Quite suddenly we got our marching orders to a three-roomed hut in the Hankow Barracks area and which faced onto the main road. The Japanese believed in keeping us all on the move and in making constant searches of men and rooms. It is to say the least annoying, when as a result of a sudden move, a man becomes parted from his prized possession. This was to say, bricked up in a wall and later, alas, inaccessible. This sort of thing did happen!

Every day, at roughly the same time, a tiny speck would appear in the sky over us, and it was christened 'Albert'. If I could not see it I could hear the drone, and occasionally when the sun shone directly on it there was the brightest of lights. 'Albert' was I gathered, an American reconnaissance plane, and he brought joy and comfort on every visit. We were alone no longer; there were friends up there, high in the sky, and probably taking pictures of us.

Yes, we were all sure the Americans knew just where we were, and keeping tabs on us, surveillance! Morale rose higher and higher with each succeeding visit but nothing seemed to happen until, eventually the enthusiasm died down, though the wish to be 'up there' with him remained! Then, one day, things were a bit different. 'Albert' did not come alone. We saw him high in the sky and shortly afterwards there was a drone of many aircraft and great excitement amongst the sentries. All the inmates were ordered into their huts, while the sentries blasted off ammunition at the plane thousands of feet in the air. Then there was crunch, crunch, as the bombs came raining down on the oil installation at Lai Chi Kok, which was some 1,000 yards from where we were. Lai Chi Kok fuel installation was, like Shamshuipo camp built on reclaimed ground. There was a patch of water between us which was waiting the attention of the 'reclaimers'. The blanket bombing was a success, and soon we could see columns of black smoke hundreds of feet in the air, and the fires did not go out for some days. From what I was able to see, the bombs had blasted the major part of the oil storage tanks, but many bombs had fallen into the sea between us, and uncomfortably close. We expected the bombers to return to complete the task, but perhaps they were satisfied with the days' work here. Their run also took in other oil installations on Hong Kong Island as well.

Now we felt we were very much part of the war; and my Middlesex friend was elated, as indeed we all were! The Japanese did not like this bombing, while our morale was increased, theirs correspondingly waned. The loss of the oil was a severe blow to them and they showed it by their actions. Things were getting just that bit more difficult for them, and in a different way for us! All kinds of rumours spread round the camp and hopes in some quarters were raised to unrealistic levels, with thoughts such as 'out next week'. From my point of view I thought we had a very long way to go. One bombing, like one rose, or one fine day, did not make a summer. But it did make the day of reckoning just that bit nearer! Towards the middle of 1943, and on the orders of the camp commandant, the entire stock of stationery held by the canteen was removed by the Japanese, without giving any reason, or where the money was to come from to reimburse canteen funds. A few days later the camp commandant enquired what stationery it was desired to hold in the canteen, and he was given a list. Surprisingly, the items on the list were delivered by the contractor about three weeks later, but nothing was said about whom was going to pay for the items removed. However, some months later the Japanese decided to make a free issue of prisoners of war stationery, and that removed by them earlier would be paid for by them. They also stated that future issues to the camp for correspondence purposes would be free, and the sale of stationery in the canteen would cease forthwith, except in the case of ink and pen nibs! Later still, the canteen contractor gave a credit note for the total value of stationery purchased from him in May 1942. The effect of this was that stationery was brought to the position of a free issue ever since its use in camp.

As can be imagined the money for the stationery already sold was not traceable to individuals, many of whom had left camp, so the central fund benefited accordingly. The reasons for this strange manoeuvre are not known and are left to the imagination of the reader, but at least the paper for writing letters home was not provided by our hosts!

Air raids and aerial activity were increasing, and we were enjoying the warm, clear and sunny days, and in particular those on which the planes came from Kweilin. The sight of them, and the aerobatics they performed were, we thought, being displayed for our own special benefit and entertainment! So convinced were most of the inhabitants that the Americans knew just where we were, that it was more than a shock when three planes flew low over the camp and sprayed it with cannon fire. The planes seemed to come over the brow of the hill from the direction of Tolo Harbour, and straight down the main road through camp, dividing what had been Hankow and Nanking barracks. Japanese guards began firing indiscriminately all over the place, at the same time driving the prisoners into the nearest hut, and then opening up on the invading aircraft that were, by that time, well out of sight! When the planes had gone their track was plain to be seen. Our hut fronted onto the main road, and I retrieved a bullet which had gone through the roof. It was only a yard or so from where we were sitting. Another bullet had also come through the roof of our store, where the chief clerk and his assistant were at that time. Fortunately there was, I think, only one casualty and he was only very slightly hurt. This particular raid did us good in many respects. It gave us all more confidence, but it also showed just how little we counted. The Kowloon peninsula was dotted with prison camps of various kinds, and although I had no doubt the pilots who came to see us would be well briefed before they left base, by the time they were over their target, would not have the time or the inclination to consider just where those ruddy prisoners were. I am sure this particular raid had a salutary effect upon us all. The three aircraft flew away into the sunshine, and we were left wondering as to the purpose of their visit. I did not believe it had anything to do with us! Then, to our surprise we found that there was a Japanese ship anchored some few hundred yards from our camp and about halfway between us and Stonecutters Island. These particular aircraft had passed right over this ship and had no doubt given it a broadside as they flew over it. We had not known of the existence of this ship as it was hidden from our direct line of sight by Jubilee Buildings. However, very shortly after this first raid there was another, but this time a bombing raid. It appears that the ship was fully loaded with ammunition, and determined efforts were being made to sink it. The Japanese had no doubt placed the ship in that particular position deliberately, perhaps in the hope it would not be seen, and would be afforded some protection by its proximity to Shamshuipo prisoner of war camp. What we were to see, from only a few hundred yards distance, was a most accurate display of high level bombing. The planes made a number of runs causing a series of explosions, and then, ultimately, the complete crippling of the ship. The crunch, crunch of each stick of bombs as it dropped on, or very close to, the target! So close in fact were they, to our observation position that even the ground under us shook, and so did the buildings! We could not see very much, but what we did see was most heartening. The news we were able to glean from the Chinese newspapers smuggled into camp was very good, but what we had just witnessed with our own eyes, was doubly so.

17

Christmas 1943

In December 1943, the Japanese were still intent upon sending more and more men to Japan for work there. They had just formed a further draft of 500 men, which included eleven members of the Royal Army Ordnance Corps. Now they certainly were 'scraping the barrel' for many of these men were far from fit by any standards, except those applied by the Japanese. As a unit we were now getting a bit out of balance. I had hoped to keep the unit in equal proportions; half in Hong Kong and half in Japan. The Japanese would have none of it, and there was little that could be done except to protest, and draw attention to the poor physical state of these particular men. How they would make out in the land of the Rising Sun gave me much concern. Maybe they would be better off for food than those who remained. The Japanese would not get much out of them unless they did receive extra nourishment. It seemed an 'even money' bet, that as from a food point of view we were again on the downgrade in Shamshuipo. The men were all well aware and informed about what they could and could not take to Japan. As they stood on the main road just prior to leaving camp for their ship the Japanese were busy carrying out the usual routine search. One of my sergeants (he had been my representative in the British Legation in Peking in 1940) seemed to be having a rough time. This NCO had never been very fit since entering camp. I found out afterwards that he had amused himself by extracting from the *New York Times*, etc the weekly recipes. The papers were, as the reader may well remember, given to us as latrine paper. The sergeant had carefully cut out the recipes and formed them into little books. No doubt he received much satisfaction and licking of lips in anticipation of the good food which lay ahead, once we were 'out', and his intention to try out his 'statements of ingredients'. I, too, had also resolved that once free, I, too, would eat well; just as well as I could afford of good plain English food. No lobster Thermidor or smoked salmon for me; after this incarceration, roast beef and Yorkshire pudding would be the height of luxury, and all I would ask. Well, the Japanese found his 'recipe books' and he received a liberal amount of slaps across the face, etc. Apparently the Japanese thought his 'books' were a diary of events in Shamshuipo, though they obviously were newspaper cuttings which had been supplied by them. Yes, they were none too anxious that anyone should keep a record of their conduct and treatment of their prisoners, and so they suspected everything, even innocent cut out recipes, which they took away for further examination. The Japanese succeeded in some things, particularly the abasing and humiliating of their captives; but not in breaking their will. This draft, which comprised both British and Canadian elements, took with them their share of central funds: and a packed of cigarettes each as well.

It was nearly Christmas; the second we should spend in prison – for that is what it was! The thoughts of all of us turned to our families. We wondered what they would be doing and eating, and of our wives and children, and of the presents that would be exchanged. I know, and hoped that mine were safe and sound in Australia. Mother would take care of the two children, and when the great day came there would be presents from their father, though he would not be there! I missed them all, just as surely as all the others with me missed their kith and kin. But there is no point in becoming morbid or sentimental. Christmas is a time for rejoicing and happiness, and where we can, of forgiveness. Christmas in Shamshuipo 1943 was unlikely to be a very happy one, from a material point of view. Food for the body we most certainly needed, and food for the soul as well. Sometime in November a suitable opportunity occurred to speak to the camp commandant about Christmas, so I told him that I and some of the other officers would like to give small presents to their men. We wondered if he would allow, and arrange for the purchase of some eggs and a few cigarettes, which we could finance from our monthly pay? He would consider our request. The great day was fast approaching and so far nothing had happened, so the interpreter was asked if the camp commandant had come to any decision on this matter, and if so would he please let us know.

Yes, he gave his approval and suggested that he would make the ration truck available for this foray. He also suggested that duck eggs could be obtained quite readily at one of the markets in the New Territories. The eggs would be cheaper, fresher and better from there than if purchased in the streets of Kowloon. (He may well have had an ulterior motive in this suggestion). However, a few hundred excellent duck eggs were obtained and so were a few cigarettes, and these were shared between participating units. As a result, each man of No. 6 Section, RAOC was given eggs and a couple of cigarettes as part of their Christmas festivities. In addition, the central fund provided each man in camp (other than those paid as officers), with a tin of beans and a packet of cigarettes. The small additions to the diet were undoubtedly enjoyed, and helped make a slightly better Christmas dinner than the Japanese were likely to provide. Materially the men had little money with which to buy what was on offer in the canteen, while the officers were in receipt of a monthly pittance from the Japanese authorities. I, too, had a pleasant and unexpected surprise on Christmas day, when a small deputation came with two small gifts. One was a handmade cigarette case while the other was a matchbox holder. The cigarette case had been fashioned from a small piece of a teak beam taken from one of the huts, and inlaid with a small piece of wire in the shape of a large letter 'V', which enclosed a letter 'E'. The matchbox holder had been made from a piece of aluminum which had been cut from someone's mess tin, and carrying a tiny RAOC badge (taken, I think from the centre part of an officer's collar badge used before the 1939 war), and engraved with my name and 'Camp "S" 1943'. Both items represented hours of work on the part of the donors, using improvised tools, in adverse conditions. I treasure them, and hope, one day, they may find a place in the Royal Army Ordnance Corps Museum, for they were made by my partners in misfortune, during the dark days of our captivity.[1] There is nothing more that need to be said now, except perhaps, that Christmas Day 1943 has a special significance for me; as this particular day has for all of us!

The only contact we had with the other prison camps and the hospital at Bowen Road was on the occasion of the transfer of someone from one to the other; an infrequent happening. The recent return of a couple of patients from hospital provided an opportunity to catch up on news from there. No. 6 Section, RAOC had, to my knowledge, only one inmate at Bowen Road. He was an oldish man who had been unwell for many months while he was a resident of the 'old men's home' in Shamshuipo before his transfer to hospital. As soon as it was convenient the new arrivals were asked for news of this man. They told me he had passed away in October 1943. The old men's home was a Japanese idea for giving the older people (over sixty years) special treatment and privileges. All this amounted to was not having to go on parade (Tenko) for roll call. This man's son was also in camp; the new status meant they were parted, so that one could not help the other. There were constant changes in the staff of the camp commandant's office; it appeared to us that as the tide of events became worse for Japan, so the type of men to 'overlord' the prison camp changed – a seemingly more reasonable and considerate sort of individual moved into the local Japanese hierarchy.

The latest arrival was of a rank and type not seen before. They called him a sergeant major, but he was in fact of a slightly higher order when compared to British standards. He had more power. I figured out that he equated to a junior subaltern, or perhaps a 'commissioned warrant officer'. He was a tall, light, and good looking chap, while pleasant in conversation and with a friendly smile. The impression gained was that he had a job to do, and would do it, and he left no one in doubt about that, but it seemed he intended to be reasonable; and so far as workshop and store matters were concerned, that in fact is how I found him. Of course he was not able, nor were the Japanese then capable of satisfying our needs, their shipping was taking too much of a hammering for that, but I got the impression he would 'try' to do his best for us! So it seemed we got the worst of all worlds; when they could have provided what we wanted, then they refused. When they had little or nothing in the kitty, then they claimed they would very much like to supply, but could not do so on account of shortages. Once or twice I got the inference that it was the fault of the American fleet or American aircraft. Well, under such circumstances we got less, and enjoyed it more, well knowing or sensing the reasons for the shortages. We were also sustained by the news we gleaned from the local papers smuggled in by the working parties; it was good, sometimes very good. It was pleasant to 'improvise' in such circumstances. No one announced any changes in the organisation, but got the impression [that] the new sergeant major would have special responsibility for my 'outfit', and other specific matters as well. He spoke a little English, possibly a little more than was apparent so did not always need the services of an interpreter. What was more, when shown a problem (and we had plenty) he had the ability and authority to try and do something about it. I now had a feeling that our case was put to the camp commandant more fairly than it had been here-to-fore. I had felt, for a long time that the interpreters often conveniently forgot to put our case forward. A spirit of ill will as it were. As a result I had been timing my audiences to occasions when 'The Little Man' was present and could hear what was being said, even if 'No' was the answer. Dealing with the Japanese under any conditions was difficult. In the situations in which we were trying to work, practically impossible. Getting blood out of a stone would usually be just as fruitful.

18

Ladder Bombing

In April 1944 the Japanese prepared a further small draft of men for Japan, and with this party went one man of the RAOC. Like their predecessors they took with them an allocation from the central fund of MY250. This was the last party to leave. Now we were left with only the sick and infirm.

The position of No. 6 Section, Royal Army Ordnance Corps in May 1944 was as:

	Officers	Rank & File
In Formosa	1	–
Argyle Street	7	–
Shamshuipo	2	23
Died	–	4
Taken out of Camp by		
Japanese and not returned	–	2
Japan		60
Total	10	89

Of those who remained in Shamshuipo nearly all were in very poor health and condition, but all who were fit enough were doing light work in camp. Although the food had become progressively worse as Red Cross supplies came to an end, there was no rapid or sudden deterioration or decline in the condition of those remaining. By now they had become more accustomed to the diet and were able to assimilate it. During the last year only one had died of illness. One or two were permanent residents in the camp hospital, and all those who were out and about had some complaint or other. Mostly the troubles were dysentery, pellagra, sores of various kinds, eye troubles, malaria, and of course malnutrition, which was common to all. (In my own case, which was typical, I was suffering from occasional bouts of malaria, but there had been a slight improvement in my eye condition). However, by May 1944 we had become reconciled to our own individual problems. If our health was poor, our morale was high. There was hardly any sign of men 'giving in' so I felt quite sure that those of the unit who were left would survive, for a while at any rate. But what of the position of those in Japan, where approximately two-thirds of the unit now were? During the preceding twelve months there had been a slight improvement in the supply of goods from Japanese sources.

Soap, of extremely poor quality, and quite insufficient for our needs, toothbrushes, tooth powder, talcum powder, minute hand towels, and Fandoucis (loin cloths) had been received at irregular intervals and issued to the men. Intermittently, small quantities of shirts, caps, canvas shoes and socks had been supplied, but these were intended for men who went out on working parties or on drafts for Japan, so it was not possible to make a general distribution; nor were the quantities large enough. In the event many items found their way to those who were in most urgent need of them. Many of the men were literally in rags, and in particular short of adequate footwear, socks, eating utensils, and very many other items as well.

'Improvise' was still the key word in our existence, and how overworked this word was both in action and meaning. We had been able to meet our target in the manufacture of winter trousers, so that all ranks now had something to keep them warm. The Red Cross windcheaters had been a godsend, and I am sure it is to the Red Cross that we owe our very existence. The tailor's shop had functioned very well indeed. They had made over 600 pairs of warm trousers (Shamshuipo pattern) and kept many more garments in useable condition. No mean feat when considering the poor state of practically every garment the men had. The stitch in time service continued to be a great blessing. In fairness to the Japanese it must be recorded that they had supplied sufficient cotton and needles for both manufacture and repair of garments. How and why, is another matter.

Work in the shoemaker's shop had continued, but the task of keeping boots in any sort of repair was becoming more difficult than ever.

Red Cross supplies of:

Soles	319
Rubber heels	346
Thread balls	24
Nails (lbs)	31

had been invaluable, as were the shoe repairing tools which came at the same time. The Japanese did continue, in their erratic way, to supply some materials. The NCO in charge of the shoemaker's shop said:

Approximately 25% of the leather soles sent in were so thin that it was impossible to nail them to the boots. The shape of the soles had been stamped out to the pattern of Japanese boots and were much narrower than the British pattern, consequently the sole could only be used for patching, and any boots larger than size 7 could not properly be repaired.

Wax for thread was made in workshops from pitch with candle grease and dubbin mixed.

The bookbinders were still hard at it trying to preserve the volumes that were still left, and keep them in circulation. They also made books, etc from newsprint. Theirs was a continuous and never-ending task; not much to see, but the efforts of these men brought much comfort to the sick, who had the ability to read, but were not engaged on tasks that required any physical effort. The work of the spectacle and watch repairers was diminishing. Either the items were broken beyond repair, or the numbers of men in camp had reduced. For whatever reason there just was not the amount of work of a year ago. Just the same, some work went on constantly. There never is any end to this kind of commitment. The Cornish plumber and his two mates were in constant demand, either taking down piping or putting more up, often in a different place. They now seemed to have a stock of various lengths of piping that would have done credit to the Naval Yard, but their appetite for more was insatiable. If it wasn't pipes, then it was taps they wanted; if not taps, then joins or bends of 'T' pieces. Neither I, nor the Japanese, could keep them down, and they were such a likeable team they nearly always got their own way. I sometimes wondered which side of the fence they belonged, for they were so often 'out'; scrounging for the good of the camp, of course. They had now fixed up showers in every place where they might be needed, but there was no choice of hot or cold, or mixed. In the matter of showers, everyone was treated alike, with a cold one! The sprays needed constant, (almost daily) adjustments, for they were made from empty tin cans with holes bored at strategic places. Yes, the plumbing was under control if the plumbers were not! They did a magnificent job.

Not to be outdone, the tinsmiths were hard at it retrieving every empty tin can they could lay their hands on, so their little corner had the appearance of a refuse dump without the smell, for every can was scrupulously clean. In a Japanese prison camp all tins are licked clean, and with a liberal use of fingers, until not a vestige of food remains. I am sure that, like the Billy goat, most would have devoured the tins as well, if they could. In camp, if you wanted a new eating utensil, something to put your teeth in, a baking tin, or a container in which to bury a hidden diary, then ordnance tinsmiths would meet any needs. For the carpenters, the re-fitting of doors, etc and the never-ending task of sandal making still went on. We had not got round to making coffins again, stopped alas so long ago, due to the shortage of both wood and nails, and now by reduced requirements. Many in camp were past caring whether it was a box or a blanket they would be buried in, or if it would be a burial. They also knew there would not be any flowers, just kind thoughts and sympathy, from friend to friend, as they were gently laid to rest. Like everyone else the carpenters were kept busy, but I never heard them singing 'I like my job as a carpenter, there's nothing I'd rather do'. They did not have any demarcation disputes, nor become bedeviled in 'Who does what'. In their quiet way they kept going, doing good work for the camp; like others they were in constant demand in cookhouses, hospital, ablution rooms, latrines, bakery, etc.

The fitter's shop was really a misnomer, for it bore little resemblance to the conventional workshop with benches, overhead lights, and tools spread all over the benches and floor, and complete with smell of oil. Paradoxically it was the working home of the bricklayers as well. You see the elite of our craftsmen, armament artificers of all kinds had become bricklayers early on, but they reverted to being 'fitters' whenever there was a demand for them in that capacity. The Japanese knew them as bricklayers. I can hardly say, or list, the intricate jobs they handled, for they were many and varied, and of all descriptions. They were the only authorised users of the cherished hacksaw blades, and their head man was my advisor on all matters technical, like the bakery oven, etc. Between them they kept our cookhouses, bakery and hospital going and in constant working order. Naturally, they had a vested interest in seeing that the [ovens, in which] the cooks prepared food, in the oil drums they had cut in two, and housed in the brick settings they had also made, worked. On call most days, they were permanently engaged in rebuilding or improving the cooking facilities. The work these men did was invaluable. The day was bright, warm and sunny, and the camp commandant had agreed to us making a further search of Jubilee Buildings for some items which might be of use to us; such as floor boards, piping, perhaps a cistern, etc. To carry out this raid a small scouring party had been assembled to await the arrival of the interpreter and sentries. When they arrived it was suggested that I could go with this party, and I was quick to accept this unexpected invitation. I had not been over to Jubilee for a very long time, but quite apart from taking part in the selection of items we wanted, I should be able to enjoy the excellent views to be obtained from there, in particular from the upstairs rooms which faced the sea. It would be something akin to a Sunday school outing except that there would be no pop or sweets, or packed lunches. We did a quick tour of the various flats looking for spoils, and then the different men commenced the task of dismantling the items we wanted. As I moved together with the interpreter into the front of the building, which commanded an excellent view of part of the harbour, and a large number of anchorages, I was surprised to see how full of ships the harbour was. The interpreter too seemed unprepared for the sight which met our gaze, and, being caught unawares, did not appear to know what to do. For me the scene looked much as it did in the piping days of peace, when ships from all over the world tied up in this beautiful and natural harbour, possibly one of the finest in the world. I was just trying to work out if my sight was deceiving me, or if what could be seen was a Japanese convoy newly arrived from Japan with supplies, or if they were vessels which had been driven into Hong Kong harbour for shelter by the Americans' naval action. There were a very large number of merchantmen, and in the distance a couple of destroyers and some other small naval craft. Still the interpreter had not uttered a word, which surprised me more than ever, as for a long time there had been hardly any shipping to be seen in the harbour.

Perhaps I had been brought over for some special reason. I was still surveying the peaceful scene, when, all of a sudden, and coming over the hills on the island I could see an awful lot of aircraft making their way in our direction.[1] Then, over so quickly, they dived on their respective targets, one by one, in what was understood to be ladder formation. They released their small bombs and then, if they could, rose quickly and disappeared over the hills at the other end of the island. It was a most impressive sight, but my heart sank as I saw some of the small planes hit, and then dive into the sea, or make valiant attempts to get away. Never before had I seen anything like this exhibition, for some of the activity was literally only a few hundred yards away. As I saw these brave pilots sacrificing their lives I felt very humble indeed, and hoped, with all my heart, that they would not fall into the hands of the Japanese.

All this action happened so quickly, and the interpreter still did not know what to do; whether to leave me and round up the others, or take me with him, or if it would be safe to do so. The first phase of the attack was nearly over when reinforcements came from the guard room.

What I had witnessed was an unforgettable display of dive bombing. From a distance it did not look very effective, though undoubtedly it was, as certain ships were lower in the water than they had been, while others were developing definite lists. At least one was lying in the harbour bottom upwards.

Eventually, we were all escorted back to the main part of the camp, while the excitement on both our side and the Japanese, was at fever heat. We were all confined to our rooms, but I stayed with some of the staff in our compound, which still commanded a view of part of the harbour. All was quiet now; we wondered if this attack was a prelude to another in which we might play a part, while we conjured up ideas about what might happen next. We did not have long to wait! These small aircraft were obviously carrier based, and the main fleet probably only a few miles away. The second attack was similar to the first; suddenly one plane peeled off from the others, and with a tremendous screeching noise came down in the sea quite close to us, between Stonecutters Island and Jubilee Buildings. (afterwards it was learned that the pilot had been captured and was being dealt with by the gendarmerie). Down came the planes, one after another, and seemingly only a few feet apart, while the Japanese naval vessels blazed away constantly. By about 4pm the final attack had been completed and all was quiet. Success was obvious; from our vantage point only one merchant vessel was seen to be still afloat! We counted eleven planes brought down, while others had just limped clear, and had probably come down in the sea on the other side of the island. The Japanese naval craft appeared to be still afloat; perhaps the attack was not concentrated on them, and they would be dealt with by superior American warships when they dared to leave harbour. This was the most effective piece of bombing I have ever seen, and it made us think very deeply. We wondered if this attack was a prelude to a landing from the task force, as we had read they had done in other areas, so again we thought up our plans for such an eventuality. I did not think so. Had this been the American intention, then surely they would not have attacked the merchant ships, but far more likely the naval craft would have been the target.

As I saw it, there could only be one purpose in the Americans taking Hong Kong, and that would be to make use of the harbour, so they would not render the harbour useless by such an attack as we had just seen. Surely, if Hong Kong was wanted for strategic purposes then an attack by one of those mythical Chinese armies supposed to be about 100 miles away would be more likely? The destination and aim of this convoy seems to be much further south, where the Japanese troops must be running short of ammunition and other essential supplies – the sinews of war – their mainstay, was now cut! The next batch of local newspapers, which were smuggled into camp by working parties, was read with great interest; they bore out what we had witnessed, but of course the number of planes brought down was enhanced, to show what a wonderful victory it had been for the defending forces. Members of the working parties had also seen a good bit of the raid, and we compared notes. Undoubtedly the raid had come as a complete surprise to the Japanese, as it did to us.

19

Return of Friends

We had long become accustomed to the interminable changes which took place in camp when batches of men were moved from one lot of huts to others; resulting in the taking down of doors, moving of cookhouses, facilities, etc. On nearly every occasion these moves had taken place after the departure of drafts for Japan, but this move was different; it was taking place before there was any sign of a draft, in other words, before the event. The men in camp were being moved into the huts where they would not have so much room; they would be housed much closer together. It was also noticed that everyone was being congregated into an area west of a very deep mullah, which had been built to drain away surplus water, usually after typhoon conditions. On all previous occasions our carpenters, bricklayers, plumbers, etc had been engaged on taking down doors, relocating cookhouses, etc; but this time there was no demand for them, it seemed odd, very odd, and quite the opposite of the usual pattern of events. The unusual sequence of events was very intriguing, and even more so when the Japanese declared the empty area out of bounds to us all. Many were the predictions as to the reason for all the activity and secrecy, but all proved to be wrong. Just as suddenly as the departure of most of the officers to Argyle Street had been, in April 1942, just over two years ago, so was their unexpected return in

May 1944. We could hardly believe our eyes when they, and their baggage, came into camp and were deposited on the road by the now vacant buildings. Most of us were elated at the prospect of having them with us once again. Many had close friends who would not be only just across the wire; we would be able to see and speak to them. The officers who had been left behind in Shamshuipo, Camp 'S', had a lonely and responsible time trying to care for and look after the men of their unit, though without any control, other than moral control, over them. Now perhaps, these responsibilities would be shared. Unfortunately, the new arrivals had been warned, just as we were, that there would still be two distinctly separate camps to be known as Shamshuipo Camp 'S' (men) and Shamshuipo Camp 'N' (officers). There was to be no fraternisation, visits, talking, or any communication with one another, and guards (sentries) were patrolling along the Dannert wire, to enforce these orders. It is not very difficult to see, or imagine, the kind of difficulties this sort of a situation would provoke.

We, on our side of the barrier, did not believe that this line of demarcation could last very long, or that the Japanese would be able to enforce the rigid and unnecessary rules they had laid down. It was not very long before notes were passing backwards and forwards, short and hurried conversations were taking place, and visits one to another were undertaken. As time went by the traffic backwards and forwards became easier; the sentries were not so vigilant, and there did not seem to be so many of them. All this of course tended to make communication less difficult than it had been. There was a purpose behind special visits, and no sense at all in random or unnecessary ones. I cannot remember anyone actually being caught 'on the wrong side' or for that matter any 'beatings up' by sentries. When the day of my birth came around I was surprised to receive from my friend and Chief Inspector of Naval Police (an inmate on the other side), birthday greetings and a special boiled pudding which he had made so that

I could celebrate the occasion. It was hardly of the quality his cook in the naval yard used to make for us on our weekly visits to his establishment but was a most acceptable present under any circumstances. Who, but such a kindly man would have thought of such a thing, and who but a very special friend would have wanted to carry it out? Yes, friends, some very good friends, were now no more than a few yards away, albeit kept apart from each other by a few strands of wire, the symbol of Japanese inhumanity. In camp it was very well known that events were not going well for the Japanese, as the American forces crept nearer to Hong Kong and to the Japanese mainland. As a result the camp commandant and his staff were becoming extremely touchy, and their ability to fill anything more than our very basic minimum needs was contracting. So far as materials were concerned, supply had never been better than very meager and infrequent. Now it was non existent! My constant requests, through the interpreters to 'The Little Man' fell on stony ground. He did not want to see me and made this position quite plain. I was constantly being told that we were better off than the Japanese themselves, and there possibly was a ring of truth in some of these statements. 'The Little Man' seemed to be away from his office quite a lot, and on enquiry, he was said to be 'unwell'. Rumour had it that he had been to Canton, and that he had been there to look for a camp to which we could be transferred 'so that we should be safe from the Americans if every they dared to make an attack on Hong Kong'. All very good stuff and quite uplifting. Even rumours are taken seriously in a prison camp, and so many of them had, in the event, proved to be right, or have some foundation. As a result we gave consideration to the possible implications of such a move. The hiding places of diaries, etc and an assessment of those who would, and would not, be able to stand up to such a transfer; and how far any of us could walk, possibly with our kit. It was a useful exercise, and provided us with the opportunity to review our 'contingency plans'.

For some time the change in the attitude of the Formosan sentries (or guards) had become very apparent. They were not so keen on doing their job, and many of them had taken to fraternising with the prisoners. Now apparently, they wanted to talk and to be friendly! All these were straws in the wind from which we could, and did, profit. As the reader will by now be well aware, the Japanese guard room was only a few yards from our store and work-shops; so, in their off duty time they had taken to paying visits, often quite frequently, to our compound. They did not seem to want anything in particular, but just to talk, and perhaps to learn a little English. Nevertheless, I did not trust them and told my chief clerk so. It could be, and in fact was, inconvenient having the 'enemy' constantly popping in and out, and able to see everything that was going on. I was suspicious they might be reporting back to 'The Little Man' and his sergeant major, so we kept a very close eye on them. On January, 9, 1945 the RAOC suffered a further casualty. This particular non-commissioned officer collapsed in the Bath House where he was employed, and he died from a blood clot on the brain.[1] He had been with me in Tientsin and was an ammunition specialist, and I relied on him for advice where explosives were concerned.[2] In camp he had led a rather quiet and unobtrusive life and had never, so it seemed, come to terms with our present situation. His quiet way of going about things had kept him out of the limelight, and though he was not at all well, had led a useful life in camp.

In the early months of 1945, my roommate, and ex-laundry manager, was transferred from Camp 'S' to the Officers Camp 'N'[3] (together with a number of other officers) which was just across the wire. His departure was sudden and unexpected. He had been employed, though not with me, on looking after the ablution facilities with the sergeant, now alas dead. They had both done very good work. As the summer months of 1945 were approaching, we did a recapitulation of our position so far as clothing, footwear, etc was concerned. We were in a bad way; we had virtually no stocks of anything that the men needed, and little hope of getting any. In turn, the items in possession of the men were deteriorating rapidly, and there was little we could do about it. Very few men had adequate footwear, hardly anyone had any kind of waterproof clothing, and only relatively few, chiefly officers and warrant officers, had greatcoats. Shirts and socks of those who had them, were rapidly wearing out, and for eating utensils the men were still using the empty cans from Red Cross parcels. If we had to contemplate another winter without further additions, then the situation so far as wearing apparel was concerned would be very grim indeed; and should a move to Canton, or anywhere else be envisaged, our position would be desperate. But winter was in the distant future, we were concerned first about the coming summer months. A careful examination was carried out of the living quarters (huts) to see if they were likely to stand up to the ravages of a typhoon. The doors were mainly makeshift, while nearly all the windows had been bricked up. For a very long time; since in fact Shamshuipo had first become a prison camp, we had been helping ourselves to the beams from the huts, systematically taking down alternate ones, and then constantly repeating the process. The beams were required for the making of wooden sandals and other essential uses. In addition the men had taken the timbers for making 'small fires' on which to cook the produce they had grown in their own gardens.

As a result the roof structures had been weakened to such an extent that if we did get a respectable 'blow' from a typhoon, it seemed probable that many buildings might finish without a roof at all. The situation had become progressively worse, as with succeeding years more and more timbers were removed. There was nothing we could do about it now except to hope the weather would be kind to us. In the tailor's shop there was practically no cotton left with which to repair those garments which were capable of being renovated. Most of the garments in use were, by now, so well worn they needed to be replaced. Certainly most were beyond our capacity.

The position in the shoemaker's shop was even worse; there were literally no facilities at all. We had run out of material. There was however, a slight bonus, as will be seen from the extract by the non-commissioned officer in charge:

> In March 1945 the Japanese started to send in the camp guard boots for repair, separate material being supplied for their repair, and by rendering a number of them unserviceable some material could be used on the prisoners of war footwear, thereby saving a good percentage from becoming unserviceable.

There seemed to be no lessening of the work in the bookbinder's shop. The more the books were read, then the more upkeep they needed. The small, very cheerful and efficient staff of unfit men kept things going. The camp I know was very appreciative of their efforts.

Work on plumbing inside such a camp as Shamshuipo was never ending. It was a constant daily repetitive task as cookhouse installations were moved (on Japanese instructions). The plumbers were on top of the job and capable of providing cold water wherever it might be wanted, including copious sprinklings from overhead in the bath house. The work of carpenters, fitters and bricklayers was always with us, though the wherewithal to perform the task was more often than not, lacking. It was not possible to go to the nearest ironmonger's shop for nails, screws, hinges, etc. You made them or 'improvised', or did the job some other way, or did without. The reduced numbers in camp had helped, and [we] were satisfied that, for the foreseeable future our simple needs could be met. We still had a reasonable stock of empty tin cans in the tinsmith's shop which were capable of serving their purpose and most would hold water, or a cooked ration of a few ounces of rice. Gradually both spectacles and watches in possession of individuals became 'beyond repair' so far as our facilities were concerned. There was therefore less and less work for the repairers to do, but so long as there was hope for a timepiece or glasses the job was tackled, sometimes with remarkable success.

Good news, very good news continued to be brought into camp by outside working parties, and this was backed up by the Chinese language newspapers they obtained. (Of course they could not buy them, it was understood they were just 'found' in some convenient places, or had been deliberately dropped, by sympathisers). The contents of the papers were eagerly devoured by those who could read them, and the tidbits of news passed on to their trusted friends by word of mouth; while they, in turn, relayed the good news to others. The camps became agog with excitement and amazement at the accounts of island hopping, and of saucy bombing raids. Even the Japanese press could not completely disguise the facts. There was eagerness, even urgency to get out of camp and onto an outside working party, and thus become the purveyor of good news. The Portuguese, most of whom could speak Cantonese fluently, being the main source. It soon became quite obvious that the war in Europe was rapidly drawing to a close. What would happen then?

How could anyone not be excited and uplifted by these events, and the possibilities inherent in them? Even when times were grim we never doubted that hostilities would end in our favour. Any other ending would be quite inconceivable. However, in the Far East it seemed we still had a long way to go. Just the same, I looked once again, at the names and forecasts pencilled on the walls in early January 1942, 'Over in six weeks' or 'six months'. The sentries were undoubtedly becoming less vigilant, and in off duty periods, and even when on patrol inside camp, many of them found their way round to our compound, and were another source of news. The camp commandant's staff I feel sure did not like it, but apparently could not stop it. Then, news leaked into camp that two of the Formosan guards had deserted, and taken their arms with them. If I remember rightly, the Japanese camp staff did not disguise their loss, and even carried out a full dress search of the camp, presumably just in case we were hiding them.

20

Money Matters

Towards the end of our captivity I was made aware of what could be a plot by the Japanese to get rid of us. The available evidence was therefore examined most carefully by me in Shamshuipo, Camp 'S' and with two brother officers, and others who might 'need to know'.

The conclusions drawn were such that required us to take immediate precautions, and to prepare plans of action to counteract what we feared might happen. Plans were formulated and explained to the senior officer in Shamshuipo Camp 'N' who took very seriously the information evidence and suspicions we had, and gave his approval to the action we proposed to take which, in the event, did not materialise. There were two matters which, though of no direct concern of mine, did have considerable effect on the unit as a whole, and therefore some mention ought to be made, from time to time, about these activities.

Money

Since most of the officers departed for Argyle Street Camp, there had been a steady flow of money, subscribed by them, for the benefit of the men in Shamshuipo. In the first place this cash was subscribed to back the scheme for credit trading by other ranks; and afterwards, when this ceased, for the amenities fund which was used primarily for the benefit of the sick in hospital, cookhouses, etc and for medical and nutritional necessities. There were all kinds of complications; for instance, initially most of the officers left in Shamshuipo did not subscribe because they were usefully employing their money on the needs of their own units, and at the time there was no shortage of cash in the amenities fund. In addition, the Canadians, Royal Navy, Royal Artillery, etc all had separate funds which were applied to their own units. Added to this the contributions from Argyle Street were becoming less and less as the months passed by, finally ceasing by the end of 1943. Most of the men who were fit had the opportunity of going on working parties for which they received the pittance already described. At the end of 1944 the financial situation in camp was peculiar, because the prices of all items had risen greatly in the last quarter of the year, the main results being:

a. The limit of daily cash sales in the canteen, (which had been set at MY1,500 per day by the Japanese military authorities represented a much smaller volume of goods.

b. The canteen profits, and the cash available for the camp fund from other sources, sufficed to purchase very little.

c. Those in possession of any realisable commodity were able to obtain large sums for it, and were the 'New Rich'.

d. There was no shortage of money in camp, but those few in possession of large sums could not spend them.

e. Those receiving parcels, and those with opportunity to grow food, were not comparatively well off.

f. The pay received by officers was of little significance.

The general policy of the Amenities Committee was to allocate money for various minor items, such as, sports, entertainments, etc and then divide the available balance between the main cookhouse and the hospital cookhouse, in proportion to the ration strengths.

Rock salt was now the only main item remaining within reach of the fund's resources.

During the early months of 1945, the financial situation changed rapidly due to the sale, through sentries, of articles in possession of the prisoners.

It is believed that, through the summer, blankets would realise about MY800, and by August, cheap towels about MY100 while stockings fetched MY150.

Gold was reported to be over MY195,000 a tael (1 1/3 ounces). Articles of jewellery realised MY15,000 to MY20,000, and might bring in the equivalent of £1,000. Over and above all these, amounts of money were coming in a steady flow from the Red Cross, etc.

Most of the money was, of course, spent in the canteen. I had not realised at the time, just how much money did come, but the following (which may not be absolutely accurate) gives some idea of the extent to which money was received from the sources shown.

Date	From	Amount	Distribution
December 1942	Canadian Government	MY10	for each Canadian
January 1943	International Red Cross	MY40,000	MY16 per man
April 1943	do	MY19,800	MY10 per man
July 1943	do	MY50,000	MY24 per man
August 1943	Red Cross	—	MY30 for each Canadian

November 1943	Red Cross	MY15,190	MY10 per man
February 1944	British Red Cross	MY21,240	MY20 per man
February 1944	Canadian Red Cross	MY10,000	MY8.50 a head to all in camp irrespective of rank
March 1944	British Red Cross	MY17,385	MY15 to all ranks in camp
July 1944	do (?)	—	MY17 per man
August 1944	Red Cross	—	MY25 per man
February 1945	International Red Cross	—	MY25 per man including officers

Pig & Poultry Farm

Much earlier I described the start of this project and the following will, perhaps, bring the reader up to date with the position as it became known to me. The information given may be sketchy and undoubtedly incomplete, but at least it will show, I hope, how much benefit accrued to the camp as a whole from this source. If, at the start, the pig and poultry farms were born under a cloud, and at the behest of our captors, the project proved to be quite successful. Undoubtedly the person who was responsible for the actual day to day running was the lance corporal of the Hong Kong Volunteer Defence Corps, and much of the success should therefore be attributed to him. The start of the 'farm' was made at one of the rosier stages of our existence, when we had just received large quantities of Red Cross supplies and in consequence, coupled with the large number of sick people who could not assimilate the rice ration, there was a quantity of spare rice and a reasonable amount of swill.

Both the pig and poultry farms were financed from the amenities fund, and both were proving to be a success, especially the former.

Rough financial statistics up to the end of 1943 showed:

	Pig Farm	Poultry Farm
Net outlay	MY 610.80	MY 1042.20
Stock	75 Pigs	92 Birds
Produced for camp	1,408 lbs Pork	2,558 eggs & 128 birds

In April 1944 it became necessary to reduce the stock of pigs as there was insufficient swill with which to feed them all, so the camp commandant agreed that a number should be killed. This was sufficient for pork meals to be provided for the whole camp twice a week for a period of three weeks. As a result 2,811 lbs of pork was issued and consumed during April and May 1944, and the stock of pigs was halved. At about the same time it was decreed by the camp commandant that 150 eggs per month were to be handed over to the hospitals, while the balance was to be sold at 30 sen each, proceeds to the amenities fund. By the end of 1944 the position had become acute, as there had been considerable difficulty with the feeding of the pigs owing to the shortage of swill; so there was a killing in prospect for Christmas dinner!

In the meantime, the officer's camp next door had enquired about the purchase of pork for Christmas. The number of animals was twenty-eight, and at the direction of the Japanese military authorities:

a. 6 pigs were sold to the officer's camp for MY 1,500.
b. 12 small pigs were sold outside camp by the Japanese for MY 1,000.
c. 5 large pigs were killed for consumption in camp.

    d. The proceeds of a and b were placed in a special pig
       fund, instead of the camp fund.

The MY2,500 set aside by Japanese order for the pigs
fund was expended at the suggestion of the Amenities
Committee, on the purchase of sweet potatoes, as those
were much cheaper than using rice, and the swill had fallen
almost to nothing by early January 1945. Purchase of food
for the pigs was necessary. (The money was also depreciat-
ing) I have no idea what the final outcome of this project
was, but the hospital patients got considerable benefit from
the eggs and birds produced, and the camp as a whole (and
No. 6 Section RAOC) from a much-needed supply of pro-
tein. At the time of the surrender, and while the Japanese
remained in nominal control of the camps, the pig and
poultry farms began to be looted by the sentries, so it was
necessary to remove the remaining stock to the officers
camp to prevent total loss.

Japanese Surrender

In spite of the very poor and inadequate food, the morale of No. 6 Section, Royal Army Ordnance Corps, and the camp in general, was at its highest for a very long time. There was much less lethargy and despondency, and a smartness of step. Even the hospital patients seemed to have a new interest in life. Most of us were thin and weak and in very bad shape, but the spirit was good. Obviously all now intended to 'make it', as we fed on a diet of good news (if not on turkey) nearly every day. In the compound we carried on the normal day to day work, just as it did in the cookhouses, bakery, hospital, etc. Bookbinders were forever busy with the endless task of repairing damaged books. The tailors attended their place of work, but thread was almost exhausted; while the shoemakers were busily employed on the oddments they had been able to 'win' from the Japanese. There was less and less work for the bricklayers, fitters, carpenters, tinsmiths and plumbers to do, while the stormed spectacle and watch repairers were practically out of work. Our task was rapidly coming to an end. No one said very much, no one wanted to tempt providence, but the animation was there for all to see. The working parties brought back news of fresh American advances, and Japanese defeats. Events which previously seemed to proceed so slowly were now gaining momentum, as each succeeding day brought us nearer to the end. To what end? We joked, once again, about needing the barbed wire fence not to keep us in, but to keep the Chinese out.

The working parties also brought back news of a deteriorating situation in town, so there was worry and anxiety for those who had wives, families and relatives in the colony. I wondered how the men of No. 6 Section, RAOC were progressing in Japan. If they were any better off than we had been, and how they would fare in events with which they would most likely have to deal. On reflection I thought it was perhaps a good thing they were in Japan. Surely the food would be better there, and so might the conditions. I should be glad, at some future date, to compare notes. The guards seemed less and less keen on their job and showed it. Visits by them to the compound were quite regular, and though the news they were able to impart was often already known, it was still useful to hear what they had to say. The working parties were able to acquire more and more newspapers and got them into camp without any trouble. It appeared that everyone outside camp could see signs of the war coming to an end as the Americans advanced nearer and nearer to the Japanese mainland. Many outside relatives and friends shouted, quite openly, cries of hope and encouragement, while messages were passed to their loved ones inside camp. There was obvious despondency and apprehension on the part of the Japanese camp staff. Except for roll call 'The Little Man' was hardly ever seen, while for quite a long time the 'Fat Pig' had not been seen in camp. But there was no jubilation inside camp; we might have trials yet to come, so we carried on just as we had become accustomed over the past years. It was better that way. As the days passed we became increasingly concerned that our discipline was right, and that we had some chance of coping with the unknown. So, once again, I took a good look at the RAOC when on parade, and how, in certain circumstances, they might acquit themselves.

I did not need such convincing that they were in good heart, even if their physical condition was poor, and would give a good account of themselves whatever the problems we might have to face. Discipline within the unit had always been kept at a satisfactory level, and we still had a well known chain of command. If I fell by the wayside my chief clerk would take over, and after him, the 'bricklayer' warrant officer, and then downwards to some excellent senior NCOs. Our small band had always turned out on parade clean, (as well as they could be), orderly, and as correctly dressed as circumstances would allow. The spirit was alright and equal to any eventuality; only the flesh was weak. Yes, I was quite sure they could all be relied upon should they ever be tested. They too, were well aware of their responsibilities and what might be expected from them – I had not thought it wise to place any reliance on the RAOC officers just across the wire being available; they might well be whisked away again, just as suddenly as they had been brought back from Argyle Street to Shamshuipo, and for that matter I might not be available myself. We, in the men's camp, were near to the main camp gate and to the camp commandant's office and guard room, while the officer's camp had no separate entrance. Short of cutting the wire the only way out was through the men's camp. Yes, I was satisfied we could and would give a good account of ourselves, if we had to.

I was rather surprised that the Japanese authorities were still taking out working parties, but probing the Japanese mind was never straightforward. Presumably, if they stopped the working parties then we would know something was wrong; perhaps they intended to brazen it out, or maybe they did not care what we knew. For our part the working parties were in a good position to produce news, and we wanted all that we could get. In the direst few days of August the working party came back with a most remarkable story about a mighty fire bomb which had been released on the Japanese mainland, causing enormous casualties and damage.

The details were confused, having been passed by word of mouth, and no one seemed positive about what had really happened. Maybe the whole thing was being exaggerated out of all proportions. When all is said and done it would not take much in the way of fire to obliterate whole townships of the traditional type of wooden dwelling customarily used in Japan. But the working party was adamant that this was something different. Everyone was talking about it, but so far there was nothing mentioned in the newspapers. At this stage I was becoming confused, but a friend of mine was due to go out on the very next working party, so I looked forward to his comments on his return. Later, I gathered from him, that there had been something in the papers about a tremendous explosion at Hiroshima, with many casualties.[1] It seemed that the Japanese propaganda machine was in disarray, and did not quite know what they should be saying. That the fire bomb was something unusual was, however, now beyond doubt, and they were playing it down. Locally, amongst the Japanese staff it was not possible to deduce anything. A day or two later came news that a further bomb had been dropped on Nagasaki[2] which had completely wiped out the whole town, and rumour had it that the Japanese were suing for peace. Japanese wanting to surrender; incredible, yes, quite incredible.

Still there were no reactions from the camp commandant's office, but we watched them carefully, very carefully, for any sign of possible hostility, or any unusual action on their part, but everyone on the Japanese side seemed dejected, and so overwhelmed [that] they did not know what to do, or say. Perhaps they were waiting for orders to destroy us. We were even more vigilant, many hardly sleeping, while others became so excited that sleep was impossible.

Next morning we heard, I think from a guard, or camp staff, that the Emperor was making a personal broadcast to all his troops and that all camp staff, guards, etc would be assembling, under the camp commandant, to hear in person, the Emperor's voice and what he had to say.

Obviously this unusual course must have tremendous significance. It was not customary for the Emperor to personally address his troops; in fact I understood that it had never previously happened.[3] So the address must have been highly important. Would it bode good or ill for us? I waited in our compound, but a few yards away from the Japanese office, while the assembled company heard what their august master had to say. We saw the guards return to their guard room; they looked dejected, dazed, forlorn and dumbfounded. I had previously given instructions to the men who worked for me to keep away from the Japanese and Formosans during these most difficult times for them, and for us, but to carry on with their work as usual. The enemy might have aggressive intentions. We did not have long to wait before a sentry on patrol came into the compound and told one of the staff the gist of the Emperor's broadcast. Formalities apart, the war now seemed to be over, and we were still alive!

The whole turn of events was beyond our understanding; it seemed impossible that the dropping of two bombs had miraculously changed the situation and brought a quick and unexpected end to hostilities. I went over the wire, (now well trampled down) which separated us from the officers camp, and gave a report to the officer in charge there. He seemed surprised and incredulous. I undertook to keep him informed of any future happenings and assured him we would be vigilant and careful. Meanwhile the 'Tenko' (roll calls) still persisted. So far as I can recall, it was from workers in the camp garden who heard Chinese, on the other side of the wire, calling to them 'Japs surrender', and this news probably came from other sources as well; but the camp commandant would have none of it. When challenged by the officer in charge of the officer's camp he denied there had been a surrender. Later however, this officer ordered the Japanese out of camp, and surprisingly, they went, and I took over some of their arms and held them in my store. A ceremonial parade was organised, when both camps were reunited, and a Union Jack was raised on the flagstaff which still stood outside the old guard room in Nanking Barracks, while we sang the national anthem. This was a very simple and most moving service. We were making a new start, we hoped into a better world, with dark and evil days behind us. Soon we should be going home to our loved ones, and a new world we did not understand. But even more our thoughts were of those who would not be returning with us as a result of war and captivity.

The Japanese had gone, and we had the camp to ourselves. There was a different kind of work to do now and lots to talk about, while visits were made to the camp by relatives and friends. One who came to camp with his wife to see their son told me of a harrowing account of water torture he had endured. Yes, the civilians who were not interned suffered the Japanese wrath just as we did. New duties were undertaken, like the taking over of the wireless station, communications with the internees camp at Stanley, and the hospital at Bowen Road, civilian government matters, and many other assignments like forays for food and medicines.

I made one such journey over to the island, looking for food and prepared to pledge HM Government for any items that could be obtained. I walked down the centre of the road, the same route we had come, carrying our kit into the unknown, three years and eight months ago, and over to the island on the Star Ferry. A strange and weird journey. The Chinese did not speak, surprised perhaps at seeing such an apparition. The Japanese gendarmerie were in evidence, while odd bunches of Japanese troops were making for the collecting point where they were congregating to await the arrival of the relieving forces. Alas, my journey was fruitless. There just was not any food in quantity available; the cupboard was bare, and it seemed we should have to await the relieving forces for those extra rations so badly needed; in the meantime devouring with friends our escape rations and tit-bits that others brought into camp for us. The staff in the RAOC compound were busy tidying up their respective workshops and store, and getting rid of items which others might want, or could make use of.

Then there was the job of recovering from hiding places, tools, instruments, diaries, documents, maps, personal effects of those no longer with us; in fact anything that had been secreted away from the prying eyes of the Japanese. Some of my staff gave me reports on their respective activities which would be useful to me when I made my report. This, too, was an opportunity to thank each individual personally for the work they had done. We had just one more task, to prepare and put out markers on the parade ground to assist the Americans who would be dropping some supplies from the air.

The Americans came at the end of August and dropped supplies on our parade ground, a most welcome sight. In preparation for the arrival of the relieving forces the officer in charge of the camp asked if there were any particular matters to which their attention should be directed, and for which special action was required by them. Imprinted on my mind was one of prime importance, to find out the whereabouts, and what happened to, those men who had been removed from camp by the Japanese and were never brought back. I gather that other officers in charge of units involved also tabled similar questions. A month after our first hearing of the dropping of the atomic bomb, we were on our way home, mostly on [board] the SS *Empress of Australia*. A motley crowd if ever there was one. Undoubtedly saved by the atomic bomb! Fit, and around 12 stone 4 lb in December 1941, I was leaving a sick man of about 6 stone 8 lb, suffering from malaria, eye troubles, malnutrition and other sundry disorders. And I was one of the lucky ones. Many officers and men required immediate hospital treatment and were evacuated by hospital ship.

The men who had been employed in the RAOC compound had been a very mixed bag comprising different nationalities and a variety of arms, units, regiments and corps. Royal Navy, Dockyard Defence Corps, Merchant Navy, Royal Engineers, Royal Scots, Middlesex Regiment, Royal Army Ordnance Corps, (including many who had been in REME since 1942, but unknown officially to us), Royal Army Education Corps, Hong Kong Volunteer Defence Corps, and others who I cannot now remember. These men, of a variety of ranks and backgrounds, gave their services in the common cause for the benefit of others. They had no union; they came to serve and expected nothing in return. In writing this account I have been ever conscious of the loyalty and help these men, of widely differing backgrounds, gave to me, and of my debt to them. Nor is it possible to measure, in any way, their contribution to the general welfare of the camp, but it was substantial. I hope those who were there, and though they are nameless in this account – for whatever success was attained was entirely due to them, and them only. The spirit they brought and the service they gave, was second to none. To those members of my own unit, No. 6 Section, Royal Army Ordnance Corps (including subsequent members of the Royal Electrical and Mechanical Engineers) I should like to thank them publicly for the ingenuity, courage and loyalty while they were prisoners of war of the Japanese. Future generations of our corps may be justly proud of them.

appendix 1

Report by Captain Ebbage, RAOC

8 Dec. 41	Evacuation of stores from Hong Kong to Ridge.
9 Dec. 41	ditto
10 Dec. 41	ditto
11 Dec. 41	ditto; Captain Ebbage and Lieutenant Wardle proceeded to Ridge. Lieutenant Wynne and Markey were already there, and from this time until
15 Dec. 41	Considerable receipts of stores took place, the Depot of Hong Kong being emptied of all important stores.

Similarly on 13/14 Dec the stores at Lyemun had been evacuated to the Ridge. This latter move was carried out by Mr Walker under very considerable shell fire. In all cases volunteer RAOC[1] drivers took the lorries from place to place. Most of the stores had by 17 Dec. been put under cover in additional accommodation taken from the residents.

On 14 Dec DADOS[2] Lieutenant Colonel McPherson and Captain Burroughs arrived at the Ridge. On 13 Dec. a bomb was dropped on the Ridge below No. 5 house but no damage was done except to houses 4 and 5 where all windows were broken and plaster brought down.

19 Dec. 41: Work proceeding normally but it was observed that the navy were sinking their ships by burning them in Deepwater

Bay. Mines were also being blown up and at approximately 10am a Japanese officer was seen waving a sword at the top of Wong Nei Chong Gap. He and his party were not immediately fired on as it was seen that Canadians were on the other side of the hill. Later, fire was opened from the Ridge with two Bren Guns and seemed effective.

At 11am a message was received from HQ that Canadians were in possession of Wong Nei Chong Gap, but they were as far as we could see on the lower side leading to Little Hong Kong. By noon they were retreating along the road to Mount Nicholson in a lorry, and to Little Hong Kong on foot. A message was received from HQ to say that the DADOS had the general's permission to burn down the Ridge when he considered this course necessary. The Japanese on Wong Nei Chong Gap were digging in and a party were also half up Mt. Nicholson. At approximately 4pm Captain Atkinson RA and a party arrived from Post Bridge and were given rations, two Bren Guns and ammunition and they returned to Post Bridge. They also tapped our HQ telephone line and we made an attempt with directions from them to inform CRA[3] of the result of artillery from (should read on) Mt. Nicholson. After an hour CRA said they were unable to shell the target due to angle. During the afternoon some lorries of navy ratings had been mown down by machine-gun fire approximately 500 yards higher up the road. It was understood that they were from the 'Thracian'. The gun site was not visible from the Ridge nor was the gun able to fire on us. We received periodical machine gun fire until darkness. After dark Major Hunt RA arrived with a party of 100 with instructions to take Wong Nei Cong Gap. Just before dark we had seen two parties, one on the path from Little Hong Kong, and one on Mt. Nicholson steadily making their way towards Wong Nei Chong.

Major Hunt was told of this, and of the party at Post Bridge. Late at night a party of RE, RASC, RAOC and HKVDC,[4] arrived under command of Lieutenant Colonel Fredrick, RASC.

20 Dec. 41: Ridge was machine gunned about 9am. After dawn all RE, RASC, RAOC and HKVDC under Colonel Fredrick RASC left for Shouson Hill.

Information was received from HQ that Wong Nei Cheong Gap and Cross Roads were in our hands.

About 9.30am some of the party returned. Others had made their way to Shouson Hill and others were in 'Twin Brooks', 'Monto Verde' and nearby houses. They had been badly ambushed at Cross Roads. Mr Haynes had shrapnel wound in both legs as a result of hand grenades. Information was received that Captain Bonney had had a portion of his face blown away, and Lieutenant Wilson had escaped into the hills.

It was also reported that there was a very strong concentration of Japanese at Cross Roads, and that they had approximately sixty prisoners at Deepwater Bay. With additional personnel, approximately 280, the Ridge was prepared as much as possible for defence, and troops were divided between all houses with a proportion of officers.

We had also been joined by the remnants of a Chinese battalion under Major Mayer. At approximately 2pm there was heavy machine-gun fire from Wong Nei Cheong and water catchment, and a number a casualties. Private Taylor was killed at house No. 5.[5] There was (sic) a total of thirteen seriously wounded. ADMS[6] was asked to send ambulances and a plan was drawn up for all personnel to leave that night and proceed to Little Hong Kong or onwards to Aberdeen. Reported houses 4 and 5 hit by mortars. After all plans made to evacuate and burn down the Ridge (this had already been provided for) instructions were received that Canadians were coming. Lieutenant Colonel McPherson received a bullet through the arm when trying to get from house 2 to house 1 and Lieutenant Colonel Fredrick, RASC, a minor cut on the nose.

Later instructions were received from Brig. Wallis (shown as Wallace) area commander, that the Ridge personnel were to be divided into four parties:

8 Officers and 80 Ors to take Cross Roads.
8 Officers and 80 Ors to proceed to Middle Spur and storm water catchment.
Lieutenant Colonel Fredrick and a party to make Repulse Bay.

Balance to remain until road was clear, burn Ridge and follow to Repulse. Parties left after dark, the storming party being under command of Lieutenant Johnston, Canadian Royal Rifles. Lieutenants Markey and Wynne were in this party. Rations and water was very low. Two ambulances arrived 4.30pm and were greeted by a hail of machine-gun fire. Left with wounded after dark for Stanley. Quiet night but more stragglers, RAF and Navy, etc came in.

21 Dec. 41: Considerable activity on water catchment, machine-gun fire, sniping, etc. It was impossible to go out of houses but fire was returned on all possible occasions with some success. Told to stay at Ridge, as further Canadians were coming to take Wong Nei Cheong. Canadians, approximately sixty under Major Young, Canadian Royal Rifles arrived during the night, but took up positions on 'Altamara'.

22 Dec. 41: Joined by Canadians who had found Wong Nei Cheong impassible [impassable]. Received instructions in French (line had been tapped for some days) that if we could make Repulse Bay Hotel by midnight we could get through to Stanley. Prepared accordingly. Early afternoon heavily attacked with machine-gun fire. At least five machine guns were used from close distance and also heavy mortar fire. Captain Burroughs in house No. 4 reported several direct hits on Nos 4 and 5.

Ridge also shelled with light field guns and there were some casualties. Position bad, enemy had range and mortar hit by a shell. Very heavy machine-gun fire. Fire was returned when possible with some effect, but Ridge was a perfect target and quite unsuitable for defense [defence] with the enemy in command of all positions.

5pm after extremely severe bombardment Lieutenant Colonel MacPherson decided to surrender, but first telling all houses that those who wished should try to make Repulse. Major Young and available men from House No. 5 slid down the bank, similarly house No. 4 under Captain Burroughs and house No. 3 under Captain Davies HKVDC also went when they could.

Impossible to leave house No. 1, which was continually riddled with machine-gun fire. At dusk white flag put out from houses but machine-gun fire continued, and during one burst Lieutenant Colonel Macpherson got a large wound in the thigh.

At dark all houses visited by Major Phippance [Flippance] HKVDC and all ranks told that the remainder were making their escape to Repulse. Told to follow at 10 yard intervals. Captain Ebbage led party who left at 7.40pm, followed by Sergeant Major Neale, Mr Collinson, Quartermaster Sergeant Cooper, etc.

Party continued down to road near Nullah thence up into hills by Tebbuts House. Only three reached Tebbuts House: Captain Ebbage, Sergeant Major Neale and Quartermaster Sergeant Cooper. These three made for Repulse Bay Hotel and arrived at 12.15pm but found it quite impossible to get through to the hotel. Many wounded in hills, mostly parties who had previous left the Ridge, and who had been ambushed twice.

Following night Sergeant Major Neale [was] lost when an attempt was made to get round the back of Repulse Bay Hotel. Dead body of Sergeant Major Neale seen 8am, 24 Dec., near 'Eucliffe'. Captain Ebbage and Quartermaster Sergeant Cooper continued in the hills where signs of Captain Burroughs and/ or Staff Sergeant Palmer had been there were evident. Captain Ebbage and Quartermaster Sergeant Cooper subsequently surrendered 8.30am, 28 Dec. 41.[7]

Captain Ebbage and Quartermaster Sergeant Cooper returned morning on 26 Dec. 41 to stream near Ridge as they were without food and water.

appendix 2

Report on RAOC whilst Prisoners of War of the Japanese in Shamshuipo Camp, Hong Kong. By Capt.V.S. Ebbage, RAOC who was the senior RAOC Officer left in this Camp

On 30.12.1941, the RAOC who remained after the surrender of the colony were taken by the Japanese to Shamshuipo Camp where they were interned along with the personnel of other units.

A Nominal Roll of all who entered this prison camp is attached.[1] The RAOC were under the command to [of] Col. G.R. Hopkins, OBE, RAOC who was ADOS[2] China Command and OC[3], RAOC, China. Col. Hopkins remained in Shamshuipo Camp until 18.4.42 when the Japanese removed approx. 300 officers to another camp and left behind approximately fifty, the way the selection was made was to herd all the officers together and then pick out two from each unit who were to be left behind to look after their respective units. Capt. Ebbage and Capt. Ramsey, RAOC were the two who remained behind of the RAOC. The effect of the removal of officers from the camp was badly felt. What organisation there was destroyed and a new system had to be set up. I spoke to the whole of the corps and asked for their support, pointing out that they were subject to Mil. Law[4] and the fact that the remainder of the officers had been removed made no difference, and that if I and Capt. Ramsey were to be taken away then the next senior RAOC Warrant Officer [WO] would take command and that I expected them to give that WO or NCO[5] their full support and loyalty. This they all promised to do. All members of the RAOC who were under my direction I am very glad to say have conducted themselves in an exemplary manner as I expected that they would and were a credit to the unit to which they belong[ed]. This report is intended to be solely a Regimental report, and the Corps activities from a Departmental point of view are the subject of a separate account.

The RAOC were accommodated in rooms of their own, and their food was drawn from a combined RASC/RAOC cookhouse.

Armt. S.M.[6] Read, RAOC who was the senior RAOC WO was appointed a sort of Section Sgt. Major, and until the departure of this WO for Japan carried out his duties in a most efficient manner. Although the spirits of the corps were high the health of many began to deteriorate badly, and in May 1942 I forbade such energetic sports as football, hockey, etc so that what strength the men had they would conserve. This was done with the approval of the unit MO[7] Coombes. It was about this time that the camp was visited by a diphtheria epidemic which lasted some months and which carried off a large number of men. A number of the RAOC were affected but I am glad to say we lost none, though there were two or three who had narrow shaves. In June 1942 S-Sgt.[8] S. Addington was taken out of camp by the Japs in connection with the guns at Stanley.

He suffered much at their hands but gave nothing away. His conduct was exemplary. During the period May to October the health of the camp was frightful and alarmed all OCs and MOs alike. The ones who were able to assimilate the diet of rice and veg were able to struggle along but those who could not soon became in a very bad way. All became very thin and worn looking and there was considerable apathy among everyone. A visit to the hospital (so-called) was a most depressing experience, but the MOs who were doing their best were helpless without medicines and dressings, which were non-existent. It was at this stage that we had our second casualty (S.Sgt. Ackerman had died soon after entering camp on 13.1.42 of internal stoppage) and Pte. Patterson died of Dysentery. This man gave up the unequal struggle and in spite of all that could be done for him did not really seem to have sufficient interest to pull round. Everyone wondered who would be next and a look round the unit made one feel there were quite a number of possible starters.

The corps, however, turned out on parade daily, looking as clean smart and properly shaven as was possible under the circumstances. On May 24th, the Japanese required each man to sign an affidavit that he would not escape. Many refused to do this in spite of the fact that we were warned of the dire punishment that would be meted out to those who did not sign, and the threat that the camp would be punished collectively. However after some days everyone was forced to sign. After signing the men were given soap. Their first for six months except that which I had been able to buy from limited funds available. On July 24th, 1942 there was considerable excitement in camp as an attempt to escape by digging a tunnel had been discovered by the Japs. I was quickly informed that two RAOC men were involved and had been arrested by the Japs along with 7 or 8 others.

I immediately had the two men's kits and bedding searched and found much escape impedimenta, which I had removed and hidden prior to a search of the kits by the Japs. The other OCs did the same. Our two men Pte. Dunne and Pte. Stopforth were taken out of camp on 5.8.42 and have not since returned. Their plan did not appear to be a particularly good one and I did not know that they were making any attempt. Conditions about this time in camp were very bad indeed and it was some relief when the Japanese arranged for a draft of some 500 details to leave the camp for Japan, where they were told conditions would be much better. None of the RAOC left by this party.

Another draft was formed to go on the ill-fated *Lisbon Maru*[9] and I was warned by the Japanese camp commandant that I was to be in charge of this party. I therefore decided to take the majority of the RAOC with me (if I could) but it was later decided that 50 or so officers were to be brought from Argyle Street and Lt Col.[10] Stewart was to be in charge. As a result neither I nor the RAOC went. The *Lisbon Maru* was torpedoed with the loss of very many lives.

The health of everyone of the corps was now poor or bad and there was hardly one who did not suffer from beriberi, pellagra, blindness or what was perhaps worst of all 'aching feet' to say nothing of dip., dysentery and skin diseases. Cpl. Reason, an auxiliary died from dysentery and enteritis on 1.11.42.[11]

A further draft was sent to Japan in Jan 1943. This was to be a 'Propaganda Draft' to go on a luxury ship and with this party went 45 RAOC in charge of S-M[12] Read. There were no officers sent. The corps were now divided into two parties and whatever the future held in store I felt that at least some of us had a chance of getting out of it alive. S-Cdr[13] Haskins then took on the job of S.M. for the remainder. There was a more cheerful atmosphere about this time, large supplies of Red Cross goods had been received and we were soon to feel the benefit of them. The health generally improved, there was a better spirit. The supplies were spread over a lengthy period so that the maximum benefit could be obtained from them.

A further small draft of RAOC left for Japan in Dec. 1943 and one man in April 1944. By this time most of the corps men had become accustomed to the diet and all of them were working on camp work inside the camp. Col. Hopkins had decided in the early days that easy work should be found for all corps men as all were better in health and mind if they had 'something to do'. I carried on this policy and until the closing of the camp all corps men were employed on light work. S-M Haynes died in Bowen Rd. Hospital in Oct 1943.[14] He was an oldish man and had been unwell for many months in Shamshuipo before he was transferred to the main hospital.

1944 was a better year from a health point of view and though the food got worse and we had no further casualties. On Jan 9th, 1945 Sgt. McCulloch collapsed in the Bath House where he was employed and died. (Blood clot on the brain.)[15] This was our last casualty and we were released in Aug. 1945. The corps men kept up their good name to the last and I cannot say too much in praise of their conduct during captivity. Particularly outstanding were S-M Read, S-Cdr Haskins and Q-M-S[16] Nichol. S-Sgt.[17] S. Addington.

Endnotes

A Brief Military Biography

1 Interview by Andrew Robertshaw with Miss Joyce Ebbage,
6 January 2011.

2 1911 Census.

3 Interview by Andrew Robertshaw with Miss Joyce Ebbage,
6 January 2011.

4 Ibid.

5 Ibid.

6 Royal Army Ordnance Gazette (RAOCG), November 1990,
p.231.

7 Ibid.

8 RAOCG, December 1921, p.691.

9 RAOCG, September 1923, p.1330.

10 RAOCG, November 1990, p.231.

11 RAOCG, February 1924, p.1479.

12 RAOCG, May 1925, p.1899.

13 Typescript 'The Hard Way', V. Ebbage, Author's Note, p.1,
Archives of the Royal Logistic Corps Museum and History of
the RAOC, p.318.

14 RAOCG, October 1925, p.2036 and December, p.1894.

15 RAOCG, June 1926, p.2259.

16 RAOCG, March 1927, p.2512.

17 RAOCG, April 1927, p.2548.

18 RAOCG May 1920, p.165.

19 RAOCG April 1930, p.177.

20 RAOCG March 1931, p.99.

21 RAOCG January 1930, p.33; February 1930, p.74; April 1931, p.140; April 1933, .p.139 and May 1934, p.182.

22 RAOCG July 1934, p.265.

23 RAOCG, December 1933, p.436.

24 RAOCG, February 1936, p.59.

25 RAOCG, December 1936, p.440

26 RAOCG, January 1936, p.27.

27 RAOCG, April 1938, p.143.

28 RAOCG January 1938, p.24.

29 RAOCG, August 1938, p.298.

30 RAOCG December 1938, p.436.

31 RAOCG January 1939, p.19 and April 1939, p.153.

32 RAOCG, August 1940, p.321.

33 RAOCG, March 1940, p.93.

34 Typescript 'The Hard Way', V. Ebbage pp.13–14, Archives of the Royal Logistic Corps Museum and History of the RAOC, p.318.

35 Ibid. p.6.

36 Ibid. p.15.

37 Ibid. p.7.

38 Ibid. pp.26–28 and pp.31–32.

39 Ibid. pp.35–37 and History of the RAOC, p.318.

40 Typescript 'The Hard Way', V. Ebbage p.47.

41 Ibid. p.54

42 Typescript 'The Diary of Lieutenant James Sutcliffe', J. Sutcliffe, p.2, Archives of the Royal Logistic Corps Museum. Interview by Andrew Robertshaw with Miss Joyce Ebbage, 6 January 2011. Commonwealth War Graves Commission register, 66420, Burroughs, Sydney Gilbert, Captain, aged 50, Sai Wan Memorial.

43 The Diary of Lieutenant James Sutcliffe, p.5.

44 Typescript Report by V. Ebbage, p.1, Archives of the Royal Logistic Corps Museum.

45 Ibid.

46 History of the RAOC, p.321.

47 Typescript Report by V. Ebbage, p.1, Archives of the Royal Logistic Corps Museum.

48 Ibid.

49 Ibid. p.2.

50 Ibid.

51 Ibid.

52 Ibid.

53 *Not The Slightest Chance: The Defence of Hong Kong, 1941*, Tony Banham, p.205, Hong Kong University Press, 2003.

54 Typescript Report by V. Ebbage, p.2.

55 Ibid. p.3 and Commonwealth War Graves Commission register, 1417920 Neale, Reginald Arthur, Warrant Officer Class 1 (Armt. S. M.) aged 36, Sai Wan Memorial.

56 Typescript Report by V. Ebbage, p.3.

57 History RAOC p.324.

58 Typescript, 'Shamshuipo', V. Ebbage, Author's Note, Archives of the Royal Logistic Corps Museum.

59 RAOCG, November, 1945 p.243 and interview by Andrew Robertshaw with Miss Joyce Ebbage, 6 January 2011.

60 Interview by Andrew Robertshaw with Miss Joyce Ebbage, 6 January 2011.

61 RAOCG, November 1990, p.231.

62 RAOCG, January 1948, p.212.

63 RAOCG, August 1949, p.12.

64 RAOCG, September, 1956, p.92.

65 RAOCG, May 1966, p.485.

66 RAOCG, December, 1965, p.281.

67 RAOCG, August 1978, p.68.

68 RAOCG, Gazette, November 1990, p.231.

Preface by Capt. Ebbage

1 The camp in Hong Kong where the author was a prisoner of war from December 1941 to August 1945.

2 The author volunteered for the Royal Army Ordnance Corps (RAOC) as a Private 7576720 on 1 March 1920. He was commissioned as a lieutenant on 12 February 1940.

3 RAOC – Royal Army Ordnance Corps.

4 The Royal Army Ordnance Corps became part of the Royal Logistic Corps in April 1993. As part of the amalgamation the museum and archive of the RAOC was merged with the newly created Royal Logistic Corps Museum. The typescript and associated documents are now held in the archives of the museum and can be consulted by appointment.

5 In compliance with the author's wishes, it is planned to make a donation from the royalties of the book to the Red Cross and forces' charities.

6 This is a quote from the author's commission as an officer.

7 GOC – General Officer Commanding.

8 In 1940 the garrison of China comprised two British and two Indian battalions, three regiments of artillery (and later an anti-aircraft regiment) and ancillary services in Hong Kong, two infantry battalions in Shanghai, one infantry company in Tientsin and in Peking, the legation guard. In addition to maintaining this force the RAOC equipped the Hong Kong Volunteer Defence Corps', the Second World War 1939–45, Ordnance Services, The War Office, 1950 – Hong Kong, p.294.

9 The shipping line was Jardine Matheson & Co.

10 Not so different for ships off Somalia in the early twenty-first century.

11 See Biography, pp.15–16.

12 Amah – nurse or helper

13 It is no coincidence that two British members of the Shanghai Municipal Police, Eric A. Sykes and William E. Fairburn were to develop the famous Fairburn-Sykes fighting knife for the army during the Second World War.

14 Suzhou Creek also called Wusong River is the river that passes through the Shanghai city centre.

15 The Shanghai International Settlement was wholly foreign controlled through the Shanghai Municipal Council (SMC) and maintained its own fire-service, police and military reserve, the Shanghai Volunteer Corps. From 1937 the International Settlement was surrounded by Japanese forces and under attack from Chinese revolutionaries. However as the settlement remained Sovereign Chinese territory, unlike Hong Kong, when Britain declared war on Germany and Italy in 1939 their nationals were able to operate alongside their 'enemies' with the territory.

16 Tientsin –Tianjin.

17 Peking – Beijing.

18 Tsingtao - Qingdao, in Shandong was ceded to Germany in 1898 as a port and naval base. In 1914 the town was besieged and captured by a combined Anglo-Japanese force. The name

Tsingtao is used on a type of Bavarian-style beer which has been brewed in China from 1903.

19 Chefoo – Qufu, home of Confucius in Shandong province.

20 Wei Hai Wei in Shangdong province was leased by the British from 1898 until October 1, 1930. It was a summer station for the British naval China Station and it was also used as a sanatorium. It became one of two major ports for ships of the Royal Navy in the Far East. The other was Hong Kong in the south.

21 Taku – Dagu located by the Hai River (Peiho River) estuary.

22 Tientsin – Tianjin.

23 See Biography, p. 16.

24 OC – Officer Commanding.

25 The Boxer Rebellion was the Chinese uprising of 1900 against increasing foreign domination of their affairs. The International Legation in Beijing was besieged until relieved by force which included Russian, British, French, German, United States and Japanese troops.

26 Shanhaikwan – Shanhaiguan on the coast.

27 Ch'ien Men Gate – Qianmen or Front Gate to Beijing.

28 See Biography p. 14.

29 Mex – For historic reasons the major unit of currency in Shanghai at this time was the Mexican Dollar.

30 Chinwangtao – Qinghuangdao.

31 Gulf of Liaotung – Gulf of Liaodong.

32 Decauville railway was a type of narrow-gauge track which was used for both agricultural and industrial purposes in addition to being employed by the military of many nations.

33 Peitaho – Beidaihe a beach resort.

34 'Crossing the Bar' signifies having left the notional end of the river course and entered open sea.

35 ADOS – Assistant Director Ordnance Services.

36 A ball game.

37 GOC – General Officer Commanding

38 DADOS – Deputy Assistant Director of Ordnance Services.

39 Shum Chum River – Shenzhen River, Hong Kong.

Chapter 1 - Chaos

1 Murray Barracks is in Stanley on the southern side of Hong Kong Island and close to where the author must have surrendered to the Japanese.

2 The author had surrendered at 8.30am the previous morning having taken an important part in the heavy fighting against the Japanese on the Ridge on Hong Kong Island. He had evaded capture for three days without food or water and was believed by his comrades to have been killed in the fighting or in the massacre of survivors that followed the surrender.

3 The author's family was at this time in New South Wales Australia and only received conformation that the author was alive and a prisoner of war in July 1942. Letter from Australian Red Cross and telegram in the collection of the Royal Logistic Corps Museum.

4 Star Ferry, which still runs, connects Kowloon with Hong Kong Island.

5 The author was forty-one years old and had just endured a week's intense fighting plus three days of trying to evade the Japanese Army.

6 This is a reference to Nanking (Nanjing) Massacre of December 1937 in which tens of thousands of Chinese had been killed by a victorious Japanese army during the Japanese invasion of northern China to which the author was an eye-witness.

7 This quotation is taken from the wording of his commission which clearly meant so much to the author.

8 A Nullah or Nulla (Hindi, also Nallah in Punjabi) is a water course. In Hong Kong, a nullah is typically a concrete-lined channel designed to allow rapid run off of storm water from high ground.

9 The general was Acting Major General C.M. Maltby commanding British troops in China.

10 Argyle Street Camp, which had been a British barracks, became the main camp for officers in April 1942.

11 It is not known quite whom the author is referring to as 'Dahn Omers' even to Cantonese speakers. However the diary of Lieutenant James Sutcliffe, RAOC provides more information about the process. 15 January 1942: 'Private

supplies may be handed over the wire by friends through the Japanese at the guard room. This indeed a boon and our party (Captain Ebbage, Lieut. Hanlon, Pte. J Stopforth and self) are benifitting (sic) from it', p. 36. This is in the collection of the Royal Logistic Corps Museum.

12 The diary of Lieutenant James Sutcliffe, RAOC, provides a number of harrowing accounts of the treatment received by those who attempted to help the prisoners in the camp.

13 The staff sergeant has been identified as 758833 S/Sgt W.R. Peters, REME, and the original envelope is now as 2176/7708. It is framed together with an account of the history. The account was used when the History of the Royal Amy Ordnance Corps 1929–45 was written, and also in *Craftsmen of the Army: The Story of the Royal Electrical and Mechanical Engineers*.

Chapter 2 – Some Order out of Chaos

1 Lt Col Henry William Moncrieff Stewart, OBE, MC, CO, 1st Battalion, Middlesex Regiment.

2 Small boats of traditional Chinese style normally propelled by oars.

3 This was Colonel G.R. Hopkins, the senior RAOC officer.

4 Clearly the author's time during the fighting on the Ridge and on the run had taken a physical toll. He was forty-one years old at this point and not a young soldier.

5 Although not a term used in Britain other nations use 'intendant' to describe a form of administrative office.

6 Miss Ebbage has informed the editor that her father did not speak any Japanese. It can be surmised that his previous experience of working with the Japanese army in Beijing and his 'holiday' in Kobe suggested him as an ideal candidate for this post.

7 The author is referring to the massacre of the survivors on the Ridge after the surrender, and the death of Lt. Colonel MacPherson.

8 Lieutenant James Sutcliffe suggests in his diary that the officer was 'the Japanese Paymaster' and that he arrived 'just after 8 a.m.', p. 39. Collection of the Royal Logistic Corps Museum.

9 Lieutenant Sutcliffe suggests in his diary that this event happened on or just before 18 January: 'Ebbage left with the Japanese Paymaster Lieutenant at 8.30 a.m. and was able to bring back from the Ridge what the Japanese had left of our clothing store – a few brushes, table knives, a couple of forks and hair brushes; also few under-pants. Ebbage also brought back a 50 tin of Pall Mall cigarettes at $3.50. He tried hard for sugar, but had no luck. The Japanese officer took him to Taikoo Sugar factory, but the Naval Landing Party were in occupation – no luck', p.39.

10 According to Lieutenant Sutcliffe the author was using his trips with the Japanese officers to purchase food for the men in the camp. Some of the men may have questioned the author's motives in so doing. 16 January: 'Captain Ebbage went out with the Japanese again – sudden call, – had tea and toast with Colonel of the Japanese Pay corps (they control Pay, stores and Food) and visited Po Shing Shoe company with him. They are still talking of helping us with clothing and food. Ebbage asked permission to buy some sugar and milk on return trip. Given O.K. Called in at Sunny Farm, Nathan road – proprietor very astonished and dubious, as a Japanese was also there. Bought 12 large tins of milk, 9 large jars of honey (clear) in lieu of sugar, 1lb of Ricksha tea (now $10 a pound, before about $3), 12 buns, about 6lb Kraft cheese, 2x1lb tins S. & W. coffee. We retained a reasonable amount and gave the balance to the troops and Col. Hopkins. The Japanese made him a present of cheese. Very successful outing and we were so excited we had difficulty in controlling ourselves', p.37.

17 January: 'Ebbage was able to buy a lot while out with the Japanese – 48 tins of milk, 6 jars of honey, 4lbs. of cocoa, 4lbs. of coffee, and 1lb of boiled ham. We kept 12, 2, 1 and 1. The ham was a rich change. To the others it was the taste: to me the look. I've never seen such beautiful looking ham – rich, red and lean. Ebbage has his for his evening meal and for breakfast next day', p.37.

11 The hotel opened in 1928 and was and remains a luxury establishment.

12 Lt Col Reginald David Walker, OBE, MC, commander of the HKVDC Field Company Engineers.

13 Contents of the latrines.

14 Lieutenant James Sutcliffe indicates in his diary that the author's trips out with the Japanese became less frequent by the end of January. On the 28th he records '28/1/42: We have a few luxuries on hand milk, cocoa and honey – which Vic Ebbage brought in when he was taken out by the Japs. He hasn't been allowed out lately; evidently because the Japs require no more information and have little intention of supplementing in the equipment and clothing line', pp. 50–51.

15 The author and some of his fellow officers were able to obtain items from outside the camp. Lieutenant 'Mick' Hanlon and he had a windfall at the beginning of February. According to Lieutenant Sutcliffe's diary of 8th: 'Mick and Vic had parcels today. Mick had his usual few tins, 1lb butter and a large loaf of bread. Vic had obtained a contact from somewhere and it's still a mystery. We're pleased he got it, all the same, as he received a sand-bag full of good stuff, including among being (sic) a large loaf of bread and a tin of butter, a large tin of biscuits and many tins of meat and fish.', p.66. Clearly Lt. Sutcliffe was in a similar position to many others in the camp but benefited from the author's generosity. 15th February: 'Although I am not now in a position to obtain anything from outside I am still left with the initiative where food and meals are concerned. I have cooked every meal which it has been necessary to cook since our arrival. My conscience is fairly easy about accepting their hospitality as I am still supplying money to Ebbage and Mick', p.73.

16 Roughly 30 US dollars or £3.15 shillings (£3.75).

17 According to the original receipts the author contributed a total of 210 Yen to this camp fund between 30 June 1942 and the end of the war. Collection of the Royal Logistic Corps Museum. See Chapter 4.

Chapter 3 – 'Improvise'

1 See Chapter 13 for details of these workshops in the camp.

2 One example of this coincidence is provided by the diary of Lieutenant James Sutcliffe of 31 January 1942. 'Another coincidence was Ebbage's shoes. Some 12 months ago he had a pair of shoes made to measure which were not a success. These he put in his desk drawer and forgot. When we took

over Queen's Road depot as a billet after surrender, and we assumed Ebbage to be dead, the troops looked around for kit and found Ebbage's shoes. Hoping that Ebbage would reappear, I took charge of the shoes and deposited them in drawer in my desk. On leaving for Murray Barracks 2 days late I left them behind as too much lumber. We eventually arrived in sham Shui Po together with Ebbage, who had no kit whatsoever and we decided to fit him out. Much to our surprise, Private Dinner – one of our Batmen – produces the shoes as a pair we had found and would likely fit', p.59. The archives of the Royal Logistic Corps Museum.

3 Treadle sewing machines are foot operated.

4 Colonel Takanuga – 'the Fat Pig', officer in charge of Hong Kong's POW camps.

5 Note that despite the treatment received by the author he is prepared to compliment those of his captors whose conduct was 'correct'. See also Note 1, Chapter 13 for name of Cardiff Joe.

6 In his diary Lt. Sutcliffe provide a little more detail about the first of these interpreters 'Two days ago a Jap Methodist (?) parson came to our service. We suspected he came in the capacity of a spy. This may or may not have been so. From what we gather he has been sent from Japan by the Government to act in a liaison capacity between ourselves and the Jap military. He has met Ebbage on a job of work and gives him greetings whenever he passes during roll-call. This is appreciated… Ebbage is now waiting the opportunity to invite the Jap parson up here some evening for a chat and a cup of cocoa', 30 March 1942, pp.98–99.

7 Staff Sergeant Leonard Ackerman died on the morning of 3 January 1942, Lt. Sutcliffe provides the details. 'Staff Sergeant Leonard Ackerman, R.O.A.C. died at 4 a.m. I was informed about 9 a.m. and had to make all the arrangements for burial in the absence of Captain Ebbage who was called by the Japanese Paymaster just after 8 a.m.', Sutcliffe report, p.34.

8 7581855 Ackerman, Leonard Albert Gardner, RAOC, aged 42, Stanley Military Cemetery, Grave 6. C. 20 CWGC.

9 The author spent a great deal of time gardening in his retirement.

10 Numerous examples of this sort of brutality were witnesses at Shamshuipo camp and elsewhere in Hong Kong. Despite the

dangers family members and local Chinese took enormous risks to keep the prisoners supplied with food, luxuries and information.

Chapter 4 – Exodus to Argyle Street

1 Batmen are soldier servants in the Indian army although the term is often applied to all men so employed.
2 The siege of Kut in Mesopotamia by the Turkish army occurred in 1915. The British garrison surrendered in April 1916 and was an example of a comparable military disaster in a previous war. General Townsend's lack of concern for the British prisoners in Turkish hands was obviously a lesson to be discussed at length.
3 Approximately 3 shillings or 14 modern pence.
4 This halved the value of the Hong Kong currency against the Japanese Yen.
5 Lasts are wooden formers for the uppers of shoes.

Chapter 5 - Affidavit

1 Colonel Takanuga.
2 This author's friend has been identified as Captain Hugh Spencer Badger, 1st Battalion Middlesex Regiment.
3 The Great East Asia Co-Prosperity Scheme was the term used by the Japanese to justify their Imperial expansion before and during the Second World War.
4 RAPC – Royal Army Pay Corps.
5 According to the original receipt this is a transcript of the author's own contributions to the camp fund. It is signed by Major Roger Digby Buck, Royal Army Pay Corps. Collection of the Royal Logistic Corps Museum. See Chapter 4.

Chapter 6 – Letters Home

1 Colonel Takanuga.
2 Hari-Kiri (Harakiri) refers to a form of Japanese Seppuku or ritual suicide.

3 For an account of the deaths that resulted from this epidemic see *We Shall Suffer There, Hong Kong Defenders Imprisoned, 1942-45*, Tony Banham, Hong Kong University Press, 2009.

4 The original of this card is not in the archive collection handed to the Royal Logistic Corps Museum.

5 The original telegram is in the collection of the Royal Logistic Corps Museum. Also shown in the plate section of this book.

6 ditto.

Chapter 7 – The Steam Oven

1 The identity of this man is provided in *Craftsmen Of The Army: The Story of the Royal Electrical and Mechanical Engineers*, Brigadier B. B. Kennett, CBE and Colonel J.A. Tatman, REME, 1970. He was Artificer Staff Sergeant Saddington. The information was provided to Brigadier Kennett by the author.

2 The Aldershot Oven was a simple system of steel plates that could be quickly assembled and covered with bricks or clay and fired with wood, charcoal or coal to create an effective means of baking bread or cooking.

Chapter 8 – The Party System

1 It is clear that the author is being modest about his skills as a musician. Lieutenant Sutcliffe records in his diary on 7 February 1942: 'We have a large, and improving repertoire of songs, not only from the Community book (about 60 only) but from memory. Vic Ebbage and Mick Hanlon know nearly every song which has been sung on a Music Hall stage this last 40 years. Both have phenomenal memories and have the aptitude for picking up that type of song. Since yesterday's evening meal I have recorded the titles of every chorus sung in the room on the distempered walls, the chorus must be sung properly with correct words and tune before I'll accept it. The score is 72 in less than one day and is likely to mount rapidly.' p.61.

2 The original copy of the will is in the collection of the Royal Logistic Corps Museum.

3 It identifies the witnesses as Captain Harry S. Badger and Captain C.G. Webber?, both of the Middlesex Regiment. See p.130.

4 Basrah (Basra) in Iraq. See biography p.14.

5 Sen are the sub units of the Japanese Yen. There are 100 Sen in one Yen.

Chapter 10 – SS *Lisbon Maru*

1 Lt Col H.W.M. Stewart.

2 The author took a photograph of this hut when he revisited the site of the camp in 1966. It is included in this book in the plate section.

Chapter 13 – Pig & Poultry Farm

1 Cardiff Joe was Matsuda-san. A generally well-liked individual, he had been the Cardiff manager for Uyamashita Steamship Company until late 1940.

2 Propaganda photographs staged by the Japanese. Not shown here.

3 Amyl Acetate – a solvent used in the camp for the repair of spectacles.

4 Hankow Barracks was part of the Shamshuipo Camp. On the opposite side was Nanking Barracks.

Chapter 14 – Propaganda Draft

1 Gowdowns – Name used in the Far East for Dockside warehouses.

2 Biography, p.16.

Chapter 15 – Term Report or Salt Pans

1 The death rate in No. 6 Section RAOC does appear to be lower than among other units in the camp. For details see *We Shall Suffer There, Hong Kong Defenders Imprisoned, 1942–45*, Tony Banham, Hong Kong University Press, 2009.

2 Dannert wire – a type of barbed or razor wire.

3 The Royal Electric and Mechanical Engineers (REME) were

formed in October 1942. A fact which the men in the camp who had been transferred to the new corps were not aware.

Chapter 16 – 'Albert' or Intelligence Tests

1 Will Hay was a popular British Music Hall and cinema comedian of the early twentieth century.
2 Both Korea and Formosa (Taiwan) had been invaded and occupied by the Japanese. The guards recruited from these areas were subject people of the Japanese Empire but of dubious loyalty.

Chapter 17 – Christmas 1943

1 The items described by the author are in the collection of the Royal Logistic Corps Museum.

Chapter 18 – Ladder Bombing

1 This air raid is almost certainly that of Monday 16 October; *We Shall Suffer There, Hong Kong Defenders Imprisoned, 1942–45*, Tony Banham, Hong Kong University Press, 2009, pp. 174-75.

Chapter 19 – Return of Friends

1 The Corporal was 7588090, David Murray MacCulloch, RAOC, who died on 9 January 1945, he is buried in Stanley Military Cemetery. CWGC
2 Biography, p. 17.
3 Camp 'N' – North Point POW Camp.

Chapter 21 – Japanese Surrender

1 The first atomic bomb was dropped on by a US military aircraft on the Japanese city of Hiroshima at 8:15am on 6 August 1945.
2 The second bomb was dropped on 9 August 1945.
3 The announcement made by Emperor Hirohito of the surrender of Japan was the first occasion his people had heard his voice.

Appendix 1 – Report of Captain Ebbage, RAOC

1 RAOC – Royal Army Ordnance Corps.

2 DADOS – Deputy Assistant Director of Ordnance Services.

3 CRA – Commander Royal Artillery.

4 RE – Royal Engineers, RASC – Royal Army Service Corps, RAOC – Royal Army Ordnance Corps and HKVDC – The Hong Kong Volunteer Defence Corps.

5 Private, 7609583, David Alexander Taylor, RAOC, died 22 December 1942, aged thirty-three, Sai Wan Memorial, Hong Kong. CWGC

6 ADMS – Assistant Director Medical Services.

7 See Captain Ebbage's Military Biography on pp. 20–21.

Appendix 2 – Report on RAOC as POWs

1 Now held in the archives of the Royal Logistic Corps Museum.

2 ADOS – Active Duty Operational Support.

3 OC – Officer Commanding.

4 Mil. Law – Military Law.

5 WO or NCO – Warrant Officer or Non-Commissioned Officer

6 Armt. S.M. – Armament Sergeant Major

7 MO – Medical Officer

8 S-Sgt – Staff Sergeant

9 The *Lisbon Maru*, with over 1,800 British prisoners of war, aboard was torpedoed on 1 October 1942, by the American submarine, *Grouper*, off Shanghai. Over 800 POWs died.

10 Lt Col. – Lieutenat Colonel

11 Corporal Harry Reason, RAOC, died 1 November 1942, aged forty-eight. Sai Wan War Cemetery. CWGC

12 S-M – Sergeant Major

13 S-Cdr. – Senior Conductor, Warrant Officer.

14 Haynes, Frank Henry William, Civilian, RAOC, died 27 October 1943, aged fifty-seven.

15 Sergeant McCulloch, RAOC, no details available from the Commonwealth War Graves Commission.

16 Q-M-S – Quarter Master Sergeant

17 S-Sgt. – Staff Sergeant

Bibliography

Published Sources

The Second World War 1939–45, Ordnance Services, The War Office, 1950

History of the Royal Army Ordnance Corps, 1920–1945, Brigadier A.H. Fernyhough, CBE, MC, Royal Army Ordnance Corps, 1967

Craftsmen of the Army The Story of the Royal Electrical And Mechanical Engineers, Brigadier B. B. Kennett, CBE and Colonel J.A. Tatman, REME, 1970

The Story of the Royal Army Service Corps, 1939–1945, Bell and Sons, 1955

Not The Slightest Chance, The Defence of Hong Kong, 1941, Tony Banham, Hong Kong University Press, 2005

We Shall Suffer There, Hong Kong Defenders Imprisoned, 1942–45, Tony Banham, Hong Kong University Press, 2009

The Sinking of the Lisbon Maru: *Britain's Forgotten Wartime Tragedy*, Tony Banham, Hong Kong University Press, 2006

Unpublished Sources
(held at the Royal Logistic Corps Museum)

2176/7708: Envelope which contained a copy the RAOC War Diaries returned after his captivity in Hong Kong by 758833 S/Sgt W.R. Peters REME

2994, 3044, 3045 and 3046: Folders containing the typescript of *The Hard Way* and associated documents, drawings and photographs.

The Diary of James Sutcliffe RAOC during Japanese hostilities in Hong Kong from 7th December to 14th August 1945.

Explore other titles published by The History Press

Surviving Tenko
PENNY STARNS

The Story of Margot Turner

978-0-7524-5553-2

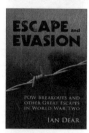

Escape and Evasion
IAN DEAR

POW Breakouts and Other Great Escapes in
World War Two

978-0-7524-5581-5

Treblinka Survivor
MARK S. SMITH

The Life and Death of Hershl Sperling

978-0-7524-5618-8

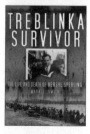

Barbed Wire Disease
JOHN YARNALL

British and German Prisoners of War, 1914–1919

978-0-7524-5690-4

Visit our website and discover thousands of
other History Press books.

www.thehistorypress.co.uk